LEO J. BRUNING
11549 Circle Way
Dublin, California 94566

GAMES, ASTERISKS, and PEOPLE

Memoirs of a Lucky Fan

GAMES, ASTERISKS, and PEOPLE

Memoirs of a Lucky Fan

by FORD C. FRICK

Crown Publishers, Inc., New York

Second Printing, May, 1973

© 1973 by Ford C. Frick
Library of Congress Catalog Card Number: 72-96644
ISBN: 0-517-503468
Printed in the United States of America
Published simultaneously in Canada by General Publishing Company Limited

Dedicated to my wife, Eleanor, who for more than fifty years has put up with the crazy machinations of a dyed-in-the-wool sports buff, and has never lost her sense of humor or her faith in the guy she married.

CONTENTS

Picture inserts following page 52 and page 212.

INTRODUCTION

This is a book of sports memories—memories born through more than half a century of association with baseball and the personalities it has created.

It is in no sense a formally documented or official history for dedicated researchers or literary perfectionists; memories do not lend themselves to that sort of treatment. Rather it is a series of memory vignettes, set down as they came to mind.

It deals, naturally, with some of the great names in baseball—players, owners and officials. There are memories, too, of some of the unsung figures whose contributions have been large, though unrecognized—writers, television announcers, umpires, statisticians, bat boys, and even concessionaires. And, of course, the fans—big and small, bleacherites and presidents, the famous and the unknown—for fans are the most important figures of all. Without their loyalty and support, professional sports could not exist.

This is not a controversial book, though from time to time controversial questions are discussed, and opinions expressed. Such opinions are my own; they do not represent the thinking of baseball's management or officials.

From time to time, too, I wander from my immediate subject to indulge in a bit of personal philosophy, or recall an offbeat story or incident. That is the way memory functions. For such digressions I offer no apology. Like it or not, philosophizing is a senior citizen's privilege, whether writing or dreaming of "days that were."

Occasionally, too, you may feel I have overstepped reality in my praise of an individual, or in describing the thrill of some dramatic event—or that I have been overly enthusiastic in my defense of baseball, and baseball's rules and practices. I plead "guilty," proudly and without excuse. It was intentional.

And that's the story.

This is a book written by a "lucky" fan, for fans everywhere. I hope it is a happy book. If fans get half as much pleasure in reading it as I got in writing it, then I will be happy indeed.

June 1, 1972   FORD C. FRICK

GAMES, ASTERISKS, and PEOPLE

Memoirs of a Lucky Fan

PROLOGUE

"Through the sycamore, the candlelights are gleaming
On the banks of the Wabash far away."

Baseball is a game of fans, and fans develop in strange and devious ways. Indiana youngsters of my generation were born to baseball. We couldn't avoid it.

In my little country village every vacant lot, every stubble field, every bit of pastureland, was a potential diamond. Every school building was a ready-made clubhouse; every nearby farm village an enemy stronghold, ripe for conquest. Basketball, just coming into prominence, we considered a mere time killer, to be tolerated only as a filler-in between baseball seasons. Football required too much equipment and too many players. To field an adequate squad would have required the entire juvenile population of at least three or four villages like ours.

As for golf, that was a game for wealthy old men, or dudes, or sissies. No self-respecting farmer would for a moment consider sacrificing good corn acreage for so silly a thing as a golf links. If grown men were so keen for that sort of outdoor exercise, let them get it at the handle of a plow, or on the business end of a hoe at corn-planting time.

No, sir! For us it was baseball by default—and we loved it.

1

If a boy could throw a ball across the diamond (even on one bounce) or run ninety feet without falling flat on his face, he had it made. For those who couldn't handle a glove or swing a bat, there was always a place for a ball-shagging outfielder. Provided, of course, he was willing to accept our rules and remain a perpetual retriever. Such an unfortunate was admitted to full gang membership with all rooting interest—but no batting privileges.

There was one general exception. The kid who was lucky enough to come up with a real league ball, or a "store-bought" bat, automatically became team captain. He held that post as long as the ball remained playable, and the bat unbroken. Caste system? Sure. But we loved it, and accepted it gladly.

Although I've never been able to figure out why, some people regard my generation as underprivileged youngsters reared in an old-fashioned era, under archaic conditions. We were, they say, unfortunate victims of a self-centered society that failed to recognize the psychological importance of a planned, organized, and supervised recreation.

Maybe they're right. After all, we did have to make do as best we could with nothing but fresh air and sunshine. There were lakes to fish in, and dusty roads to explore. There were open fields where we could run, and jump, and play—and perhaps fight imaginary battles as knights of old, or cowboys, or Indians, or bank robbers, whatever fancy might dictate. And, of course, there were acres of shady woodlands where a boy and a dog could establish a private kingdom in kinship with the squirrels, rabbits, and all the creatures that lived therein.

Somehow, despite some modern psychologists, we didn't feel underprivileged. We were perfectly happy with our lot. We were entirely content to create our own amusement, and our own heroes, from the material at hand, without envy, or even passing thought, to the world outside.

Baseball, historians point out, was born and nurtured in the broad rural areas of an infant nation. Undoubtedly, that's true, and the northern Indiana I knew as a youngster was typical of such rural areas throughout the nation.

It was a land of lush meadows and waving grain, of sunshine-spattered dirt roads. These roads twisted and turned through golden fields, and on into the shadow of oak groves, and woodlands of hickory and black walnut. It was a land of rivers and lakes; of hazel bushes and wild raspberries and pawpaws; of blueberries and butternuts and wild strawberries in season. It was a land of open spaces and bronze pasturelands, ready for juvenile occupancy. All we needed was a tape measure to mark off the base lines; three grain bags, cut to size, and pegged down for bases; and a shingle set in the ground to serve as home plate. We were in the baseball business.

More important, it was a land of farm villages and hamlets as physically alike as peas in a pod, yet as completely distinctive as a Dali painting or a Brahms lullaby. These villages, intensely proud and violently competitive, were the battlegrounds of our baseball wars. Each hamlet had its loyal rooting section, and each village its local hero. In Brimfield, Indiana (population 250), our reigning demigod was a tall, lean, broad-shouldered baseball divinity named Ed Morley. In our eyes, Ed was a better pitcher and a more bona fide idol than Cy Young or Amos Rusie, or any other of the outland heroes whose names were frequently bandied about by our elders when they assembled each evening at the railroad telegraph office to get the major league scores.

It was not that we didn't appreciate the greatness of these fabled giants whose names are today enshrined in Baseball's Hall of Fame. We did appreciate and honor them. But Ed Morley was different. He was "handy-by." We could see him in the flesh. We could touch him. We could talk to him. He was our own personal property.

Ed was a pitcher—a long-armed, loose-jointed chap, who had a fast ball to make opposing batters' eyes pop, and a good curve to go with it. He was the best bass fisherman in our county. And, too, he was the editor, publisher, and printer of our local four-page weekly newspaper, which he turned out single-handed on an antique hand-operated Franklin press.

It was in his shop that I first got the smell of printer's ink in my nostrils, and the lure of news reporting in my heart. Writing your first story is always a thrill. But when you're permitted to hand-set the type, and then read galley proof on your own copy—then you have reached a pinnacle in boyhood dreams.

Ed Morley never reached the big leagues—never even played in Organized Baseball. But he did travel to Toledo, and Dayton, and

Fort Wayne, and South Bend to pitch for semipro clubs. He was paid twenty-five dollars, plus round-trip railroad fare. To us youngsters that was the clincher. To earn that kind of money, he had to be a star.

We had another authentic hero in those days, too. He was an idol whose fame reached beyond the confines of village and county, across state lines into Illinois and Ohio, and even into faraway Pennsylvania and New York. He was a burly right-handed pitcher named Burt Inks, and he pitched in the National League from 1890 to 1896. He played with Brooklyn, Baltimore, Louisville, and Cincinnati, and established a pitching record of 50 victories and 33 defeats in big-time competition.

Not a great record, really, but sufficient to enshrine him in memory as our first real and personal contact with the shining world of grown-up professional baseball. Bert knew John McGraw and Hughey Jennings and Connie Mack and Ned Hanlon personally. He called Wilbert Robinson and Willie Keeler and Kid Gleason by their first names. He told us tales of the pitching prowess of Cy Young and Amos Rusie and Kid Nichols, and of the batting genius of Hughey Duffy and King Kelly.

Believe me, Burt Inks was "big stuff." He rated first rung on the ladder with Levi Crume, the local Civil War hero, who fought at Shiloh and Chickamauga. Burt was some notches above Albert J. Beveridge and Tom Marshall. After all, they were only political figures, and probably wouldn't know the difference between a curve ball and a change of pace.

The crowning touch to a youthful fan's dream came a few years later. In the summer of 1907, the champion Chicago Cubs stopped off in Kendalville (our local metropolis) for an exhibition game with our Kendalville Blues. Club houses were unheard of in those days. Visiting players donned their uniforms at the local tavern, then walked the short distance to the ball park through an excited honor guard of juvenile hero worshippers. You can be sure that I wasn't going to miss that.

Among the last players to come along was a smiling, darkly handsome chap. He spotted me, big-eyed and mouth agape, watching in awed silence as the athletes walked past. He grinned, and beckoned.

"Hi, kid," he said, "want to go to the ball game?"

I gulped, and managed to convey the idea that I would.

"Tell you what to do. Just carry these shoes for me, and when we get to the gate you just walk in with us. Maybe the gateman will let you by."

I did exactly as he told me, and the miracle happened: I walked right into the ball park with the players. Furthermore, I was permitted to sit on the ground alongside the players' bench. I could see Mordecai Brown and Ed Ruelbach in person. I could hear Schulte and Tinker and Chance and Evers and Steinfeldt talking on the bench between innings. What a moment.

Years later, I had the opportunity to meet and chat with the Crown Prince of Japan. On another occasion, as a newspaperman, I spent several days with the then Prince of Wales, when he attended the international polo matches at Meadowbrook, Long Island. Through the years, I've been privileged to chat with Presidents at the White House; to hobnob with renowned figures in sports, in finance, science, and all phases of public life. But these were routine workday assignments, to be taken in stride as part of a newspaperman's days. That ball game was different. For the rest of the summer, I lived in a dreamworld. I was the hero of the village, the envy of every kid in the community, the hometown boy who, for a few fleeting minutes, had hobnobbed with greatness.

It was not until 1937, thirty years later, that I had an opportunity to meet and talk again with my hero of the shoes. Older, grayer, and heavier than I remembered, he still retained that same friendly smile. There was the same warm, friendly twinkle in his eyes that I recalled from the day of my biggest boyhood thrill. He didn't remember the incident, but seemed to enjoy the story.

One thing sure. That day in 1907 convinced me that baseball was the greatest game in the world, and he its greatest player. Now, more than half a century later, mature judgment and the leavening experience of years dims somewhat my childish enthusiasm. In my mind I know that there must have been others greater—but in my heart he will remain forever the greatest catcher who ever lived.

His name? Johnny Kling.

1

HOW IT ALL BEGAN

Baseball, in a historical sense, is "without pride of ancestry" or documented historical precedent. Like Topsy, it "just growed," without benefit of birth certificate or genealogical family tree. To historians, the emergence of the game has been an eternal puzzle. After all, a battered old baseball, the early memories of an elderly man, and the casual findings of a self-appointed "ad hoc" committee constitute a pretty tenuous foundation on which to base the origin of a national institution.

The real story of baseball's beginning and early development is not to be found in any historian's documentation, but in the folklore of a sports-loving people. Long before our own game was ever dreamed of, long before communications had extended beyond the local level, long before records and documentation had become an integral part of athletic accomplishment—wandering minstrels sang of the athletic prowess of their heroes. In their songs they topped the political, religious and world-influencing stature of their heroes with a halo of physical greatness that common people could understand and love.

Sir Francis Drake, it is said, held up the sailing of an English fleet, in order to complete a game of bowls. Only then did he set forth to settle the destiny of an empire through the defeat of the Spanish Armada.

The battle of Waterloo, says tradition, was won on the playing fields of Eton.

These stories, and myriad others like them, have no documented basis of fact. But people love them, and all the learned research of a century of historians cannot dim their luster, nor prevent their repetition. Somehow, it is folklore which often better reports the spirit of a people than a thousand sermons.

So it was with baseball.

Our forebears were venturesome people, intent on building a fresh new nation in their own image. They loved challenge. They worked hard; they prayed hard; they lived hard; they played hard. They faced constant daily perils that could be conquered only through community effort. Consequently, in their leisure hours, they sought competitive games, based on community participation, and demanding community pride.

Baseball offered such a challenge. It was a game everyone could play. It required little equipment. It adapted easily to local whims and local conditions. It provided opportunity for team effort, without hidebound traditional rules to hamper individual enterprise. Small wonder then that a migrating people carried the game with them across the country, even as they carried their traps, their rifles, and their household belongings.

During the early years, baseball was a hit-or-miss operation. In New York, it was "Townball." In New England, it was "Massachusetts Ball." "Anthony Over," and "One Ol' Cat," and "Tag Ball" had their own adherents in rural villages along the Eastern Seaboard. Then a couple of miracles and a war, coming in rapid succession, set off the fireworks.

In 1839, the game had no standard rules, no agreed-upon competitive procedure, and no particular indication of future greatness. That summer, folklore has it, a teen-ager named Abner Doubleday was playing "Two Ol' Cat" with other youngsters on the pasture lots of a little upstate New York village called Cooperstown. The game they played was inadequate to accommodate all the boys who wished to participate. So Doubleday, says the story, picked up a twig and outlined in the dirt a daring new concept.

He drew a square, with a stone placed at each of the four corners. These, he explained, would be the bases. To count a point, it would be necessary to touch each of the four bases in succession. The runners would be in peril of extinction if they were "tagged" in the process of advancing. The additional bases, Doubleday pointed out, would enable more boys to play on a side. It would also increase interest by affording the defensive side more opportunity to cut off runners before they could score.

Many skeptics through the years have questioned the Doubleday legend. They are still questioning it. But to me the argument is unimportant. Whether Doubleday should actually be credited with establishing the first diamond, or whether that honor rightfully belongs to some other genius, both unknown and unsung, is immaterial. The important thing is that the diamond was instituted. What had been a simple, rural pastime became overnight an appealing competitive game, and that game caught the national fancy as has no game before or since.

The new game was instantly popular. The standardized diamond added a new dimension. In less than ten years (circa 1845) another unsung genius added the crowning touch by establishing the base line distance at a standard 90 feet.

Maybe that unknown was an engineer, a mathematical genius working with slide rule precision. Maybe it was all sheer luck and happenstance. In any event, it worked. To perfection. Today, more than a century later, the 90-foot base line still exists, offering perfect balance between offense and defense; between the speed of the runner and the power of an accurate throwing arm; between safe and out. Certainly if the establishment of a diamond is to be credited with starting baseball on its way to greatness, then equally certain, the establishment of the 90-foot distance between bases must be recognized as the greatest contribution to perfect competition any game has ever known. It is that specification on which our hitting and fielding records are based; that unchanging measurement of success or failure that has set the guidelines for heroes; the great reason why baseball, through the years, has qualified as the most mathematically perfect game ever devised by humankind.

Again, folklore and tradition credit one Alexander Cartwright as the genius who established the 90-foot distance. So far as I know, there are no existing records to prove or disprove the authenticity of such claims. Nor is it important. Alexander Cartwright's contribution to the early development of baseball is so many-faceted that one more honor, more or less, cannot dim his claim to greatness.

Cartwright was a tall, burly man, with a roving foot and a great love for athletics. He took up the new game most enthusiastically. He had great ability as a player, and even greater ability as an organizer and supporter. He was a prime mover in the establishment of clubs in New York and New England. He later joined the great pioneer movement to the Mississippi and the Rockies; he participated in the California gold rush; and he made the long windjammer trek to Hawaii and was among the first settlers in that island crossroads of the Western world. And wherever he went, he carried baseball with him.

He was followed by others. The greatest tragedy of the nineteenth century was the Civil War, which threatened the very existence of the new and struggling nation. But out of that war came a stronger and better union, and out of that war, too, baseball emerged as a truly American game.

The men who had learned, firsthand, the horror of war, learned at the same time the value of recreation and friendly competitive play. In their idle moments, soldiers played the new game. They played in training camps, prison camps, and convalescent areas. City men found athletic counterparts in boys from farms and villages. It was all in fun, and they loved it. At war's end, when they headed for home, they took baseball with them. Overnight, it became the national game, both in geographic scope, and in the affections of a reunited people.

With the end of the war came organization of rules and procedure. Interested and dedicated men gave of their time and money to develop teams and arrange schedules. High schools took up the game, and established an organized form of local competition. Semipro teams, operating successfully in larger towns and cities, gave evidence of the widespread spectator interest that became the basis for the professional operation which endures today.

Professional baseball, it seems to me, was inevitable. The right of man to make a profit under a national economy based on free enterprise and initiative is inalienable. Our great corporations, our railroad systems, our public utility complexes, our oil giants, all were created on that concept. Baseball, representing our entertainment and recreation desires, was a natural. Yet professional baseball arrived through evolution rather than explosion. As early as 1859, players were being paid. But British standards were still observed. The early pros, like the college athletes of a later era, were paid "under the table." The halo of amateurism was maintained pro forma, if not de facto.

In 1869, the first acknowledged professional club came into existence. Harry Wright, one of the great players of his time, teamed up with "money-man" A. B. Champion, a Cincinnati lawyer, to organize the professional Cincinnati Red Stockings. He arranged a schedule of "championship" games that took the team from the Atlantic westward to the Mississippi, and back again.

The tour was an artistic success. The team played 57 games, winning 56 and tying one. In the process, they traveled nearly 12,000 miles and played before more than 280,000 paid customers. Financially, the tour proved to be another story. Total gate receipts were $29,726.26. Salaries and expenses totaled $29,724.87. Net profit—$1.39. Hardly the sort of figures to appeal to business tycoons, or "quick-buck" promoters.

The professional idea caught on; in the next ten years new clubs sprang up in profusion, but without organization and without any central control. The result was chaos. Proselyting, gambling, player piracy, umpire baiting, bribery and thrown games became commonplace. Baseball, its popularity as a sandlot game undiminished, became completely discredited as professional entertainment. What promised to be a merry life, threatened instead to become a very short one.

Professional baseball needed help desperately. It got it from William Hulbert, Chicago businessman and baseball buff, then president of the Chicago club. Hulbert himself was no paragon of sportsmanlike virtues. He lived in an era of rugged individualism, when might made right. He was an arrogant man, quick-tempered and self-centered.

In newspapers of his day, he was accused of being ruthless. He was. He was accused of being power mad. He accepted the charge as a compliment. Boston newspapers called him a "pirate" and he was flattered. In fact, it was the "theft" of four players from the Boston club that enabled him to field a championship team in Chicago.

When Hulbert conceived the idea of forcing an organized league, the man he chose as his partner and supporter was another of the same ilk—A. G. Spalding. Spalding himself had been guilty of breaking his Boston contract under the lure of Hulbert money.

After a mixture of "round-the-corner" conniving and political strongarming, Hulbert was ready. He called (commanded is probably more accurate) a meeting. It was held on February 2, 1876, at the old Broadway Central Hotel in New York City. Present were representatives of eight clubs—Chicago, Boston, Cincinnati, New York (Mutuals), Philadelphia, St. Louis, Hartford, and Louisville. When the meeting was called to order, Hulbert proceeded to lock the door and put the key in his pocket.

"Gentlemen," he said (according to A. G. Spalding in *The National Game*), "I have locked the door to prevent any intrusions from without, and to make it impossible for any of you to get out until I have finished what I have to say to you."

He then went on to outline the selfish need for organization if professional baseball was to be a financial success. He reached into his pocket and produced a proposed constitution, which he had previously prepared, and moved for the formation of the National League of Professional Baseball Clubs, Inc.

If there was an inclination for argument or dissent, that locked door was an effective deterrent. The hour was late, and the assembled "magnates" were hungry. The vote was unanimous. Professional baseball, as we know it today, was off and running.

Perhaps William Hulbert was all the things his critics said he was. Certainly his methods, measured by our modern regulatory system, were arbitrary and illegal. But they followed the business "ethics" laid down by other, and more important, empire builders of his era. Certainly, Messrs. Rockefeller, Carnegie, Frick, Vanderbilt, et al., were not exactly plaster saints either. They set up the rules. Hulbert proved to be an apt pupil.

The objectives of the new league, as written into the Constitution read at that closed-door meeting, have never been changed. They remain today as starkly simple and eloquently apt, as the day they were written:

First—to encourage, foster and elevate the game of Baseball.

Second—to enact and enforce proper rules for the exhibition and conduct of the game.

Third—to make baseball playing respectable and honorable.

No game, no industry, has ever had its goals and its obligations spelled out more simply or more effectively.

I cannot but feel that Fate must be given an assist, if not full partnership, in the development of modern professional baseball. Hulbert furnished the drive—but the timing of his drive was happy coincidence.

There were no monopoly or antitrust laws in those days. There was no socially minded Congress, scrutinizing every move that business made. There were no Supreme Court decisions to bar or restrict. Public consciousness had not yet been aroused to individual rights and privileges. Paternalistic industrialism was the standard economic principle; industrialists had the economic bit in their teeth, and baseball could ride the coattails of business in its operation.

If a community failed to support a team, the solution was easy—move to a greener pasture. Franchise shifting was as much a part of normal procedure as expansion has become today. When a problem arose, a rule was passed to solve it. No questions asked. If a given rule failed to work it was replaced by a new one, with little fear of questioned legality or public condemnation.

It was in that atmosphere that the now controversial "reserve clause" came into being. Though the reserve clause has received a lot of publicity in recent years, very little has been written of its organization. Shortly after the league was organized, there was a plague of contract jumping and player pirating. Players left clubs in midseason under the inducement of higher salaries elsewhere. Successful club operators, without a qualm of conscience or thought of public reaction, abetted the practice. As a result, competition was destroyed, and public confidence in the integrity of players and owners was shaken.

In 1879, the first reserve rule was passed, permitting clubs to reserve five players for the coming season. That helped, but didn't solve the situation. Oddly enough, the greatest objection came from the players themselves—not because they objected to being reserved but "because the player who was not reserved was thereby discredited as a performer, his reputation injured, and his standing with the fans destroyed." The reserve list, as a result, was increased to eleven, then to twelve, and eventually to include the entire club roster.

The new plan worked. Contract jumping and piracy ended. And, despite the fears of some players, salaries increased as competition between clubs was improved and public confidence in player integrity restored. By the time legal questions were raised, and monopoly and antitrust laws passed, the reserve clause had proved itself. Its value, even its necessity, in preserving the integrity and the competition, had been essential to the game's success.

Twenty-five years of unhampered trial-and-error operation enabled baseball to establish the ability of a professional sport to operate as a self-governing body, under a code that modern laws never would have allowed to develop.

One cannot defend the "buccaneering" methods of business and industry in those free and easy days of a past century. Nor can one decry the laws and regulations that the courts and a wise Congress have imposed to guarantee the rights of its citizens. At the same time, one wonders what would have happened if today's laws had been effective in those days.

Perhaps there would have been no great railway systems, or oil empires, or vast steel corporations. Perhaps, too, there would have been no professional baseball, self-governing and self-policing, and no professional football or basketball or other team sports. Today those other sports have ridden home free on the coattails of a code established by baseball in its infant era of "free enterprise and rugged individualism."

A newspaper friend of mine, nearly half a century ago, penned this cryptic line: "Baseball must be a helluva game to survive all these years despite the guys who run it." Maybe he was right.

2

THE PROS TAKE OVER

Modern professional baseball really dates from the beginning of the twentieth century. It was at that time that newspapers opened their pages to sports as part of the daily news diet. Records, hitherto a hit-or-miss recital of sports highlights, became an authentic part of the game. In those early years of the century the American League came into being to create a competitive two-league system. An organized minor-league structure was set up to make the game truly national in scope, and the World Series first brought sensational climax to a long summer of competitive struggle.

Most important, sportswriting became an honored profession, and sports pages a priceless inspiration to a sports-minded public. Without the interest and support of these writers, without their sturdy defense when warranted and their severe criticism when justified, baseball would have been the loser.

With the coming of organized competition, there came, too, a hardy group of men willing to devote their time and their money to promoting the game, in anticipation of a lot of fun and some hope of future profit. Club owners and officials have, through the years, contributed much to the success of the game—yet by the very nature of their jobs they were born to be whipping boys. They couldn't help themselves. The public nature of the game inevitably makes them public targets—their every move open to public discussion, every decision subject to public argument. It was in this early part of the century that a newspaperman wrote: "Baseball must be a helluva game to survive all these years despite the guys who run it." Yet baseball has survived. And despite criticism, no small part of that success is due to the fact that owners have, on occasion, been ruthless, and selfish, and tyrannical.

Strangely enough, some of the practices and procedures that are accepted policy in private trade or industry, in politics and in government, become public scandals when they occur in baseball. That has to be a high tribute to the integrity of the game, and to the place it holds in the esteem of the public. If the time ever comes when fans no longer exert their right to "boo" happenings on the playing field or in the front office; if sportswriters ever surrender their policing rights, or become blasé to the machinations and manipulations of individuals and leagues, then baseball, and the entire sports world, will be in serious trouble.

Baseball people have made mistakes. They have been guilty, at times, of selfish ruthlessness. They have, on occasion, cut a corner to attain a personal end. From time to time they have refused to adopt progressive measures that would benefit the game, perhaps because they saw it as a threat to their personal profit or merely because they didn't want to upset the status quo. For such action, they have been criticized.

But it always seemed to me unfair to use baseball as a scapegoat for national sins of commission or omission. Baseball never posed as a self-appointed leader in social and economic reform. It does not attempt to set legal precedents or standards of human behavior. In its sins and its virtues it only reflects the spirit of the times, a cross section of contemporary life. Because of its popularity with the masses, it does afford a perfect sounding-board for public expression. It should not be used as a whipping boy for governmental and business shortcomings, or as an alibi for a hurting national conscience.

Even from the professional and business angle, the "Lords of Baseball" are the products of their era—no more money mad, no more piratical, no more ruthless and selfish than their peers in contemporary religion and government, business and communications.

Entering the new century, the National League was sitting pretty. They had the professional field to themselves. Most of their serious problems, they thought, were behind them. The league, after years of turmoil, was fairly stabilized. Competition had either been assimilated or ruthlessly eliminated. The corner saloon atmosphere of earlier days had been done away with. Open park betting had been brought under control. The league smugly prepared to settle down and enjoy life—and profits—with a complacency born of complete domination and public approval.

But, fortunately for the development of the game, the dream proved only a fantasy. Out of the West came trouble, in the person of a young Cincinnati newspaperman named Byron Bancroft Johnson. Johnson had a deep love for, and an abiding faith in, the future of the game. Even more important, he craved a share of the fame and the profits he was convinced were ready at hand.

His American League, organized the year before, was thriving. He had financial support. Charles Spink and his newspaper, *The Sporting News*, were in Johnson's corner. What he sought was recognition, and major league status.

In the beginning, Johnson's approach was entirely friendly. He appeared at a National League meeting, hat in hand, to discuss the possibility of securing eastern franchises for his already flourishing organization. Instead of hearing his proposition, the National League sneaked an adjournment, and left Johnson twiddling his thumbs in the hotel foyer. To take action like that against any man is rude. In the case of Ban Johnson, it also proved to be the spark that set off a war.

First, Johnson cut his minor league ties by abrogating the National Agreement. Then he raided the enemy's ranks with devastating sweeps. Of 182 American League players that first season, 111 came directly from the National League. Included were such stars as Cy Young, Larry Lajoie, Jimmy Collins, and Clark Griffith.

A few withstood Johnson's efforts, including a fiery little Irishman named John McGraw. In fact, while Johnson was luring National League stars to his new league, McGraw deserted Johnson's ship to go to New York to manage the New York Giants. McGraw's decision started one of the most famous and longest lasting feuds in baseball history. From that time on, McGraw and Johnson were bitter enemies, and remained so throughout their lives.

But a feud or two wasn't going to stop Ban Johnson. He carried his fight to the field, and to the clubhouse. He fought through the newspapers, and through an excited public. It was the shortest and most successful fight in baseball history. By 1902, Johnson's league was firmly established as a major league. By 1903, he had invaded the East successfully, including McGraw's own New York territory. At the same time, he had forced the National League into the first World Series in history. He needed only one thing more, and he got it when his Boston team defeated the favored Pittsburgh Pirates in that World Series.

The following year, McGraw got a modicum of revenge. When his New York Giants won the pennant in the National League, he refused to play the American League champions in the World Series, calling them upstarts. By the next year, an agreement was reached, and the World Series was played. The National League team—led by McGraw—beat Philadelphia four games to one, with every victory a shutout. Three of the victories were recorded by Giants immortal Christy Mathewson.

Johnson was humiliated, of course. He hated to lose, and especially to McGraw. But he had won the war, and baseball was off and running, in a new century of new goals and new accomplishments, with Ban Johnson the dominant figure in the game.

Johnson was a driving man, arrogant and ruthless at times. He made worthwhile friends and then, because of this arrogance, saw them turn against him. But he was a good captain. He was the first executive in baseball to insist on discipline on the playing field; he eliminated rowdyism from the parks and clubhouses; he insisted that players had an obligation to the public off the field as well as on—and he made his rulings stick.

It was Johnson who first took up the cudgels for the downtrodden umpires, backing them to the limit. He cloaked them with authority, which permitted them to establish dignity and respect for their profession.

From 1901 through the First World War, he ruled with an

iron hand—not only his own league, but pretty much all baseball. He never ducked a fight. He was never neutral. He was unforgiving in his enmities, and blind to any shortcomings in his friends. He was intolerant of opposition and enraged by criticism.

In my years of contact as a newspaperman, I never once heard him mention the American League as such. It was always "The g-r-r-eat American League." Nor did I ever hear him mention the National League by name. It was always "that other league."

The end, of course, was inevitable. His own arrogance and ruthlessness caught up with him. The White Sox scandal of 1919 left him dazed. He couldn't believe it. His world of rule and discipline was upset. He resented the ensuing appointment of Judge Landis as commissioner, and challenged his authority at every turn. He fought hard—but for the first time in his career he was overmatched. His lifelong friend, Charles Comiskey, deserted him. Colonel Ruppert, of the New York Yankees, Frank Navin, of Detroit, and other American League owners sided with Judge Landis. The cards were stacked. The American League he had created had outgrown him. Either Johnson must surrender, or the league would fall apart. There was no other choice. Johnson had to be retired, and he was.

I never knew Johnson intimately during the years of his strength. At the time I knew him well, he was an old and broken man surrounded by enemies, and alienated from his friends by his own vindictiveness.

I did cover the meeting in Chicago when he was retired from office. It was a long meeting, and outside the door waiting newspapermen speculated that he might still win out. Finally, the door opened, and a league representative read a short announcement. Ban Johnson, he said, had been granted retirement under pension provisions acceptable to him.

We asked to talk to Mr. Johnson. He had left the meeting, the spokesman said, and was not available. I never saw him again.

A few years ago, on a trip to Indiana, I happened into Seymour and paid a visit to his grave. It was weed-grown, and not well cared for. A simple, chipped stone marked his resting place. It read "Byron Bancroft Johnson. Founder of the American League."

Nothing more. Just a small line to memorialize a lifetime of dedication.

Yet there is another monument to his memory that thousands see each year. It hangs in Baseball's Hall of Fame, surrounded by other plaques immortalizing other and younger men, whose deeds and accomplishments have added luster and stature to baseball throughout the years. Ban Johnson belongs in that array. In his time he was baseball's greatest emissary—and his own worst enemy.

Sic transit gloria.

Those years from 1900 through the First World War could well be called the Ban Johnson era. Certainly he dominated the scene. But if he was the aggressive leader—a flaming comet in the baseball skies—he did not stand alone. He was surrounded by able and determined men who rallied to his banner when the going got tough—men like Charles Comiskey, president and owner of the Chicago White Sox; Connie Mack and the Shibe brothers, of Philadelphia; and Clark Griffith, the famous old pitcher who managed the New York American League club at its inception, and then moved to Washington and became a sports landmark in the nation's capital. They were among the greats who sat in the council of the American League during its fight for recognition and greatness.

Meanwhile, in the camp of the opposition National League, were other greats who fought to keep Johnson's domination in balance, and build up the healthy league rivalry that exists today. To recount in detail the battles and skirmishes that added zest to a growing rivalry would require volumes, and serve little purpose. Today, they are largely forgotten. But the true story of professional baseball and its development cannot be told without a low salaam toward men like Pittsburgh's Barney Dreyfus, Cincinnati's Garry Herrmann, John McGraw, Brooklyn's Charley Ebbets, Arthur Soden, of Boston, and others of the National League who helped carry the torch of baseball through a dark, and sometimes bloody era. Fortunately, that era was as brief as it was violent.

It's interesting to note that about the only names of that era that arouse a flicker of recognition among today's fans are those of the men who won fame on the field, and not through front-office bickering—McGraw and Mack, Mathewson and Young, Cobb and Wagner, to mention a few. By 1905, when the first official World Series was staged, the players had taken over the headlines; batting and pitching records displaced league meetings in public interest; and the "Lords of Baseball" passed into a semioblivion that has never been entirely dissipated. The game was the thing—and the role of the front office, like that of the maligned umpire, was one of silent unobtrusiveness.

From Carnegie, Pennsylvania, a giant bowlegged Dutchman named Honus Wagner rode into baseball immortality on the power of his bat, and his good right arm; from Lehigh came a handsome college boy named Christy Mathewson to capture the public's fancy; from Royston, Georgia, emerged a fiery, young Tyrus Cobb to set new standards, and leave behind him, like so many broken sticks, most of the marks in the record books. Out of Coffeyville, Kansas, came Walter Johnson to add a new dimension to pitching speed and control. A Larry Lajoie deserted his cab in Rhode Island, and from the campus of Columbia University came an agile Eddie Collins. Both were to dazzle fans and writers alike with the magic of their wizardry around second base.

In Chicago, Frank Chance and his Cubs won four pennants and two World Series over a five-year period, first of the great teams to capture the imagination of the fans. Among those who reacted was a writer for the *New York Globe* named Franklin P. Adams. He wrote a piece of verse entitled "Baseball's Sad Lexicon," which sang the praises of the Cubs' double-play combination—Tinker to Evers to Chance. Almost single-handedly that poem was later to carry those three players into baseball's holy of holies, the Hall of Fame in Cooperstown.

Baseball began its first expansion era. It was to bring increased rivalries on the field. The demand for playing strength created rivalries off the field, too, and a new dimension came to front-office operations. In the villages and small towns, on the farm and the city sandlots, there grew a diverse group of self-appointed "bird-dogs." As age robbed the game of its stars, these men dedicated themselves to the finding of successors for the retiring heroes.

The work of these pioneer "bird-dogs" was, in the beginning, largely a labor of love. Old-time ball players, watching sandlot games in their communities, would contact their favorite clubs with a tip on a likely prospect. Bartenders and grocers vied with school teachers and bankers in combing the countryside. All wanted to find that young man who could either "hit the ball a country mile" or "knock a squirrel from a tree with a stone three times out of five, at twenty paces."

Tradition has it that John McGraw picked up at least three of the star players of his early championship teams on the recommendation of the barber who gave McGraw his daily shave. Whether this is fact or folklore, I can't say. But in later years I did hear Miller Huggins say, on many occasions, that Rogers Hornsby was first brought to the attention of the St. Louis Cardinals by a fan who saw Rog doing his thing on a sandlot diamond in Winters, Texas.

In any event, these unknown and unsung enthusiasts made great contributions to the game during these hectic times. They also laid the foundation for the present vast and organized scouting systems, the greatest ever devised for any sport anywhere—a systematic manhunt procedure that must at times have made the late Mr. Hoover and the FBI turn green with envy.

That's why I have to smile at the complaints that baseball is so organized today that many youngsters are denied professional opportunity. Bunk! The scouting system as operated today is almost foolproof. Because the scouts are professionals, they do not advertise their coming and going. They do not boast of their signings, or pop off to their friends about the great prospects they have discovered. But they're on the job, scouring the sandlots, high schools, colleges, junior leagues and semipros, for hidden, unknown talent. This is true not only in the fifty states, but in South and Central America, Canada, Japan, Australia—wherever baseball is played.

If a youngster can run and throw; if he can hit a ball and catch it; and if he has the competitive spirit, chances are that he will be looked at not once, but often. And not by one scout, but by several. If he doesn't want to be looked at, he's in big trouble. Maybe, in that case, he ought to move to Timbuctu. He'll be safe there. Reasonably safe, anyway.

During those two decades of original expansion, two crises arose, that for a time threatened serious disruption of the game. One affected the organizational structure, and brought the Establishment back into the headlines with a vengeance. That was the formation of the Federal League, with the attendant raids and contract jumpings.

This threatened to wreck the whole baseball structure on the heretofore submerged legal reef of antitrust laws, and their application to the "reserve clause" under which baseball operated.

It was a short war, but a tough one. Huge financial losses brought individual clubs to the brink of bankruptcy. But while the owners bled, players and public had a field day. There was excitement galore: more places to go, more heroes to admire, more enemies to condemn, more issues to argue publicly, more dollars to spend. It is an old adage that no one ever wins a war. That is broadly true. But out of war frequently comes change and reform that rebounds to the benefit of both combatants and sideline public. That was true with baseball.

The two major leagues, bitter in their enmities, were forced to join together to fight for a common cause. They learned, the hard way, that cooperation was better than personal feud, and mutual respect more productive than public deprecation. For the first time since its inception professional baseball became united in a true joint venture for the benefit of the game.

The players profited, too. Salaries, disgustingly stagnant through the years, moved upward. Playing conditions were improved. Better hotels and better living conditions were provided. Most important, salary discussions, previously a back-room, shuttered-window affair, emerged into the sunlight of sports headlines and public discussions. The reaction was expected, but effective. Fans sided with the players, and a sympathetic public became a prime weapon against management in a majority of cases.

The fans, perhaps, benefited most of all. Owners became suddenly aware of the importance of public relations. Parks were cleaned up and made comfortable. Modern toilets were installed. Eating and drinking facilities were provided. For the first time professional baseball moved into the parlor to become a family game.

Perhaps it is unfair to baseball to attribute all these reforms to the Federal League war, and its aftermath. Probably they would have occurred through natural process and the passage of time. But the war speeded things up—and baseball was better for it.

But as Hy Turkin pointed out in his *Encyclopedia of Baseball*, the price of peace was high. It was necessary for the leagues to take over $385,000 of players' contracts. A couple of Federal Leaguers became a part of the baseball structure. Charley Weeghman was permitted to operate the Chicago Cubs, and Phil Ball stepped in as owner of the St. Louis Browns. In addition, sizable payments spread over twenty years cut deeply into baseball's coffers. (When I became president of the National League in 1934, that league was still making an annual payment of $20,000 to clear up the debt.)

Nor was that all. Darkness deepened even further over the game when the Federal League club of Baltimore, unhappy over the settlement, instituted an antitrust suit against baseball for triple damages of several million dollars. Less hardy owners might have tossed in the sponge. But they were born fighters, those old boys. They fought back. What looked like a death blow to the struggling establishment was, instead, to become its greatest blessing. The Supreme Court, with Mr. Justice Holmes writing the opinion, ruled in 1922 that baseball was a sport, and was not a business engaged in interstate commerce.

Sometimes the dice do come seven.

With the end of the Federal League it seemed baseball was off and running. There was a new spirit of cooperation between the leagues. Older owners were discarding their "public be damned" attitude in the operation of their business.

Newer owners were ready with newer ideas—ideas of cooperation with the press and public, and new concepts of their responsibility for the honesty and integrity of the game. Women and children were being made welcome to games, and extended consideration and courtesy, where once they were barely tolerated.

Players, with better salaries and increased bargaining power, took additional pride in their on-field accomplishments—and more interest in their off-field status.

All was right with the world—or so it seemed. Public interest was maintained even during the First World War. Baseball, it seemed, was highballing down an open track under open throttle. But the greatest crisis the game ever faced loomed just ahead.

That crisis, literally, broke overnight. It was the White Sox scandal—with seven members of that team accused of conspiring with gamblers to throw the 1919 World Series.

I was a kid reporter in Colorado Springs in those days, far

removed from the scene of the action, yet I will never forget the reaction of the fans when the news reached our town. They didn't believe it. It made no sense. The White Sox were one of the best—if not *the* best—teams in baseball. Their players were great stars, heroes of every kid in the land. It just couldn't happen:

Joe Jackson, Happy Felsch, Eddie Cicotte, Buck Weaver, Lefty Williams, Swede Risberg, Fred McMullin! The fans' initial shock turned into anger, then disillusionment, and vindictiveness. They had been let down by the men they most admired. Their faith in the honesty and integrity of baseball, so carefully nurtured through the years, was shattered. Their idols had been completely discredited for a few paltry dollars.

As I experienced the reaction of these fans, thousands of miles away, I couldn't help but think how much more catastrophic the news must be to fans on the scene—fans who actually watched and rooted for these men from the stands. For the first time in my life, I really became aware of the great hold baseball had on the American public. For the first time I really appreciated the faith of the public in the honesty and integrity of the game. That day I experienced firsthand the tragedy of a youngster when he first realizes that his greatest heroes might have feet of clay.

For weeks the whole future of baseball rode in precarious balance. That the public was disillusioned was obvious. The big question was whether or not public confidence, once destroyed, could ever be restored.

The newspapers, once the initial shock had passed, rallied their forces to save the game. Owners met in solemn session to establish penalties and rules that they hoped would head off, or at least discourage, future scandals. Thoughtful fans, while condemning the deed, urged an upset public to forgive and forget.

And most of all, a Kindly Providence must have had the welfare of the game at heart, to send around the clincher in restoring public interest.

For, as the dark clouds faded, and the sun began to break through,

ALONG CAME RUTH!

3

ALONG CAME RUTH

*You step up to the platter
And you gaze with flaming hate
At the poor benighted pitcher
As you dig in at the plate.
You watch him cut his fast ball loose,
Then swing your trusty bat
And you park one in the bleachers—
Nothing's simpler than that!*

Babe Ruth's formula for hitters

Attempting to measure Babe Ruth's greatness by standard rule, or mathematical formula, is like trying to thread a needle while wearing boxing gloves. Standard yardsticks might suffice for ordinary mortals. Not for Babe. He was different!

Somehow, everything he did was done in the grand manner and became etched in memory, like the harmonies of a great symphony or the impressiveness of an erupting volcano as seen in slow motion.

His home runs brought a sense of the theatrical never quite attained by a Foxx, or a Gehrig, or a Hornsby; or in later years by a Williams, a DiMaggio, a Mays or a Mantle. Even the foul balls, or so-called "pops" to the infield, seemed to soar to more majestic heights, and present greater problems than those hit by other players. As for strikeouts—and Babe had many—his "strike three swinging" brought almost as many oohs and aahs from the spectators as a drive into the bleachers by an ordinary player.

The Babe had "charisma," if I may use a modern word to describe what, in those days, we dismissed as crowd appeal. He captured the imagination of the public as no man before or since. And

27

he did it in that golden age of champions, when every sport had a special claimant for public affection.

Golf had its Hagen, and its Bobby Jones. Tennis, its Tilden, and Lenglen, and Wills. Tommy Hitchcock, a recent World War ace, was blazing new trails of greatness in international polo. Jack Dempsey, probably the most exciting champion boxing has ever known, dominated the fight world, abetted by such figures as Mickey Walker and Benny Leonard. In football, the genius of Rockne, and the talent of the Four Horsemen, vied with Red Grange for the autumnal headlines. But through it all, to the sports public, Babe Ruth was No. 1. As a newspaperman, I covered them all. I recognized that each sport's hero or heroes were deserving. But I also knew that the public was right. There was only one Ruth.

Even his coming to New York was spectacular. He came to the Yankees in a deal between their owner, Colonel Jacob Ruppert, and Harry Frazee, owner of the Boston Red Sox. The deal was labeled by New England fans as a "second Boston Massacre." Boston fans, and the Boston press, have always been noted for their low boiling points, and on this occasion they really blew their tops.

Frazee was threatened with tar and feathers. Ruppert, a bachelor, was condemned as "an immigrant millionaire brewer" without pride of ancestry or hope of posterity. For a time, it looked like another baseball war was inevitable, particularly when subsequent deals brought Ed Barrow, the Red Sox manager, to the Yankees' front office, and with him players of such stature as infielder Everett Scott, and pitchers Waite Hoyt, Carl Mays, Joe Bush, Sam Jones, and Herb Pennock.

As a matter of fact, these deals did wreck a great Boston club, and for many seasons turned Fenway Park into a baseball graveyard. It was not until Tom Yawkey bought the club, and restored the hopes of disillusioned fans, that the Red Sox regained respectability.

The whole story was summed up best by the late W. O. McGeehan in the old *Morning Herald* when, tongue in cheek, he wrote: "It's the only case in all baseball history in which a new stadium was traded for a Broadway musical production." In a sense, McGeehan was telling the truth. Frazee, a theatrical producer, got enough cash through the deals to underwrite the production of *No,*

No, Nanette, one of the great money-makers of the era. Colonel Ruppert emerged with a championship team, the beginning of baseball's greatest dynasty, and what was historically the greatest monument to one man's popularity with the fans—Yankee Stadium, "The House That Ruth Built."*

The greatest gainer of all from the bizarre deals was not the two principals but baseball itself. The cloud that hovered as a result of the White Sox scandal began to dissipate. Sports pages are basically dedicated to accomplishment rather than to defeat and failure, and deeds of derring-do are ever more appealing to sportsmen than chronicles of disaster. Fans, lured by the emergence of a new hero, flocked to the parks in increasing numbers. Sportswriters found good copy in the Babe's penchant for the spectacular, on the field and off. The scandal that had threatened the game's existence suddenly was relegated to the background as an unpleasant incident in an otherwise happy existence.

The advent of Babe Ruth should not be given sole credit for restoring public confidence in the game. The owners themselves took a couple of huge steps. First, they strengthened the rules protecting the integrity of the game. Then they brought Judge Kenesaw Mountain Landis from the Federal Court bench to enforce them as the game's first commissioner. But the Babe played an important part. He was the right man, in the right place, at the right time. Thanks to him, baseball was able to step into a new era with its head held high.

One thing sure, the game has never been the same since Babe came on the scene. Previously the home run had been something to talk about. It was a rare thrill for fans when it occurred, but it was largely regarded as a lucky accident due to a lapse in pitching skill. It was considered of minor importance in the business of winning pennants and world championships.

In those days, offensive strategy was based on the Willie Keeler philosophy, "Hit 'em where they ain't." It called for the slashing base running of a Ty Cobb; the speed and base-stealing genius of a Max

---

* In 1971, Yankee Stadium was still one of New York's great attractions, and Broadway's biggest hit was a revival of *No, No, Nanette*. Unfortunately, both Colonel Ruppert and Harry Frazee were long gone.

Carey or an Eddie Collins. The bunt, the hit-and-run, the squeeze play, were the common weapons of attack. John McGraw once fined one of his stars (Red Murray, I think it was) twenty-five dollars for taking a full swing and hitting a home run when the bunt sign was on. The pre-Ruth era was a pitcher's world. Shutouts and one-run wins were standard. A two- or three-run lead was a virtual shoo-in. Babe Ruth changed all that.

The action and power Ruth brought into the game not only won newspaper headlines for him; more importantly, it brought cash customers into the stands, and cash customers are the backbone of professional baseball. The Yankees became the biggest draw in the game—both at home and on the road. Owners prospered, and their prosperity was reflected in the players' contracts.

Joe Dugan, then the Yankees third baseman, summed up the feeling of most of the players. When a reporter asked Dugan if the other players were jealous of Ruth's home run publicity, Dugan said, "Jealous, hell. I hope the Big Guy hits a thousand. Every one he hits out of the park puts another ten bucks in Dugan's pocket."

One day the same Dugan was sitting out a minor injury, and watched the game from the Yankee Stadium press box. He listened for a while to a baseball writer dictating his play-by-play. Finally, Dugan grinned and said, "I don't know why you bother to come up here every day to send that stuff. You could do it just as well sitting at home. It's always the same. Combs walks. Koenig singles. Ruth hits one out of the park. Gehrig doubles. Meusel singles. Lazzeri triples. Then Dugan goes in the dirt on his can."

Some baseball people were not prepared to accept the message that Ruth was delivering to them. But within two years even the most stubborn owner had seen the light. Power was the thing. Scouts no longer concentrated on speed and fancy fielding. They started scouring the sandlots for the broad-shouldered boys who could lay into the ball. If the youngster showed speed afoot, or could make sparkling plays in the field, so much the better. But first of all he had to have a strong arm, and be able to hit with power. Offensive play had taken over. The way was being paved for whole new generations of home-run hitters. Tape measures would become standard clubhouse equipment. Baseball writers would find themselves studying velocity, and the mathematics of height and distance. The power of Babe Ruth's swing had truly added a new dimension to baseball.

Reggie Jackson's gargantuan blast that hit the lighting standard atop the right-center-field stands of Detroit's Tiger Stadium in the 1971 All-Star Game undoubtedly was one of the longest ever hit by any player. Ted Williams says it was the hardest hit ball he had ever seen, and Ted certainly qualifies as an expert witness. Whether that particular drive set a new distance mark I cannot say. But no one will ever convince me that Reggie's blast was hit harder than one the Babe hit in that same stadium long before Reggie Jackson or most of the other stars of today were born.

There were no double-deck right-field stands in Navin Field in those days. A concrete wall, probably thirty feet, ran from inside the right-field foul line to the stands in left center. A paved avenue (Plum Street, I think it was) led from downtown Detroit, and dead-ended at a right angle to the wall in right center. The press box in those days was high up against the roof, and scribes had a perfect view for three or four blocks beyond the wall and down Plum Street.

In the sixth or seventh inning, Babe really got hold of one—a typical Ruthian blast, golfed high in the air, with all the power of those great shoulders behind it. The ball soared high, and majestically, to clear the wall by a good thirty feet. It carried Woodward as well, and hit squarely on the pavement of Plum Street. There it took a couple of mighty bounces, and continued to roll down the concrete. From the press box we watched as a kid on a bicycle gave chase. At the end of two blocks, where houses intercepted our view, the kid was still pedaling madly, and the ball was still going strong. I don't know whether or not the youngster ever got the ball.

The next day, Harry Salsinger stepped off the distance from the wall to the spot in the street where the rolling ball and the kid on the bicycle were last seen. He figured that from home plate, the ball had traveled between 800 and 850 feet. Maybe Reggie's wallop was harder hit but, believe me, Babe's effort traveled a "right pert distance."

The Detroit ball park has long enjoyed a reputation as a "hitter's park," and nobody gave better testimony of that than the

Babe. I recall another that he hit in Detroit on a Sunday, before a capacity crowd. Back of dead center field and across the street, paralleling the ball park, there was a two-story brick building. On its roof there was a huge sign extolling the virtue of "ROSINK'S PANTS." The sign was plainly visible from the press box, and the writers used to argue about the possibility of a ball ever reaching that sign. A believer in that possibility was a droll young man from the New York *Daily News* named Marshall Hunt. Hunt once wound up his story with the observation: "Old man Rosink better put a fence around that sign, or someday he's going to be caught with his pants down."

That Sunday it happened.

The Babe connected—and the ball was still climbing when it cleared the fence in dead center field. It carried across the street with sufficient height and velocity to smack into the sign atop the two-story building. I can't say that Mr. Rosink lost his pants, as Hunt predicted, but I do know that a lot of "freeloader" spectators, watching the game from atop the building, scattered like frightened pigeons as the Babe delivered his bombastic message.

The carrying distance? Well, the center field fence was well over 400 feet from home plate. The street was at least 40 feet wide. The two-story building where the ball finally landed must have been about 30 feet high. Figure it out yourself. I'm no good at higher mathematics.

That sign is long gone, and the building with it. But so long as I live, whenever I think of Babe Ruth and his great record, and whenever long drives are mentioned, I will always think of Rosink's pants.

Maybe advertising does pay off, after all.

Two other home runs stand out in my memory—not because they were extremely long or particularly spectacular—but because they demonstrated the complete confidence of the man, and his uncanny ability to rise to an occasion. All great champions have that power. Great fighters never quit. They get up off the floor, and go on to win. In football, any ball carrier can look good when his interference clears the way to an open field. But only champions consistently come through in the clutch to battle and claw their way to that extra three or four yards that might spell touchdown and victory.

Call it "heart" or "luck," or whatever you will. Champions all have it—and Babe Ruth had it in abundance.

Both the home runs I'm talking about were hit in 1927. The first occurred in Comiskey Park in Chicago. It was a weekday game in mid-August. The Yankees were leading the league by a wide margin. They were scheduled to leave immediately after the ball game for the Englewood station to catch a 5:15 train for New York.

A mere handful of fans dozed in the stands. In the press box and on the Yankees bench, chief interest centered on getting the game over in time to ensure a leisurely ride to the train.

Mike Cvengros, a little left-hander, was pitching for the White Sox, and old warhorse, Herbie Pennock, equally left-handed, for the Yankees. The game developed into a terrific pitchers' battle. The Yankees scored a run in the second. The White Sox tied it up in the fourth. The score remained tied, inning after inning.

Meanwhile, Mark Roth, the Yankees traveling secretary, paced nervously up and down the clubhouse, as the clock ticked its way closer and closer to train time. Finally, the problem reached the point where Roth was beside himself. He went down to the bench, to tell his troubles to manager Miller Huggins.

As he walked into the dugout, Ruth spotted him.

"Hey, Markie," roared Ruth, "you look worried. What's the trouble?"

"If this game goes much longer, we're going to blow the train home. We're checked out of the hotel. The A's are checking in to-night. We're in a hell of a fix."

Ruth grinned, and said, "Hell's bells, Markie, why didn't you tell me? Tell you what you do. You have the buses moved around to the clubhouse door. I'm the third man up this inning, and I'll just hit one in the stands for you."

And he did exactly that. With a one-and-one count, he planted the ball in the upper deck, and as he pigeon-toed his way past third he waved gaily to the bench. "I told you we'd make that damn train," he yelled. Not yet to home plate, he hollered to bat boy Eddie Bennett, almost as an afterthought, "Eddie, keep out the bi-carb. I'm not feeling so good."

The other home run was one that does not appear in any record book, but is engraved in my memory far deeper than any printed word could be. The Yankees were playing an exhibition game in the old Calhoun Street park in Fort Wayne, Indiana, and my eighty-year-old Dad decided to drive in and see the game. Mark Roth took him down to the dugout and introduced him to all the players. Then he arranged a box seat right alongside the Yankee dugout. Babe was playing first base that day, as he usually did in exhibition games, and between innings he would stop and talk a bit with the old gentleman.

The game was a loosely played affair, and as the Yankees came to bat in the ninth inning the score was tied, 7 to 7. Babe stopped by Dad's seat as he came to the dugout. "Daddy," he boomed, "you look a little tired and a little hungry." Pop allowed as how he was. "Tell you what I'm gonna do. See those freight cars over there?" and he pointed toward the Nickel Plate tracks that ran along an embankment beyond the right field bleachers. "I'm gonna hit one over there for you, and we can all go to supper."

Again, Babe was as good as his word. He grinned and waved as he touched home plate, and trotted to the dugout. Pop went to supper, just as Babe had promised. That night, when I saw Dad, I asked him how he enjoyed the game. "It was swell," he said, "but there's something screwy about baseball when a man can call his shots like that. Why don't they have him hit one in every game, so all the fans could see it?"

My father lived to be ninety-four. He went to his grave firmly convinced that Babe Ruth could call his shots, and hit one out of the park anytime he felt like it. No one could convince him otherwise. After all, he had seen him do it.

Probably the most discussed, the best remembered, and the most controversial home run the Babe ever hit was the one off Charley Root, of the Chicago Cubs, in the third game of the 1932 World Series. Did he really call his shot? Did he actually point toward the stands, and then hit the ball where he had pointed? That question is still moot—and will be, I suppose, until the last surviving spectator has gone to his reward.

The situation was dramatic. Root's first pitch was a ball. The second was a called strike. On the third pitch the Babe swung at a low outside fast ball—and missed. Strike two! At that point, Ruth stepped from the box, dusted his hands, and then raised his right arm, with one finger extended, in the now famous gesture.

Root pitched. There was a crack of the bat, a white blur as the ball took off, and a moment later the Babe was pigeon-toeing around the bases, grinning broadly as he doffed his cap to the roaring crowd. On the strength of that gesture, another Ruth legend had been born.

At the moment, there was no doubt in my mind, or in the minds of any of the writers who were covering the Yankees. The Big Guy had done it again. He had called his shot, and in the most spotlighted arena imaginable. A World Series game! That's what we wrote. That's what we believed.

Later that night Charley Root questioned the gesture. That Babe had raised one finger was evident. But, Root insisted, he did not point toward the stands. The one-finger gesture was the Babe's way of saying that he still had one big swing left. Knowing Charley Root as I did, I had to believe his sincerity. He was a great competitor and a tough loser, but he was honest, too, and fully prepared to give the Babe full credit as the greatest home run hitter of all time. Furthermore, Charley's version was backed by Gabby Hartnett, Cubs catcher, who quoted Ruth as remarking, as he made the gesture, that he still had one big one left.

Nor did Babe ever seem willing to make any claim. Some days later when I was doing a bit of "ghosting," I had occasion to bring up the subject with Babe. "Tell me, Jedgie," I asked him, "did you really point to the stands and call that shot?" The Babe grinned. "Jeez, kid," he replied, "you can read the papers, can't you? You know what the writers said." That was all he ever said to me on the subject—and to the best of my knowledge he never gave any different version to anyone else.

Not that it makes any difference. Both the principals are long gone—and the records offer eternal testimony to their mutual greatness. If Ruth did point to the bleachers and call a World Series home run, it only meant one other diadem in a crown already star-studded with heroic accomplishments. If he didn't, any denial means little. The legend will continue to exist. After all, to paraphrase an old adage: "The Ruth is mighty, and shall prevail."

Babe's social life and his antics off the field were as fantastic as his performances on the diamond. He loved life, and he lived it to the hilt. From the day he emerged from St. Mary's Industrial School for Boys in Baltimore, to the hour of his death, the world was his personal oyster. Every day was a new challenge, every night a promise of a new adventure. Yet, somehow, there never seemed to be anything vicious or sordid in his peccadilloes.

Ping Bodie, old-time Yankee outfielder, was Babe's first room-mate when Ruth joined the Yankees. One day Bodie remarked to a newspaperman who was traveling with the club: "I'll certainly be glad when this trip is over and we get back to New York. I'm tired of rooming with Babe Ruth's suitcase."

Some years later William J. (Bill) Slocum, veteran baseball writer, produced a song that was the outstanding hit at the annual New York Baseball Writers' Dinner. Bill was a close friend of Babe's, and loved him devotedly, as I did. He wrote the song, not in a spirit of carping criticism but rather as a kidding recognition of those extra-curricular activities that had become such a big part of the Babe Ruth legend through the years.

The song was presented in the show part of the Writers' Dinner as a soliloquy. It was sung by newspaperman Rud Rennie, in the role of Yankee manager Miller Huggins. Here's what Slocum wrote.

> *I wonder where my Babe Ruth is tonight*
> *He grabbed his hat and coat and ducked from sight.*
> *I wonder where he'll be*
> *At half past two or three—*
> *He may be at a dance or in a fight.*
> *He may be at some cozy roadside inn*
> *He may be drinking beer or maybe gin*
> *I know he's with a dame*
> *I wonder what's her name—*
> *I wonder where my Babe Ruth is tonight.*

The song took the dinner by storm, with the Babe himself leading the applause. Encore followed encore, and at the finish nearly a thousand diners were on their feet joining in the chorus. You can still hear it sung today when baseball writers get together for a little fun and frivolity. The song brings into focus the frailties that add warmth and understanding to cold, impersonal records.

Bill Slocum recognized more than the "beer and skittles" syndrome in Ruth's character. In another song, presented at the same Writers' Dinner a year later, he used the Babe as a foil in kidding Yankee failure. The Yankees had lost their championship form in 1925, and finished a lowly seventh. The team just didn't hit. The Babe, as the bellwether of Yankee success, was the natural target for Bill's kindly kidding in time of failure. The song this time had Babe himself singing (with Rennie again doing the lyrics in the role of Ruth).

> *Little curve ball, the Yankees all miss you*
> *They miss you in springtime and fall;*
> *With swings debonair*
> *They shatter the air,*
> *They hit everything but the ball!*
> *Bob Meusel, and Wardie, and Shangie and Pipp*
> *How great is their pride and their fall.*
> *They miss you, only you,*
> *Yet they miss quite a few*
> *But I miss you most of all!*

Babe liked that one, too.

I remember best the little things about Babe Ruth—his boyish enthusiasm that never dimmed; his patience with fans everywhere; his willingness to try anything, and his ability to laugh at himself in failure. I remember the brown cap he always wore. (Joe McCarthy didn't like caps, and declared himself pointedly on the subject in a clubhouse meeting when the Babe was present. That started a feud that endured as long as they both were with the Yankees.) Most of all, I remember his love for children, and his unfailing kindness and understanding where kids were concerned. That was especially true if the youngsters were underprivileged, or ill, or in trouble.

I'll never forget an incident in Pensacola, Florida. The Yankees were playing an exhibition game at the naval base. It was a humid, windy afternoon. A dust storm raged—typical Deep South clay dust—and before the first inning was over the players looked like red goblins from some faraway planet. It was the sort of day when the only desire was to get the game over as quickly as possible. The only goal was to get back to the hotel for a bath and a good supper before boarding the train for the next day's exhibition game.

It was one of the fastest games on record. Even as the last out was called, players and writers alike were making a beeline for the buses back to the hotel. All but the Babe. As the bus pulled out, he was still standing outside the gate, surrounded by jostling, yelling kids, and autographing like mad.

The club was due to entrain at 8:30, and at 7:45 Miller Huggins was pacing the lobby, muttering to himself because the Babe hadn't shown up. "If that big guy misses the train again, I'll fine him a month's salary," Hug sputtered. "I'll call Colonel Ruppert. I'll get him suspended. I'll, I'll . . ." At that moment, Ruth walked in, still in his grimy, sweaty uniform. "Who do you think you are, you big ape," Hug roared. "Where have you been? Don't you know we got a train to make? I ought to . . ."

"Oh, Hug, don't get so excited," Babe said, patting the little manager's shoulder. "Someday you'll have a stroke if you're not careful. Some kids were playing ball outside the park, and they wanted me to manage one of the teams. I did, and we won. You wouldn't want me to walk out on them, would you, Hug?"

Another typical Ruthian episode occurred in Knoxville, Tennessee, on the same spring barnstorming tour. The Yankees arrived in Knoxville in the early morning, after a torturous overnight ride from Nashville. Most of the players, including Ruth, went directly to their rooms to rest a bit before going to the ball park. Bob Meusel, stopping for a bite to eat, was alone in the dining room when a gray-haired little old Tennessee farmer sidled up to his table. Hat in hand, the old man timidly asked Bob if he knew where Mr. Ruth was.

"Nobody ever knows where Babe is," Bob said, "but he said he was going up to his room. Why do you want him?"

The old man held up a fifty-cent "Rocket" baseball. "I thought maybe he'd be willing to sign this baseball for my grandson. He's an orphan, and he lives with his Grandma and me. All spring long, he's been counting the days until Mr. Ruth came so he could go to the park and see him play. Now the boy's bad sick—typhoid fever—and

I guess he never will have a chance to see him." The old man sighed as he turned away, "Anyhow, he'll know I tried."

Meusel, never a garrulous man, motioned the old man back. "Hell," he said, "go pound on his door. He don't need too much sleep, anyhow."

The Babe was late getting to the ball park that afternoon, missing batting practice. He came onto the bench just as infield practice was ending. No one was much concerned. The Babe frequently came to the park late, particularly for exhibition games.

It was not until three or four days later that we got the story. Not only had Babe autographed the baseball, he had taken a taxicab eighteen miles into the mountains to sit by the boy's bedside through the morning. When he finally waved a cheery goodbye, he left behind a couple of autographed Yankee baseballs, a new glove, and a couple of bats that he had purchased at a store en route.

The story never made the papers. Bob Meusel knew about it, because he had first sent the old man up to Ruth's room. But Bob wasn't a talking man. As for Babe, it was just another of those impulsive actions that were so typical. Sometime later, when I asked Babe about the incident, he didn't recall much about it.

"He was a nice kid," Babe said. "Puny though. Guess he was pretty sick all right."

"What was his name?"

"Hell, I don't know. The old man called him 'son.' Guess I never did hear his name. If I did, I disremember. Never could remember names anyhow." Then he brightened. "Hey, how about giving Gehrig a call and organizing a bridge game?"

Only recently I learned of another, and unexpected, facet of that multifaceted personality. I got it from George Weiss, one of the most efficient front-office executives in the history of the game, and now a member of Baseball's Hall of Fame. Here's the way George told it.

"I was running the Newark club at the time. We had planned a big baseball rally in downtown Newark with Ruth as the big attraction. The Lindbergh kidnapping story broke the day before the rally was scheduled to be held. It was too late to call it off. We had to go through with it but, believe me, our hearts weren't in it.

"To our amazement, a crowd of about 3,000 people showed up. The mayor introduced Ruth, and the big guy stepped up to the microphone and held up his hand for silence. He said, 'I've just been reading the papers. I guess you have, too. There's nothing much we can do for that poor little kid, I guess, except pray. I ask every one of you to get down on your knees right now and say a silent prayer that that little fellow be found and returned to his parents.'

"Believe it or not," Weiss concluded, "right there in that Square, some 3,000 people knelt with bowed heads, the Babe included. It was the most impressive thing I ever saw. After a few seconds, the Babe murmured an 'Amen,' and rose to his feet. 'Thank you,' he said, and left the platform. For him, the rally was over—the strangest baseball rally ever staged, and the most effective."

That's the story Weiss told. Emotional? Sure. Maudlin? Possibly. I repeat it here not for its drama, or its theatrical appeal, but simply because it illustrates another and largely hidden depth of character never before shown in public.

With Babe Ruth, anything could happen—and usually did!

4

THE GOLDEN AGE

Writers, even today, frequently refer to the period from the end of World War I to the Depression as the golden age of sports. Just why a decade that began with prohibition madness, and wound up with men selling apples on street corners as a sole means of livelihood, should go down in history as "golden" is beyond my ken. But it was so labeled by writers of the period, and is so remembered. So be it.

What actually occurred in that period was a complete revolution of American philosophy—a revolution that lifted our nation out of the swaddling clothes of Victorian isolation, and then dropped it, lock, stock and barrel, into a twentieth-century spirit of internationalism and (we hoped) world leadership.

It was an interesting and effervescent era, one of fun and excitement and laughter. It was an age of zany optimism, with yesterday's guidelines passé, and no plans for tomorrow. Most of us believed that we had, in truth, won "the war to end all wars." We believed, with President Woodrow Wilson, that we had in reality "made the world safe for democracy." It was a time for celebration, and when Americans start out to celebrate they do the job in detail.

Nor was it confined to sports alone. Every facet of American life felt the impact. The business and financial worlds suddenly visioned new, expanding horizons that challenged their imaginations. Politicians, heretofore concerned with local and domestic problems, glimpsed a new source of power in international development. They liked what they saw, and embraced it promptly.

The entertainment world was quick to follow suit. Caruso still thrilled the dedicated old-school musical devotees, but the real voice of America centered suddenly in the gravelly tones of a Jimmy Durante, the sentimental "Mammy" mouthings of an Al Jolson, the radio crooning of a new star named Rudy Vallee. America's dancing feet forsook the stately dignity of the ballroom waltz, and twinkled instead to the newer, livelier night club tempo of a Paul Whiteman, a Benny Goodman, a Guy Lombardo.

It was an era when a man's social standing was measured by the number of speakeasies to which he had access, or the caliber of the bootleggers he knew on a first-name basis. It was a time when headlines were made by racketeers like Al Capone and Arnold Rothstein. I've always felt that the breakdown of law and order that we lament today had its beginnings in the twenties, when reputable citizens became lawbreakers and applauded and even defended the lawless and frequently bloody antics of the gangsters, who, in turn, thumbed their collective noses at any attempt to enforce the most unpopular law ever written into the federal statutes.

It was a great age, no question about that. Nor will it soon be forgotten by those who experienced it. Certainly it will remain forever green in the memory of a young newspaperman from Colorado Springs, whose first night in New York was highlighted by an introduction to Jimmy Durante and Eddie Jackson at Jimmy Kelly's place in the Village, and whose first contact with the theatrical world was a backstage visit to the "Follies," as the wide-eyed guest of Bill Shrode, Ziegfeld's stage manager.

But back to sports.

Before the First World War baseball, boxing, and horse racing were the only sports that regularly attracted widespread interest. The annual World Series, a few stakes races like the Kentucky Derby, the Preakness and the Belmont, and an occasional heavyweight title bout were the only sports events covered by the press associations on a truly national scale. Even football, popular as it was in college circles, had not yet planted the virus that today has developed into a mania of epidemic proportions.

Golf, hoary with age and steeped in social tradition, was among the first sports to feel the impetus of postwar magic. Some unsung genius conceived the idea of municipal courses and public links. Overnight the game, hitherto confined to the stuffy, stodgy influence of social rule and financial limitation, became popular with the masses. New clubs sprang into being throughout the nation like woods mushrooms after a springtime shower.

New names began to appear in the golfing news. Walter Hagen, Bobby Jones, Gene Sarazen, Johnny Farrell, Horton Smith, and many others were heralding a new era in golfing history. They paved the way for the Palmers, the Players, the Hogans, the Sneads, and the Nicklauses of a modern era.

Bobby Jones with his Grand Slam conquest was regarded then, and still, as the greatest amateur of all time. He faced the handicap of a violent temper, and overcame it. He disliked crowds, but forced himself to accept the hubbub of notoriety with smiling graciousness. He was straightforward in his likes and his dislikes, and like all champions he was at his best when the going was toughest.

Walter Hagen was, well, he was Hagen! He was colorful in an age that demanded color; exciting in an era that thrived on excitement. He was uninhibited. He did what he pleased, said what he thought, socialized as he saw fit—with no apologies, and no regrets.

Who but Hagen, playing in the staid, tradition-laden British Open, would, after a hectic night of socialization, appear on the first tee garbed in black tie and dinner clothes to open a round of competition? Who but Hagen, playing with the Prince of Wales, would casually order; "Hey, Eddie, take the pin out, will you? I've got a hunch I'm going to sink one."

Hagen played every shot with confidence. He was a great putter, but he never wasted time around the green. Asked by a newspaperman whether or not he had any specific rule for putting, "The Haig" replied, "Yeah, 1 got one rule. Miss 'em quick!" Yet playing with this same writer a few days later, Hagen watched the scribe try futilely to sink a long putt, miss by fifteen feet, and come up with a four putt green. "Listen, kid," said Hagen, "you'll never be a golfer that way. When you're way off like that, don't try the impossible. Just imagine a two-foot circle around the cup, and putt for that imaginary circle. Sometimes they go down—and if they don't, you're sure to get off with two putts. Always play the percentage."

Golf was not the only longtime sport that suddenly found its niche in the burst of postwar enthusiasm. Football, for years the athletic symbol of ivied turrets and cloistered college halls, suddenly burst the campus barrier to establish its popularity as a game to tickle the fancy of a shirt-sleeved "subway alumni," who thrilled to the genius of a Rockne and the wizardry of a Grange. They might not have understood all the intricacies of higher mathematics or Platonian philosophy, but they did recognize colorful pageantry and hard-nosed competitive spirit when they saw it. Football, in the twenties, had it to spare.

Rockne was not only a coaching genius—he was a hard-boiled organizational opportunist as well. When he took over the coaching reins at Notre Dame, that institution was a small cow-town college, little known outside its Indiana confines. At the time of his death, not only was Notre Dame recognized throughout the nation as a great educational university and athletic citadel, but because of coaches like Rockne, Pop Warner, Tad Jones, Fritz Crisler, Howard Jones, and Bob Zuppke, to name a few, college football had assumed its rightful place as a great American game—nationwide in its fan appeal, and taking its place alongside baseball in the affections of the nation's fans.

Professional football, meantime, was struggling along as a poor substitute for the college real thing. Only the Chicago Bears, under the leadership of George Halas and the Strurdiman brothers, showed any promise of financial success. Then Red Grange, of Illinois, turned pro, with all the attendant publicity and ballyhoo. More than 50,000 people paid their way into the old Polo Grounds to witness Red's debut. Sports editors, seeing the attendance figures, licked their lips and sharpened their pencils for immediate action.

Followed by a coterie of sportswriters, the Bears and Grange undertook the toughest schedule ever staged by any sports group. Playing as many as four games a week, they toured from coast to coast. They stopped in dozens of cities, winding up in Miami in January, long after the college season was over and forgotten.

I happened to be one of the newspapermen making that trip, and I can still recall—with awe—the battering that the players took, and the punishment they absorbed. They played in the snow in Boston, on sleet and ice in Pittsburgh, on a frozen, cut-up field in Washington, and in zero weather in the Midwest. They traveled in special Pullmans, with one of the smoking rooms turned into a training quarters and first-aid station. Andy Lotshaw, the Chicago Cubs trainer, presided, and it wasn't unusual for him to work all through the night bandaging, massaging, sterilizing cuts, all the things that had to be done so that the players could be ready for another game, in another city, on another day.

Somehow those players got the job done. The future of pro football was literally built on their battered and bruised bodies. Their aches and sprains were the birth pains of a sports miracle. Now that the ordeal is long over, now that the success of professional football is forever assured, I extend to that hardy crew my congratulations. Today's stars, smug in the success of the game, possibly would be willing to stand the gaff of such a schedule, possibly, but somehow I doubt it.

Boxing, in the doldrums during the war, roared back to its greatest popularity, largely on the performance of Jack Dempsey. Jack probably was the most popular figure American boxing fans have ever known. He was the bellwether in boxing's greatest renaissance.

On July 4, 1919, Dempsey met champion Jess Willard for the heavyweight title in a jerry-built pine arena in Toledo, Ohio. Dempsey was not well known to the fans, and he had been unjustly tarred as a wartime "slacker" by harping critics. As he stepped into that Toledo ring, he was definitely an unpopular underdog.

A half hour later, his bronzed torso glistening in the hot afternoon sun, he stood over the prostrate body of a battered and bleeding Willard, listening to the plaudits of fans greeting a new champion.

Many historians and critics will argue that the rebirth of interest in boxing and other sports was a natural phenomenon of postwar letdown: that the public appetite for sports and recreation was whetted to a razor-edge by long years of wartime worry and austerity, and that the idols who took their places in the sports annals of the time were the beneficiaries rather than the creators of the sports age that men call "golden."

Maybe they're right. Maybe sports greatness exists largely in the eyes of the observer. Maybe a rebirth of sports enthusiasm is created by national state of mind and not by performance. I am not prepared to argue such philosophy, pro or con. But as a fan who saw them perform, and shared vicariously their deeds of derring-do, I feel that they were more leaders than opportunists, and that they gave full measure of performance for every laurel of public acclaim.

As a fan, I continue to believe that without the color, the personality, and the performance of Jack Dempsey—and his boxing cohorts—the golden era of boxing would be fashioned of a lot more dross and a lot less precious metal. Of course, Jack didn't do it alone. Among the others were fighters like Benny Leonard, Luis Firpo, Gene Tunney, Mickey Walker, and Harry Greb, to mention only a few. Surely if Dempsey was the Zeus of the boxing heavens of his era, these others were the demigods of his court, sharing his mantle of greatness.

The twenties brought a new international flavor to American sports, as both men and women shared the headlines.

• Bill Dwyer, who laid his rum-runner fortune on the line to bring the New York Americans into being, and bring hockey to America.

• Gertrude Ederle, swimming her way to fame via the English Channel. She set a world's record, and was paid off with a typical ticker-taped parade up Broadway. She was the first woman, and the first sports figure so honored.

• Suzanne Lenglen and René LaCoste, coming from France to challenge the tennis mastery of a Helen Wills and a Bill Tilden.

• Paavo Nurmi, carrying Finland's colors proudly as he captured the hearts of American track fans with his stopwatch middle distance running to new world records.

• Tommy Hitchcock, war ace and born Centaur, riding roughshod to fame and adulation over the prostrate forms of his opponents in international polo.

• Little Earl Sande, with leg up on the great Zev, hand-riding his mount to easy victory over Papyrus, the British challenger, in an international match race at Belmont Park.

• And the zanies—C. C. Pyle, and his "Bunion Derby"—the flagpole sitters—the marathon dancers—the Harvard goldfish swallowers—all a part of the craziest, most colorful, most interesting era the American public had ever enjoyed.

The idols of the period have, of course, long ago disappeared from the headlines. Except for a handful of immortals, they are largely forgotten. But the worthwhile changes of that hectic decade still endure, and the bad are long since discarded. One thing sure—in that so-called golden age, Americans learned to laugh, they learned to play, and above all else they learned not to take the personal business of living too seriously. Radical changes in national philosophy, they learned, can be accomplished without violence or hatred; a renaissance is not necessarily built on revolution and bloodshed. It's too bad the rest of the world didn't have the same exposure. Maybe if they had, some of the problems that beset civilization today would be solved by less bluster and more understanding; fewer frightening military gestures and more cooperation of people to people.

Baseball, like other sports, felt the impact of the postwar decade—but in a less spectacular and flamboyant fashion. For one thing, its status as America's National Game was not "up for grabs." Behind it was more than a half century of established tradition. Heroes were taken for granted, and new idols were always standing in the wings ready to take over the headlines as older ones faded.

True, the Cobbs and the Speakers, the Johnsons and the Alexanders, the McGraws and the Macks, were revered figures during the early years of baseball's golden decade. But they were in no sense products of that era. They had won their accolades earlier and were already established as stars. Even Babe Ruth, who was destined to achieve the ultimate in performance and fan adulation in the hectic years ahead, had earlier assured his place in the sun. The plans for the new Yankee Stadium—"The House That Ruth Built"—were already on the drafting board before the golden age really swung into high gear. Baseball, along with the other sports, welcomed the revival of fan interest and increased attendance, with the resultant clink of dollars at the box office. But it was the behind-the-scenes action that brought most lasting benefits to the game.

For some years prior to the war, shrewd baseball men had been concerned about player development and the diminishing opportunities for youngsters to play the game. It is axiomatic that no professional game can long endure without adequate player replacement, or without the development of facilities for succeeding generations of youngsters to play. The most enthusiastic fans are the people who learned, played, and adopted the game as youngsters. Baseball had basically developed as a small-town, rural game where vacant fields offered diamond facilities, and every small hamlet a locale for baseball war.

In the years before the First World War all that began to change. The country school went the way of the one-horse shay, and so did the country store. The advent of the paved road and the high speed motor car turned proud rural villages into mere wayside stops for buses carrying erstwhile villagers to and from their better-paying jobs in the city. Small-town diamonds gave way to filling stations and roadside diners.

The remedy had already begun before the dawn of the golden age. In 1914, the National Amateur Baseball Federation was formed. In 1925, however, the American Legion began sponsoring its summer program for high-school boys. Not only did that prove to be a great source of development for future professionals, but it showed the way for the wonderful youth programs that were to come later—programs like the Little League, Babe Ruth League, Pony League, and others. These programs were to prove invaluable to the growth of baseball in all ways, and on all levels.

All this was due to the efforts of fans themselves, not any professional enterpreneurs: the grocer, the baker, the working stiff who believed in baseball as a game; men who had played in their own boyhood, and were willing to sacrifice their time and effort—and often their dollars—to assure their sons of the same pleasure.

Professional baseball owes much to those unsung, unrewarded, but dedicated men. I am sure that there must be many red faces when the so-called Lords of Baseball contemplate the little they have contributed to the game, compared to the contribution these fans have made. If not, there certainly should be.

Out in St. Louis, a former player and manager had taken over as general manager of the St. Louis Cardinals—a club hard-pressed to keep going. His name was Branch Rickey. He was a lawyer by education, a Methodist preacher by inclination, an orator by temperament, and by economic necessity one of the shrewdest wheeler-dealers professional baseball, or any sport, has ever known.

Rickey was quick to recognize that the postwar interest in baseball was no passing fad. He was convinced that it spelled opportunity with a capital "O" to the club that could take prompt advantage of the situation. But he had problems. The basis of success first of all had to be a winning ball club, and that required player strength both of caliber and depth. Such a program, under then current procedure, required more dollars than the Cardinals could command. Undaunted, Rickey sought other means of player development.

Quietly he acquired a chain of minor league clubs, either through outright purchase, or rigid working agreement. He scoured the boondocks for likely young and inexperienced players, signed them to contracts with minor league clubs under the Cardinals' control, where he could give them intensive training under coaches and managers whom he personally selected.

The most likely candidates wound up with the Cardinals. The surplus he could sell to other major league clubs, or let them go in the draft. The draft still brought a cash return, but it was a fixed and lesser amount.

The plan worked. Before other clubs awakened to what was going on, the Cardinals were in National League contention. In 1926, they won the pennant, and defeated the New York Yankees in the World Series. Branch Rickey's farm system had proved its workability.

Common acceptance of the idea, however, didn't occur without some travail. Other clubs, caught off-base by the Cardinal maneuver, didn't like the idea of a player-control ploy to which they were not a party. They said so, and loudly, even though some of them were even then going quietly about the business of setting up a farm system of their own. Commissioner Landis didn't like the farm system, either, and for a different reason. His dream of a snug and placid baseball existence was suddenly beset with nightmares of "peonage" charges, and endless threat of legal action under the federal antitrust statutes.

In the years to come, Landis would frequently attack the farm-system baseball operation. He made one strong move against the Cardinals, and another against the Detroit club. In each case, many young players were made free agents. But, in the main, the efforts of Landis were hampered by his own position in the Bob Feller case. Here, dealing with an established star, Landis had reversed his position, and allowed the Cleveland club to keep Feller.

Despite the opposition of Landis, Rickey's farm system had worked out. For good or bad, it was in the books, a player ploy to be closely policed, but not attacked in principle, to be contained in its operation, but not abolished.

The full impact of the farm system did not come during the sports frenzy of the twenties, but later, when baseball and the nation were in the throes of a depression. The farm system, with the resultant major league ownership of minor league clubs, and the major league assumption of minor league losses through strict working agreements, saved the minor league structure.

Today, farm systems are taken for granted by major and minor leagues alike. In time of financial strain, they have proved their value. They helped solve the player development problem in the recent expansion program, making the staffing of new clubs infinitely easier. But it can be a two-edged sword. If vigilant policing is relaxed, if major league greed for players is permitted to turn minor league competitive play into mere training exhibitions—then it will become evil, and deadly dangerous. That is baseball's eternal problem.

The postwar twenties brought also two scientific developments that have changed the entire concept of baseball and all American sports. One was the advent of radio (and later television) adding a new dimension to our communications. Sports, as a living and breathing entity, came into American living rooms, business offices, and institutions, and even into the speeding motor cars of an itinerant public.

The other development was the perfection of the airplane as a means of commercial transportation. Between them, they have affected the structure of sports, not only in America but in the whole world. But that is incidental. Far more important, they have changed for all time the whole concept of human philosophy and world relations. Properly used by men of goodwill to develop better understanding between nations and people, they can only result in vast benefit to a struggling world in which old-time boundaries of time and distance have been forever eliminated. The "safety barriers" of ocean, mountain, and desert have lost their meaning. In the hands of ruthless, power-mad men or governments, they can bring untold suffering and evil.

The personnel of baseball is constantly changing, and it's difficult to classify players by decade or definite period. Recently, I was browsing through the Hall of Fame records to discover, if possible, just how "golden" that postwar decade really was in terms of outstanding performance and fan appeal. I came up with some amazing figures.

Of 108 players elected to the Hall of Fame through 1971 (managers, umpires, executives, and the like exempted) 52, or nearly half, actually performed on the field during that decade. Of those 52 players, 23 actually started their major league careers during the ten-year period.

Don't misunderstand me. I don't mean to imply that these men who played in that legendary decade were individually the greatest in their position, or deserved recognition as all-time greats. A few of them probably rate such recognition. Many do not. But they were the best of their era—and that era was the most prolific to date in the recognition of Hall of Fame greatness. If you don't think so, consider this list:

Catchers: Mickey Cochrane, Bill Dickey, Gabby Hartnett, Ray Schalk

First Basemen: George Sisler, Bill Terry, Lou Gehrig, Jimmy Foxx

Second Basemen: Eddie Collins, Rogers Hornsby, Frank Frisch, Charley Gehringer

Shortstops: Rabbit Maranville, Joe Cronin, Dave Bancroft

Third Basemen: Pie Traynor, Frank Baker

Outfielders: Ty Cobb, Babe Ruth, Tris Speaker, Mel Ott, Paul and Lloyd Waner, Max Carey, Edd Roush, Sam Rice, Kiki Cuyler, Goose Goslin, Earle Combs, Heinie Manush, Zach Wheat, Chick Hafey

Pitchers: Walter Johnson, Grover Alexander, Dazzy Vance, Herb Pennock, Lefty Grove, Waite Hoyt, Jesse Haines, Stanley Covaleskie, Burleigh Grimes, Red Faber, Ted Lyons, Red Ruffing.

Maybe you have the courage to select a "team of the decade" from that array. I can't. I've tried several times, but there are not enough places. The best I could do was a 40-man squad, and even then I had to leave out a couple of worthy performers.

And, of course, there must be a Manager of the Decade. There, too, you can take your choice.

John McGraw: John was nearing the end of his brilliant but

hectic career, but he still had enough left to win four consecutive pennants and two World Series in 1921–22–23–24.

Miller Huggins: Hug managed the first Yankee pennant winner, and started the Yankees on the road to becoming the greatest dynasty in all baseball history. Unfortunately, Miller died at an early age, but he did win six pennants and three World Series in an eight-year managerial span. Also, he was in the midst of a tight battle for another pennant when death overtook him in 1929.

Connie Mack: Connie was nearing the three-score-and-ten mark when the decade opened—an age when most men would have been willing to call it a day. Not Connie! As the decade began, he had little to build on, but he kept on swinging. He wound up with what was probably the greatest team of his career—the pennant-winning A's of 1929–30–31. That was a team that sent Cochrane and Grove and Simmons and Foxx to Cooperstown, where they joined Mr. Mack, and Collins, Baker, Bender, and Plank of another and earlier era.

Take your managerial choice. You can't go wrong. Though if it were me, I would take the easy way out. I would toss a coin to decide who was my All-Star manager, and name the other two as coaches.

Famous outfield of the Detroit pennant winners of 1907–1908–1909: Davey Jones, Ty Cobb, and Sam Crawford

Thirty years later this picture was taken at a dinner given at Toots Shor's on Sam Crawford's election to the Hall of Fame. *Seated, left to right:* Davey Jones, Sam Crawford, Ty Cobb; *standing:* Ford C. Frick

Miller Huggins and John McGraw pose for camera at start of 1922 World Series, first of many Yankee pennant wins and the start of the great Yankee dynasty.

Newspaper correspondents, New York Yankees training camp, St. Petersburg, Florida, March 1928. *Standing left to right:* Dan Daniel, *New York Telegram;* Arthur Mann, *New York Evening World;* Will Wedge, *New York Sun;* Bill Slocum, *New York American;* Ford C. Frick, *New York Journal;* William B. Hanna, *New York Herald Tribune;* Bill Brandt, *New York Times;* telegrapher (unknown); Fred Lieb, *New York Post; seated, left to right:* local scribe (unknown); Marshall Hunt, *New York Daily News;* William Henigan, *New York World;* Charles Segar, *New York Mirror;* Jim Kilgallen, Alan Gould, Associated Press.

The annual meeting of baseball leaders in the Hotel Roosevelt, New York City, December, 1934. *Left to right:* Will Harridge, president of the American League; Commissioner K. M. Landis; and Ford C. Frick, president of the National League.

The dedication of the Hall of Fame, Cooperstown, New York, 1939. *Left to right:* Ford C. Frick, president, National League; Judge K. M. Landis, commissioner of baseball; Will Harridge, president, American League; Judge William G. Branham, president, National Association of Professional Baseball Leagues.

Charley Grimm, manager of the
Chicago Cubs, and the newly
elected president of the National
League, Catalina Island Field,
March 1935.

Using the old sandlot technique, old-
timers Honus Wagner (*left*) and Eddie
Collins choose up sides for an exhibition game that celebrated the 100th
anniversary of baseball at Cooperstown, New York, June 12, 1939. Big
league stars and old-timers turned out
for the game under managers Wagner
and Collins, both members of baseball's Hall of Fame. *Press Association,
Inc.*

A light moment at an annual meeting. *Left to right:* Branch Rickey, Ford Frick, Harry Cross of the *New York Times,* and Horace Stoneham.

Sam Breadon enjoys a laugh with a couple of newcomers. The picture was taken at the 1934 league meeting, when Ford Frick was inducted as league president, and Phil Wrigley took over the presidency of the Cubs.

The baseball hierarchy during expansion days. *Left to right:* Will Harridge, president of the American League; the commissioner; and Warren Giles, president of the National League.

Two hundred ninety-five years of baseball experience. *Front row:* Clark Griffith, 60 years as player-manager and owner; Connie Mack with 75 years. *Back row:* Will Harridge and Ford Frick, youngsters of the group with a half century of official service, and Bob Quinn who served for 60 years.

Some light talk in the boxes with Joe E. Brown.

A reminder of days that were. Hall of Famers get together at the annual Hall of Fame game in Cooperstown, 1948. *Left to right:* Mickey Cochrane, Carl Hubbell, Charley Gehringer, Tris Speaker, Ed Walsh, Cy Young. Of the group only Hubbell and Gehringer are alive today.

5

FANS

We are the little people—unsung, unnoticed, too often unappreciated. As individuals we are not important. As a group we represent a good cross section of America, and all the things America stands for.

There are millions of us—good and bad—rich and poor—famous and infamous. We are black; we are white. We are Catholics; we are Protestants; we are Jews. We are Irish or German or French or Italian or whatever. We are of all races, all creeds, all colors.

We are dissenters; we are of the Establishment. We are doctors, lawyers, men of the cloth. We work at menial jobs, and run big industries.

We laugh and we cry; we praise and we condemn; we believe and we scoff; we accept and we doubt; we thrill and we agonize. We are boisterous and we are sedate; we sorrow and we rejoice.

But—we build America's stadiums—and we produce the athletes who play there. We pay the salaries and the rent. We provide the dividends that keep the owners solvent. We establish traditions, and keep green the memories that link otherwise forgotten yesterdays with brighter tomorrows. When we are happy, baseball prospers. When we criticize, management listens. And that is as it should be.

We are the fans, and in the final analysis, it is in our hands that the destiny of baseball abides.

53

In any recognition of fans and the part they play in keeping baseball in the forefront of national interest, it is only proper to start at the top. It has been a tradition through the years that the President of the United States throw out the first ball to inaugurate the opening of the major league season in Washington, and the nation. That tradition started in 1908, with President Taft officiating, and each succeeding president has kept the string alive.

That does not mean, of course, that all our presidents have been great baseball fans. They have not. It does mean that government recognizes the great place baseball holds in public esteem. The President, in throwing out the first ball, is acting as the personal representative of millions of fans throughout the nation who believe in baseball as a great American game.

Through the years, many stories have been told of the great interest Presidents have shown in the game. Most of them are legendary rather than factual. For instance, there's the fabled yarn that the committee appointed to notify Abraham Lincoln of his nomination as Republican candidate for the presidency found him playing baseball with a few cronies on a Springfield sandlot. In some versions, it is even told the future president kept the committee waiting while he took a final turn at bat, before accepting their message.

The story is, of course, without any basis of documentary fact. There is no authentic evidence that Mr. Lincoln ever witnessed an organized game, let alone played in one.

The story is often told, too, of General Grant taking time out during the Wilderness campaign to watch and root for a team from an Illinois regiment in a game against a team from Massachusetts. Pure fantasy, of course. There is no authentic evidence that General Grant, either during his military days or later as president, ever saw a baseball game or evinced any particular interest in any sort of competitive game. Grant's sports interest was horse racing—and he enjoyed several visits to Saratoga during the racing season, both during his term of office and thereafter. But baseball? Well, it makes a good story.

The first authentic evidence of any presidential interest in baseball involves President Grover Cleveland, and was vouched for by John Heydler, longtime president of the National League. During the late years of Cleveland's second term in office, Heydler was employed as a junior clerk in the Government Printing Office. As part of his duties he served as a messenger, and one evening was called upon to deliver a document to the White House. Heydler arrived shortly after the dinner hour, and at the president's request was ushered into a private sitting room, where Cleveland was entertaining a few personal friends at a postdinner "gabfest."

"Casey at the Bat" had just come into national popularity at that time, and the President asked the youthful Heydler if he was familiar with the poem. Whereupon John recited the ballad in its entirety to a surprised and appreciative audience. When he had finished, Cleveland took a small sheet of paper from his desk, hastily scribbled a few lines, and handed the note to the young messenger. Here's what he wrote: "Congratulations to John Heydler and Casey. Long may you both live! Grover Cleveland."

The memo meant much to the youthful Heydler, and he treasured it as youngsters today treasure a baseball autographed by their reigning heroes. When John became president of the National League, that memo became part of the league archives. When I succeeded Heydler, it was still there—a bit frayed and tattered—but still legible.

That memo constitutes, insofar as I can discover, the first documented evidence of interest by a president of the United States in baseball.

It is interesting to note that Warren Harding, as a young newspaper publisher in Marion, Ohio, was part owner of the local minor league club, and carried his fan interest with him when he first went to Washington as a United States senator. During those senatorial days, he was a frequent visitor at Griffith Stadium, along with Senator Jim Watson, of Indiana, and "Uncle Joe" Cannon, then the speaker of the House. Quite a trio of political wheeler-dealers, those three, and the ball park visits afforded perfect opportunity to combine baseball pleasure with a bit of political strategizing at which they were particularly adept.

Once Mr. Harding entered the White House, however, his baseball interest suffered. The demands of his office and the protocol of presidential attendance at the ball park combined to destroy the "crony" atmosphere of his sports enjoyment. Thereafter, Harding's athletic interest centered on an occasional round of golf at Chevy Chase, and the nightly poker game with friends at the "Little Green House" on I Street.

Of all the presidents who have participated in "first ball" ceremonies, Messrs. Hoover and Nixon must be rated as the most enthusiastic baseball fans. Mr. Hoover, as president, appeared at the ball park only infrequently. He disliked the pomp and ceremony that, of necessity, accompanies any presidential public appearance. Aside from the traditional opening game ceremony, he was seldom seen at the ball park.

But he followed the radio and newspaper accounts avidly—and no fan in the nation had a better understanding of the fine points of the game, or a more complete knowledge of records and personal performance than he.

It was after he retired from the White House and moved to New York that he really displayed publicly the interest and enthusiasm for the game he had so long enjoyed in private. Whenever he was in town, he never missed an opportunity to see a game. Management never knew when he would show up at the park. Frequently he would be alone, and never with more than one or two guests.

He was a silent fan, watching every play intently, with maybe an occasional comment to a neighboring fan following a sensational play or a close decision. He kept his own scorecard and did it well— but according to his own judgment rather than official decision.

One day at the Polo Grounds as I was passing through the stands, I spied Mr. Hoover sitting alone and I paused to bid him welcome. The adjoining seat was vacant, and he invited me to join him. He inquired briefly about a trade the Giants had made a day or two before, and questioned manager Bill Terry's reasoning in the deal.

"I guess Terry knows what he's doing," he commented, "but I don't think 'so-and-so' (mentioning the player's name) will hit as well here as he did in his other park. He hits straightaway, and this park was made for pull hitters."

A few minutes later the player in question came to bat, and promptly slashed a double off the wall in right center. Mr. Hoover carefully recorded the hit on his scorecard, then remarked dryly,

"Guess from now on I'd better let Terry make the trades and run the ball club. He seems to be doing pretty well without my help."

A few innings later a Giant batsman hit a hard drive through the left side of the infield. The opposing shortstop made a dive to his right, got his glove on the ball, but couldn't hold it. The ball trickled away, and the batter was safe at first. The scoreboard showed an error.

"That was no error," Mr. Hoover commented, "that ball was too hot to handle. In my book, it's a base hit."

And that's the way it went down in the ex-president's score-card. Dick Bartell, wherever he may be, will be glad, even at this late date, to learn that according to a presidential box score he is entitled to one more hit than the official records show. A true fan, Mr. Hoover—and in his quiet way a knowledgeable authority who passed his own judgments—and stayed with them.

President Nixon's enthusiasm for baseball, and for all sports, is well recognized. He is an ardent and articulate fan. Considering the vast diversity of problems and responsibilities he faces, Mr. Nixon's knowledge of baseball and his interest in, and memory of, sports events is truly amazing. Nor is his enthusiasm a phony pose adopted for political expediency. He has carried his interest in sports since he was a young boy. Like Mr. Hoover, I'm sure he will retain that interest to the end of his days. Surely he must rate as America's No. 1 baseball fan—both in stature and dedication.

These two—Hoover and Nixon—surely are tops so far as baseball interest is concerned. But there have also been presidents who proved that there was another side to that coin.

Calvin Coolidge, for instance, was a laconic New Englander who viewed any sort of sports frivolity through the jaundiced eyes of his Puritan forebears. He attended opening games, and posed for photographs, because it was the thing to do. But his heart really wasn't in it. Yet, even Mr. Coolidge had his moments. *One* moment, anyway.

Along with Mrs. Coolidge, the President attended the seventh and final game of the 1924 World Series. Just the fact that it was a deciding game of a World Series guaranteed a certain excitement. But there were additional factors. Washington had never won a world championship. The immortal Walter Johnson was pitching for the home team. The tension in the stands was almost visible to the naked eye.

It was a game that would make baseball history because of the odd way it was decided. In the twelfth inning, a routine ground ball hit a pebble, jumped over the third baseman's head, and allowed the winning run to score. Washington had its first championship.

The game was a close one, and the fans reacted to every little thing. All the fans, that is, except Mr. Coolidge. Inning after inning he sat there stone-faced and unmoving. In the press box, he became the subject of some interesting wagers by the writers who kept watching him. It was an even money bet that the president wouldn't crack a smile; 10 to 1 that he wouldn't join in the cheering; and 20 to 1 that no play on the field could bring him to his feet.

But as the winning run crossed the plate, the entire ball park went wild. It was a tremendous demonstration, but the newspapermen were familiar with demonstrations like that. We had eyes only for the president. Would there be any kind of reaction at all?

The president rose slowly to his feet, doffed his hat and grinned broadly. Then he stepped to the top of the dugout to cheer the new champions. Our last view from the press box, before the Secret Service moved in to protect him from the crowd, was of the president of the United States smiling and waving his arms in happy exultation, as he did his own personal interpretation of a stilted Vermont victory dance there on top of the Washington dugout.

That picture will remain indelibly etched in my memory as long as I live. It stands as strong evidence that even non-sports-lovers can find a bit of surcease from worry and care through an afternoon at the ball park—provided they, like President Coolidge, will relax and let themselves go.

There are other incidents involving presidents and baseball.

There is the matter of the seventh inning stretch, for instance. Today, the stretch is a traditional part of the game, yet just how it originated is a moot question. Personally, I'm not prepared to argue the point one way or the other—but I am impressed by the testimony of the late Clark Griffith, who for more than fifty years owned and operated the Washington club in the American League. Mr. Griffith insisted vehemently that credit for originating the seventh inning stretch belonged to one man, and one man only. That man, he insisted, was William Howard Taft.

Here is Griff's story:

Mr. Taft was a big man, and in his day ball park seats, though serviceable, were not planned for spectator ease and comfort—especially as concerned men of Taft's girth and stature. The President attended a game one hot August afternoon, and inning after inning he twisted, turned and fidgeted in his seat trying to make himself a bit more comfortable. Finally, in the middle of the seventh inning, he stood up to ease his legs a bit. The other fans in the ball park, anxious to get a better view of the president, stood up, too.

By a strange coincidence, the Washington club scored two runs in the last of the seventh, and won the game. And that's the way Clark Griffith says it all began. True or not, it's a good story, and as likely an explanation as any of the birth of one of baseball's most universal traditions.

President Harry Truman was interested in sports because he was interested in "folks" and folksy things. He liked the camaraderie of sports fans, and the excitement of big crowds. But, most of all, he had great respect for baseball and other sports as a great melting pot where people could meet people, unhampered by the protocol of wealth or social position.

I recall one day in the late forties when Will Harridge and I called at the White House for the annual ceremony of presenting the president with league passes. Mr. Truman asked us to remain for a few minutes' chat after the photographers had left. A few days before, an old Indiana friend of mine had been discussing world problems and come up with what I thought was a true bit of Hoosier philosophy. He said, "The trouble today is the world is too full of people, and not enough folks."

I repeated the line to the president. "That's the real truth," he said, "and don't you baseball fellows forget it. And don't you get so 'uppity' that you neglect the little guys, either. Just remember that in sports there is no 'wrong side of the tracks.'"

Harridge asked Mr. Truman what he meant by that.

"Just what I say," replied the president, grinning. "Sports is the only institution we have left where dollars, and pull, and social status don't count. If you've got the ability, you make the team. If you haven't—well, you can always carry the equipment of the man who does. And be happy doing it. Baseball also has another thing going for it. You don't have to weigh 250 pounds to make good in baseball. And you don't have to be six-foot-seven, either. I like that. I was a little fellow myself."

Maybe Harry Truman wasn't the most enthusiastic baseball fan ever to occupy the White House, but he did enjoy one distinction. He was the only ambidextrous president in history, and he loved to cross up the photographers by throwing with his left hand when they were set for a right-handed pitch, and vice versa.

On the morning after one opening game, two New York newspapers hit the street with a picture of the president throwing out the first ball. In one picture, he was pitching right-handed. In the other, left-handed. Since both pictures made page one, they made an interesting contrast lying beside each other on newsstands.

Mr. Truman got a laugh out of that. Almost as big as the one he got out of the front page of the Chicago *Tribune* that carried a headline announcing "Dewey Elected," in 1948, when all the time Mr. Truman was safely home with the California vote ensuring him a new four-year lease on the White House.

President Eisenhower was a firm believer in sports participation. He played on the varsity team at West Point, and he knew baseball thoroughly. But his greatest love was golf. No man has ever done more to arouse national interest in golf than he.

Yet, as a baseball buff, I take great pride in the fact that when a victorious Eisenhower returned from Europe at war's end, he was asked by New York's Mayor La Guardia to name any one thing he would like to do during his short stay in New York. Ike chose a ball game. His first informal public appearance in New York was at the Polo Grounds, where he watched a traditional Dodger-Giant fracas, and enjoyed every minute of it. And, as Casey Stengel is wont to say, "You could look it up."

One more Eisenhower episode. In 1953 arrangements were made for the New York Giants to make a postseason tour of Japan. The war, so recently ended, had left unhealed scars in the memories of participants, and the president was most anxious the tour be made. He was elated when arrangements were finally completed. He immediately got off a letter expressing his appreciation. It was a brief note, sent from the summer White House in Denver. Here's what he wrote:

Dear Mr. Frick:

I was delighted to hear that through your good offices the plan for the Japanese tour of the New York Giants has been successfully completed. For myself, I enthusiastically support this kind of sporting and human relationship between the people of Japan and the United States.

During the course of the tour there will doubtless be public functions in which you will be in a very real sense our American Ambassador. If, on these occasions, you would feel that a personal message from me would make a contribution to the occasion, please convey to those present my warm greetings and sentiments of friendship.

The thoughts I would express were I there myself are very simple.

The United States of America seeks the friendship of all; the enmity of none—for in real friendship there is strength, and only through strength can come the peace and freedom which mean happiness and well-being for the world.

With every good wish,

Sincerely,
(Signed) Dwight D. Eisenhower

But enough of presidents, and men of high position. It's great to have their interest, and their public support has been a great boon to all competitive sports. But baseball is basically a story of the garden-variety, workaday fans who for more than a century have given their unstinted loyalty, their support, their time, their effort, and frequently their money, without thought of reward or recognition—all because they love the game.

To name them is an impossible task. The father, home from a hard day's work, yet willing to take hours after supper to lay out a diamond so his sons could savor the joy of baseball that he had once known; the mother, when the household chores were through, spending untold hours sewing a uniform that her son could wear proudly as a member of a local kid team; the little old lady sitting beside the radio, and finding a moment of surcease from care and sorrow, as she listened to the ball game and lived in memory the thrills and excitement she had known in the days "back when."

I recall a man named Carl Stotz, of Williamsport, Pennsylvania —an ordinary sort of everyday chap, who had no dreams of greatness and national acclaim. But he loved baseball, and he loved kids. So, he started an organization he called "Little League," and by his own efforts and initiative carried it through to fruition as a national organization. Little League today is international, with offices in scores of countries, and headed by a paid organization operating on a year-round basis. You don't hear of Carl Stotz anymore. Somewhere in the business shuffle he seems to have been forgotten. But, in my book, Little League is still his baby. Certainly, the name of Carl Stotz must be rated high in the list of true fans who, solely because of their abiding faith in the game, contributed much and asked nothing.

Another man I will never forget is George Bellis, a Pennsylvanian born and bred, who for many years headed the Pennsylvania American Legion baseball program. He was above all else a fan, but he was not blind to reality. Back of his broad smile was a fighting spirit that laughed at odds, and he faced many. Pennsylvania, at that time, was not a part of the American Legion national program, and the national organization took a rather dim view of George's effort. But George held fast to his belief that a good state program that offered a full summer of play was a lot better than a national program that limited, through early elimination, the number of games a team could play in league competition. George won that one, and developed the Pennsylvania program into one of the best in the country.

On my desk as I write is a memento that I prize highly. It's a wood carving of a player in uniform, created by one of the players in George's program. It has a key in the back, and when you wind it, the player's head turns from side to side and he whistles, "Take Me Out to the Ball Game." It's a great tribute to the baseball spirit that George instilled. Eventually, it will go to the museum in Cooperstown where other kids can see and admire it.

Fans are inherently hero worshipers and not themselves averse to public attention and headlines. Some go about the job of garnering fleeting notoriety in strange and devious ways. One of the most unusual "fan characters" I ever knew operated in Cincinnati in the early twenties. Other Red fans called him "The Baker," and he always occupied a front row bleacher seat along the right field foul line in old Redland Field.

He wasn't the noisy, vociferous type; he was almost shy, as a matter of fact. His ploy was simple. He "said it with flowers." Every time a home run was hit, an attendant was on hand with a big bouquet of roses to greet the successful hitter, compliments of "The Baker." The ceremony was always the same, and timed to perfection. Always the flowers were there before the hitter had reached the bench; sometimes the attendant was on hand to make the presentation almost before the runner had crossed the plate to register his run. Where the flowers came from, how and where they were kept fresh, how the delivery was timed so perfectly—these questions stumped all the boys in the press box.

Even Garry Herrmann, then owner of the Reds, professed not to know—although I was always a bit skeptical of his protestations. Yet, through the years, we never did learn the name of the donor. He remained just "The Baker"—uncommunicative and unknown—probably the only "Mystery Fan," in a century of baseball history.

Cincinnati had another character who attained some notoriety as a baseball "nut," and not because of his shyness or any overpowering desire for anonymity in his actions. His name was Harry Thobe, a retired bricklayer. Harry missed few Red games, and he was a regular at the World Series. You couldn't miss him. He always appeared in red shoes, a red and white striped shirt, a straw skimmer with a wide, red hatband, and carrying a red umbrella. His act was always the same—a shuffling dance in full regalia atop the dugout of each team, and the larger the crowd, or the more important the game, the longer the dance. Harry craved publicity and crowd attention.

Every ball park, at one time or another, has had its favorite grandstand characters. Some of them were noted for their quiet allegiance to the home team, others because they cultivated and developed personal idiosyncrasies into individual trademarks that won them public attention.

In the list of fans who built a reputation for loyal allegiance, two names stand out in my memory. One is Harry Pearlstone, a friend of Connie Mack, and a longtime Athletics rooter. Not only did Pearl-stone attend most of the Athletics games at home, but for forty-four consecutive years he made one or more road trips with Connie and the A's. That's loyalty.

The other fan who rates kudos for dedication to a baseball hobby is Arthur Felsch, of Milwaukee. Milwaukee was a minor league town during his youthful years, and his fetish was the World Series opener. Year after year, he would arrive a week before the first game, park outside the bleacher gate, and live on sandwiches and hot dogs—all to make sure he was first in line when the bleacher gates opened.

Today, Arthur would have problems. Bleacher seats, if any, are often sold in advance. Add to that the fact that divisional playoffs mean that the World Series site may be in doubt until a couple of days before it opens. These things would work against an Arthur Felsch. But it was fun while it lasted, both for Arthur and for the press. He made the headlines he craved; the writers had a ready-made story; and the crazy record he took pride in establishing will probably endure forever.

There were others. The vociferous "let-the-tail-go-with-hide" type of fans, both male and female. There were too many to list here, but certainly there should be room for a few who stand out in my memory.

St. Louis had Mary Ott, whose loud and strident whinny would shatter the ear drums of spectators for twenty rows around when she really wound up and let go. She was particularly anathema to visiting players when she settled down behind the visiting dugout to practice her art.

In Pittsburgh, there was an unknown who could bark like a seal for nine innings and never sprain a tonsil. I never knew his name but I think they called him "The Coal Man." In Detroit, Patsy O'Toole's foghorn voice could be heard for miles in a two-tone cacophony of "Faker" and "Bum." Nor can we leave out Brooklyn's own Hilda Chester, roaming the stands with her cowbell to augment a voice that really needed no augmenting.

Every city had them, and they were all great! And unless I miss my guess, they will be remembered by baseball constituents for at least two or three generations—and in baseball circles that's a long stretch of memory.

For some reason the theatrical profession has, through the years, developed a strange alliance with baseball. My friend Horace McMahon, who was a fine actor, once said, "I think that there is an affinity among all people who make their living in front of audiences. Audiences can be great friends for performers, but they can also be tough opponents. Only those who work in front of audiences know how true that can be."

Even before the turn of the century, actors were among the most ardent of baseball fans, and at least two of them rode to fame and fortune by using baseball's growing interest in their stage routines.

One was DeWolfe Hopper. In 1888, Ernest Thayer wrote a poem called "Casey at the Bat." It was an immediate success, and Hopper was quick to take advantage of that. His recitation of the poem—even he had no idea how many times he performed it—became one of the most popular "turns" in the history of vaudeville, and the legitimate theater, too. No matter what role Hopper might be playing, audiences would demand an after-show recital of "Casey."

There is no question that no popular song with a sports theme ever achieved anything like the popularity of "Take Me Out to the Ball Game." It was to become a trademark for the game, and for a popular young song-and-dance man of the time named Jack Norworth. The song proved to be of benefit not only to Norworth, but, being completely fair, to baseball, too.

There was another actor who contributed to the history of baseball, but in a different way. His name was Louis Mann. Most of the actors in those days loved to sit in the old ground-level press box at the Polo Grounds, much to the discomfort of the Working Press. The visitors were usually considerate, and could be persuaded to move elsewhere on the big days when the press box was filled with "working stiffs."

But not Louie. He considered occupying that press box seat as a personal prerogative, and no complaint or personal invective could move him. In 1908, Mann showed up in the press box in Chicago for the World Series. Writer Hugh Fullerton arrived, and explained that the seat had been assigned to him. Mann refused to move. So, Fullerton sat down in Mann's lap, and stayed there for nine innings, covering the ball game.

That was not the end of the story. That night, the writers staged an indignation meeting against Louis Mann, and the entire group of interlopers. The result of the meeting was the formation of the Baseball Writers' Association of America. Today, more than a half century later, the BBWAA is still going strong—probably the most important attribute that baseball communication has ever known.

In all probability, such an organization was inevitable. But I doubt if it would have come about so quickly, or rules covering press box occupancy been as stringent, if it hadn't been for Louis Mann. The press box is literally a world apart in a ball park. The occupancy is not controlled by the club, but by the Baseball Writers' Association itself. Once when he was the general manager of the Brooklyn Dodgers, the colorful Larry MacPhail got into an argument with a newspaperman. MacPhail threatened to have the writer barred from the press box. The BBWAA pointed out that the writer would not be barred, and that MacPhail was allowed in the press box only at the whim of the association. If his attitude didn't change, he was going to be barred from his own press box.

Maybe the action was a backhanded compliment, but the fact remains that the baseball writers owe a big debt to a man who was once such a thorn in their sides—actor Louis Mann.

One of the most devoted of all the show business baseball fans was Jack White, the zany comic who operated the famous "18 Club" on West 52nd Street in New York. Jack was an ardent Giant fan, and each time the Giants won, Jack would hang a big sign back of the orchestra proclaiming the victorious score. If the Giants lost, another sign was posted which said, simply, "No Game Today. Rain!" Once when the club lost six in a row, Jack failed to show up for work. Patrons that night were regaled with a new sign. It read, "Sorry! Gone to a funeral."

The Yankees never had a more loyal fan supporter than Bill "Bojangles" Robinson, the famous tap dancer. Bill always carried a vial of "goofer" dust to each game. If the Yankees were in trouble, or facing a crucial series, Bill would appear in the dugout before the game and execute his own little dance as he scattered the "goofer" dust on Yankee bats to ensure timely hits, and on the players' gloves to ward off costly errors.

Bill was at his best at World Series time. He always traveled on the train with the club, usually in the press car, where he would hold court every night. He would run through his dance routines for hours on end, with an occasional break for storytelling, at which he also was a master. Many a Yankee player would sneak into the press car at such times to enjoy the show. Probably they should have been in bed, but manager Miller Huggins never seemed to mind. Bill may have cost his players a bit of sleep now and then, but he certainly kept them loose and relaxed.

From the world of politics came a very special fan in the hearts of the Yankees. Before, during, and after his tenure as Postmaster General, James A. Farley has been a Yankee Stadium regular. He is the quiet type of fan, but very knowledgeable. His straw skimmer is as much a baseball trademark as the old crumpled fedora that Judge Landis made famous.

For unbridled enthusiasm, unadulterated zaniness, and fierce loyalty, the old Brooklyn Dodgers fans had to stand out above all others.

Ebbets Field is long gone, a victim of urban progress and the lure of greener pastures. But the memories linger. Along with Hilda Chester and her cowbell, who can ever forget Jack Pierce and his "Cookie" Lavagetto balloons? Eddie Bettan with his explorer's hat and his tin whistle? Or the late "Shorty" Laurice and the strolling musical aggregation known as the Dodgers Sym-Phoney?

The fans reflected the ball club, or vice versa. Certainly manager Wilbert Robinson was every bit as much a "character" as any of the customers. Once, when the club was in a slump, Uncle Robbie happened to overhear his favorite, Babe Herman, complain about the way the club was being managed. Some managers would regard this is as insubordination and take strong action. Uncle Robbie called Herman over and instructed him to pick the lineup and batting order for that day.

Fans could present peculiar problems to the Falstaffian Robbie. The prime example of that had to be "Abie the Iceman." Abie liked to hitch his ice wagon outside Ebbets Field, while he went inside to jeer the Dodgers. He had a foghorn voice that could be heard throughout the ball park. Over and over he would yell, "Ya, bums, ya."

Uncle Robbie eventually tired of the greeting, and offered Abie a season pass to Dodger games with one proviso: "You gotta stop yelling at my boys. You're making them nervous." Abie accepted the pass happily. A few days later he sought Robbie out in the clubhouse. "Here's your pass back," he said. "I can't stand it anymore. I gotta yell. And, besides, they *are* bums!"

Robbie took the pass. "All right," he growled, grudgingly. "Maybe they are bums. But try to keep your voice down, will ya? When you holler so loud you might wake up some of the boys taking naps on the bench."

Robbie, in his own way, set the pace and pattern for Brooklyn fans. At heart he was one of them, and they knew it. Today, Ebbets Field and the Dodgers are only memories. Fortunately for baseball, the Mets have taken over where the Dodgers left off. The fans are a new generation. Their techniques have changed. Groups with banners have taken over the rooting responsibilities, and smirking into television cameras is an easier way of getting public attention than panning players or berating umpires. But the loyalty and fierce enthusiasm that built Brooklyn tradition still endures. I'm sure Mrs. Payson and her staff are most appreciative.

Before we sign off the old, and turn the camera on today, there is one other man who deserves mention in the story of fans—not only because of his fan interest, but equally because of his faith in the game of baseball. His name—Charles Ebbets, owner of the Dodgers at a time when baseball ownership was a labor of love, and profits consisted largely of personal satisfaction in a break-even operation.

Charley Ebbets was a fan by birth and nature, an owner through fate and circumstances, and a hard-boiled operator by dire necessity. In my mind's eye I can still see him, white-haired and ruddy-faced, sitting on his favorite high stool in the back of the Ebbets Field stands. He would be chatting and arguing with passing fans, discussing trades, listening to criticism, airing his plans and hopes, expounding his baseball opinion to all who would listen—a typical country squire holding court for his tenants and neighbors.

All was not beer and skittles for the Squire in those days. The going was always rough, and on occasion desperate. Certainly the fans were loyal, but loyalty alone does not take care of salaries and expenses. And a 300 or 400 home attendance is a porous fabric from which to build a cloak of confidence or an umbrella of optimism. No one will ever know how many times the Squire was forced to call on his banker for financial assistance, or the number of personal notes he signed to meet the monthly payroll to tide the club through winter periods of inactivity or to cover the expense of spring training.

But through it all he never once lost his enthusiasm as a fan, or his belief in baseball's future. In fact it was in those dark days when critics were crying that the game had lost its appeal to the public, and was slowly dying, that the Squire pulled a line that is still remembered whenever baseball people get together. Said Charley Ebbets: "The critics are all wrong. Baseball is still in its infancy!"

The critics of the game had fun with that one. Charley Ebbets became a target of these same prophets of doom. But Ebbets was convinced that he was right, and you can judge for yourself by the date of Ebbets's famous quote. It was 1914. Truly, baseball was still in its infancy.

Unfortunately, Charley Ebbets didn't live to see his prophecy come true. But if, somewhere in the Great Beyond, there is a Valhalla for baseball warhorses, I'm sure Charley Ebbets is there, still holding fans court with his cronies. And if sometimes he should look down, chuckle to himself, and indulge in a Brooklynesque "I told you so," who can blame him? That last laugh, philosophers tell us, is always the most enjoyable.

6

SCRIBES, AND A FEW PHARISEES

"The Moving Finger writes; and having writ,
Moves on . . ."

—Omar Khayyam

Sportswriters have ever been a breed unto themselves. No other group of men, through the years, has contributed more to baseball and American sports. Yet no group has received less public recognition for the job they have done or the contribution they have made.

Generation after generation they have served as the eyes and ears, even the conscience, of the American sports public. They have done their job faithfully and well. Yet, in a day when autograph hunting is America's most popular pasttime, I seldom have seen a sportswriter stopped by a wild-eyed sports devotee seeking his autograph. It's a strange paradox, one I will never understand. To the general public, the sportswriters of today remain a mystical, mysterious group of men avidly read, faithfully followed, generally believed and quoted, yet viewed as impersonally as a Fifth Avenue bus or a Coney Island subway.

Why that is, I have never been able to fathom. Maybe it is a demonstration of the truism expressed many years ago by an unsung philosopher; "In this world there's nothing deader than yesterday's newspaper." Maybe the constant flow of daily stories dulls fan appreciation of the job done by craftsmen. Perhaps the writers them-

71

selves aren't interested. Through constant close contact with a head-line-seeking gentry, they've built up an immunity to publicity. They've learned to take a tongue-in-cheek attitude toward the world of ballyhoo, learned to laugh at all the foibles of the mob, even their own. And that's a deadly sin. Laughing at yourself is a fatal process in the world of headline seeking.

I've long held the belief that the world of baseball writing could well be the subject for a serious book documenting the contribution sportswriters have made to the development of sports in America. Such a book certainly would be an important adjunct to the history of sports. But it would have to be done by a writer who has actually experienced the thrills and excitement of press box existence; who has seen firsthand the bitterness and disappointment that besets the path to sports greatness. So far, no candidate has volunteered for the task. Writers, I guess, are so engrossed in recording the accomplishments, the successes, the disappointments, and the failures of others, they have no time to document the achievement of their own craft.

Some time ago an old writing cohort of mine, Jimmy Cannon, wrote a gently chiding column about the operation of the commissioner's office. His central theme was that when Baseball chose Ford Frick they were really electing a poet as commissioner. I reluctantly plead "Not guilty" to that charge—"rhymester" perhaps, but not "poet." But I did get a kick out of Jimmy's comment. There's a bit of the poet in every sportswriter—just as there's a bit of the "eternal boy" in every sports fan. Jimmy Cannon might object to my saying so, but Jimmy has it even more than many of his associates. True, he likes to pose as a suave, hard-boiled writer who knows all the angles in the sordid business of commercial sports operation. Nor does he pull any punches in his criticism of the shady characters who too often are lured into sports through promise of easy income without work.

But given a subject he can really warm up to, whether the drama of a great World Series or the personality of an individual, the poet comes out in every line. At such times, Cannon writes not in rhyme but in glowing prose that sings its message in language as expressive as an oil painting or a great musical chord.

Did you ever read anything Cannon wrote about Damon Runyon? Runyon was Cannon's greatest idol among all the writers he knew, and when Jimmy wrote of Damon, the hidden "poet" came out and readers saw the real Cannon at his best.

Runyon also had a lot of the poet in his soul. In his early days he even published a couples of books of poetry that drew favorable comment from the leading critics of the time. But there is another poetic form, not dependent on rhyme or meter, but nonetheless lyrical in its flow of words and the sincere simplicity of the picture it conveys. Runyon often hit that chord in his daily writing.

There was, for instance, the lead he wrote for the old New York *American* the day Casey Stengel hit an inside-the-park home run to defeat the Yankees, 5 to 4, in the first game of the 1923 World Series. He wrote:

"This is the way old Casey Stengel ran yesterday afternoon running his home run home.

"This is the way old Casey Stengel ran, running his home run home, when two were out in the ninth inning, and the score was tied, and the ball was still bounding inside the Yankee yard.

"This is the way. . . .

"His mouth wide open. . . .

"His warped old legs bending beneath him at every stride.

"His arms flying back and forth like those of a man swimming a crawl stroke . . .

"His flanks heaving, his breath whistling, his head far back. Yankee infielders, passed by old Casey Stengel as he was running his home run home, say Casey was muttering to himself, adjuring himself to greater speed as a jockey mutters to his horse in a race, saying, 'Go on, Casey, go on.'

"The warped old legs, twisted and bent by many a year of baseball campaigning, just barely held out under Casey until he reached home plate, running his home run home.

"Then they collapsed."

To me, that's poetry. Not in rhyme or meter, but in the story it tells of an old man struggling for victory on spent legs that kept going by determination alone. Of course, it couldn't happen today—Runyon's piece, I mean. Time is too important, and space too valuable, to permit writers such liberties in descriptive writing. But the will is still there, the bit of the "poet" is still in every writer, and a modern generation still finds opportunity to express itself when the occasion arises.

In that connection, I think of Gene Ward, columnist on the New York *Daily News*. Gene belongs to the tongue-in-cheek school. He is hard-nosed in his criticism and skeptical in his approach to most professional sports operations. Like the majority of modern writers, he looks with jaundiced eye on the "quick buck" operators, whose professed interest in sports is measured by the size of the dollar sign in the profit column of the auditor's report. Also, Gene Ward doesn't like baseball.

But when he writes of the simple pleasures of a day in the country with his sons, when he shares with his readers the warmth of the father-son relationship, when he pictures, in a simple language, the pride that comes in sharing together the experience of sports participation—then the "poet" comes out every time.

I don't know Gene Ward well. As a writer, I was before his time. I have never met his sons. But I have clipped and preserved every one of those columns. And when, occasionally, I get fed up with all the crass commercialism, and the chicanery, and the "behind-the-scenes" maneuverings that are so much a part of today's sports picture, I reread them, and my faith in the future of sports is somehow restored.

There are others, too.

Red Smith, who usually uses a bit of humor to cloak the biting edge of criticism, needs only the lure of a trout stream to bring out the spark of inherent poetry in his soul.

O. B. Keeler waxed lyrical when he wrote of Bobby Jones. Marshall Hunt was at his best when he chronicled the feats of Babe Ruth. Harry Salsinger, usually conservative in word and manner, always added a new lyrical dimension if Ty Cobb was the subject.

Yessir, Jimmy, there's a bit of poet in every sportswriter—and any time the baseball powers see fit to elect a baseball writer as commissioner, they are likely to find a touch of poetic fervor thrown in gratis.

I have frequently been asked how I, as an old newspaperman, react to the criticism of newspapermen during my terms as a league president and as a commissioner. In both roles I was no stranger to criticism, especially as commissioner. If I told you that I liked it, I would be lying.

However, the years I spent as a reporter taught me that writers, for the most part, didn't care whether or not I liked their criticism. I genuinely feel that most of it was objective. Not all, but most.

I remember a particular day when two writers saw fit to give the commissioner a going-over. One was Dick Young, of the New York *Daily News*. The other shall remain nameless. The second one was critical but nowhere near as outspoken as Young. Still, I found Young's piece bothered me a lot less.

The reason was simple. Young had called me on the phone, and discussed with me my reasons for whatever position I had taken, and I frankly don't remember now what the issue was. I had given Dick my reasons, and he didn't agree with me. Fine. I wish he had, but I could certainly understand that he didn't. The other fellow had never given me a chance to air my side. I felt I was entitled to that. I felt that that was proper treatment when I was on the other side of the fence, too.

The art of baseball writing, in fact all sports reporting, has been a matter of evolution. The American people have ever been sports-minded, turning even the most commonplace daily tasks into competitive contests, whenever two or more men got together. Rifle shooting, rail splitting, beaver trapping, even house-raising were all grist for the early competitive mills. Back in the colonial days, the local gazettes ran frequent announcements of neighborhood racing meets and reports on boxing bouts or shooting matches between matched local champions. And in pioneer settlements, where printing presses were unavailable, news announcements were made from the church pulpits. It was not unusual to hear comments on tree-felling contests or turkey shoots, lightly dropped in between the weather predictions and the prayers beseeching God's mercy for erring souls.

Baseball emerged in the 1830s as a competitive team game—the first ever devised in America. It had immediate appeal. But it was not until after the Civil War that the impact of the game was felt by the newspapers. True, there were frequent mentions of baseball in local newspapers, and an occasional paragraph or two on an intercity game where enthusiasm reached unusual proportions—but no real indication of any regular coverage until 1869.

That year, the Cincinnati Red Stockings, the first professional team in baseball history, embarked on a national tour that attracted so much interest that newspapers couldn't ignore it. For the first time in history, newspaper reporters in various cities were assigned to cover games, and operators flashed telegraphic inning scores and final results to interested cities throughout the East and the Middle West.

It was a humble beginning, but with that tour baseball writing was born, and sports stories elevated to a regular place in the news coverage assignments.

Most of the writers who shared in those early assignments have been long forgotten. One man, however, will be remembered so long as fans keep their enthusiasm, and baseball endures. He was Henry "Father" Chadwick. Of all the contributions baseball writers have made to the game, his was probably the greatest. He devised the box score. He revised and simplified the playing rules. He established standard scoring rules and statistical procedures that unified the game whether played on city diamonds, in villages, or on cow pastures. In short, he took a rural and local pastime and, by his genius and devotion, turned it into a national institution.

Certainly Chadwick's devotion to the new game was without parallel. His contribution to baseball's development as a national institution early earned him his accolade as Father of the game we know today. Final recognition came nearly seventy-five years later when he was named unanimously to the Hall of Fame—the first, and to date the only, baseball writer ever named to that august body solely on the record he established as a writer, and without official connection, or club affiliation. Yet he was not alone in his field.

How many fans of today, I wonder, know that one of the early baseball writers was a young man from Brooklyn named Walt Whitman? Or that the erudite editor of the New York *Post*, William Cullen Bryant, was so intrigued by the game that he ordered regular reportorial coverage of an intercity series played at Elysian Fields in Hoboken? Will Irwin, himself a baseball writer during his early years, tells us that Bill Nye, the great American humorist, did a bit of baseball writing in Chicago when he first came out of the West to establish himself as a master in the field of humor.

Then there was Duncan Curry, who got his first taste of base-ball in the days of the old Metropolitans and Excelsiors, and later, as a professional writer, covered the National League in the years of its infancy. There were problems in those days, too—player strikes, re-serve rule troubles, player manipulation, contract jumping, franchise manipulation—all the things that writers face today, and Curry wrote of them all.

I was fortunate enough to know Curry in the late years of his life. He was a dapper, portly gentleman with white hair and a closely cropped moustache, he always wore the stiffly starched collars of his era, with a black watered-silk ribbon around his neck attached to the spectacles that protruded from his upper weskit pocket. A gold watch dangled around his somewhat protruding stomach, and always there were pearl gray spats fitting snugly over black patent leather shoes. Quite a Beau Brummel in his day, and quite a man about town.

He had left his baseball days far behind when I knew him, and was writing boating and yachting for Hearst's *Morning American*. But he never lost his interest in baseball. He followed the National League assiduously, thought the American League was an upstart outfit and said so at every opportunity, and shook his head sadly whenever modern players were mentioned.

"A bunch of sissies," he would argue. "Why they couldn't even carry the gloves of the stars of my day!"

Some years ago Norman Rockwell presented me with the original of one of the first sports covers he painted for the *Saturday Evening Post*. It depicted a grandfatherly old gentleman, fully equipped with spats, weskit, stiff collar, watch fob, and patent leather shoes. He stood poised, bat ready, over a temporary home plate, which con-sisted of a quartered newspaper anchored by a brick. Behind the plate a youngster, obviously the grandson, squatted, grinning as he gave the time-honored two-finger sign for a curve ball. The first time I saw the picture, it reminded me of Duncan Curry. After all these years, it still does.

I don't know who the man was who posed for that picture. I wish I did. Somehow, I'd like him to know the memories that come flooding back every time I sit at my desk and look at the painting. It's Duncan Curry as I knew him, a pioneer baseball writer who actually lived the excitement and thrills of days that a youngster dreams about, but somehow never hopes to experience.

Another old-timer of those days was Sam Crane, who spent his twilight years covering the Giants for the New York *Journal*. Sam had been a major league player during the 1880s and early '90s. He was not an outstanding star during his playing days; but he was, so far as records show, the first player to take up the baseball writing profession when his playing days were over. Sam undoubtedly was the best friend John McGraw had among the writers of his day. Sam and McGraw fought like cats and dogs at times; for weeks on end, they would refuse to speak to each other. But somehow they always managed to overcome their difficulties and remain basic friends.

Some writers felt that Sam had a real inside line on every move McGraw or the Giants made. Maybe he did. But I never knew of a single time he took advantage of that friendship to put anything over on other writers. Nor do I know of a single instance when he betrayed a McGraw confidence, even in time of deepest feud.

Sam didn't really rate among the great writers of his era, but he didn't pull his punches, and he loved the game. He was the first baseball man to urge publicly that the owners organize some sort of memorial to the greats of the game. After the Cooperstown report, he centered on that village as the place for such a memorial. Between 1917 and 1925 he made numerous pilgrimages to Cooperstown in an effort "to get something started." But, alas, he was ahead of his time, and his efforts came to naught.

Among the modern players of his day, he had two favorites. One was Ross Youngs. "Youngs will be the National League's answer to Ty Cobb," he wrote. "He can't miss. He's got everything."

The other was Frank Frisch, just blossoming into stardom. "Frisch," he predicted, "will develop into the greatest infielder ever to wear a Giant uniform. He's the best prospect I ever saw."

Today the Cooperstown shrine that Sam advocated so tenaciously is a reality. Today, Youngs and Frisch, his two favorite "moderns," are installed there. Sam would have been a proud man had he lived to be present in Cooperstown in 1939 when the doors swung open to welcome that first Immortal Five, Ty Cobb, Walter Johnson, Christy Mathewson, Babe Ruth, and Honus Wagner. He would have been doubly proud in the later years when the installation of Frisch and Youngs would make his dream a complete reality.

By 1890 sports pages had become an important part of the nation's newspapers. Baseball writing was accepted as an honored craft, though sportswriting was largely a hit-or-miss proposition without color, personality, or individual character. Writers wrote of the daily games, or course, but they were equally concerned with off-field problems. Player piracy, gambling, the constant moving of franchises, and, of course, the pros and cons of player reservation—with the attendant contract battles between management and players—demanded as much space and brought more trenchant comment than did actual play on the field.

At the turn of the century new faces appeared on the sportswriting horizon. New bylines headed the nation's sports stories. Names like Charles Spink, and Al Richter, and Cy Goodfriend, and Joe Vila, and Mel Webb, to mention a few, suddenly burst into prominence as leaders in the fight to make baseball as solid and as honest in its front office operation as it was popular in playing performance. These men may not have displayed the same writing ease that characterized their successors—but without their faith in and dedication to the game, without their willingness to fight tirelessly to protect the rights of players and fans, without their courage to criticize what was wrong, and support for what they felt was right, there would have been no American League today.

More importantly, without their constant policing in the public interest, without their exposure of chicanery and sharp practice as it occurred, there would be no public confidence, no development of public faith in baseball as a national institution. If, through the years, baseball writers have contributed much to the game—and they have—great credit must go to those early writers who pointed the way. They laid down the guidelines for sportswriting procedure; they demonstrated the power of the press to influence public opinion; they established the policing weapon of press vigilance. Those guidelines still exist today, and baseball is better for them.

Sportswriters have always been a freethinking, freewriting lot, unhampered by the style books or the "who, what, when, where, and why" of normal reportorial procedure. The very nature of their assignment allowed a breeziness of expression and an intimate approach that would be frowned on in journalism classes, or even page-one circles. I think that's because sports pages deal with success rather than failure, with happy endings rather than remorse and disappointment. Relaxation, laughter, entertainment, and fun are the basic tools of the trade.

Idols are easy to build, and heroes blossom into greatness and fade away with the regularity of changing seasons. Sportswriters have to be optimists at heart. People who go to the game and people who read sports pages look for pleasant reading and happy memories. Most writers in their daily tasks bear those precepts in mind.

Even as early as the turn of the century, baseball writers had adopted an intimate, breezy style of reporting designed to make sports pages uniquely different in the newspaper setup. Those years developed the slang school of writing. No self-respecting scribe would even consider referring to a pitcher or catcher as such. Pitchers were "hurlers" or "lancers" or "southpaws" or "sidewheelers." Catchers were "receivers" or "backstoppers." They never wore masks or protectors, but instead were arrayed in the "tools of ignorance." There was no first, second, or third base in the lexicon of the era. Instead it was "the initial sack," the "keystone," and "the hot corner"—with outfielders labeled "fly-hawks" or "retrievers" as their individual prowess might dictate. No player ever got a base on balls; he received an "Annie Oakley" or "a complimentary pass." And no player ever hit into a double play—it was always a "twin killing."

It was a period of nicknames, too. I was a kid in northern Indiana at that time. The Chicago Cubs were my idols, and the Chicago *Tribune* and the old *Inter-Ocean* my twin baseball bibles. I knew, of course, that it was Chance's Cubs I idolized, but it was a couple of seasons before I learned that his first name was Frank, and not "Peerless Leader." I was also slow to learn that "The Crab's" real name was John Evers, and that the centerfielder had been baptized "Frank" Schulte and not "Wildfire." There were others, too. Christy Mathewson was "The Big Six"; Walter Johnson, just breaking in, was already "The Big Train"; and Clark Griffith, even then, was "The Old Fox."

With a new crop of writers coming along, and with sports pages gaining daily in prestige and popularity, writing styles changed to simpler, more readable reporting. Yet, the slang-nickname style was not entirely discarded. Through the years it has been refined and polished, but it still has its place. Expressive nicknames are still a part of the baseball writing vocabulary, and slang expressions, sparingly used, add a distinctive flavor of intimacy and warmth to modern sports prose. In fact, writers in other fields now go along with the practice. Nicknames appear often these days in first-page presentations, and apt slang expressions frequently add color and spice to the staid columns of the financial and editorial pages. To my mind, that's a good thing. Score one gold star for the baseball writers on that one!

The art of baseball writing really attained its maturity in 1908 with the organization of the Baseball Writers' Association of America. At the time no one realized the importance of the move. The Association was born in anger and dedicated in pique—to rid the press box of the Louis Manns and other freeloaders—and assure the writers of a proper seat from which they could do their daily stint, without interference. It's pretty difficult to turn out deathless prose with a typewriter perched precariously on your knee, and your posterior balanced on an upturned beer case borrowed from a sympathetic concessionaire; it's doubly difficult when you face the added obstacle of freeloading spectators, yelling in your ear, stomping on your feet, and waving madly to friends, while you try to write.

So the Baseball Writers' Association was formed, and a formal resolution drawn demanding that the press box be reserved solely for the use of association members; that they be given the right to do their own policing and issue their own membership cards, without interference from clubs or officials. The demands were accepted by the two leagues without a moment's delay or a single voice of opposition. The important victory had been won. The writers had become a recognized part of the baseball picture.

The impact of the Baseball Writers' Association through the years is common knowledge. Before it came on the scene, baseball writing was a disorganized, hit-or-miss profession, and the writers were unrecognized voices crying in the wilderness. Today they are a closely knit body, proud of their professional standing, powerful in their unity of purpose, militant in their criticism of purported wrongdoing. There have been times, I must confess, when it seemed to me they were a bit too arbitrary in their demands; times when, as an official, I have resented what seemed an unnecessary arrogance in their approach to intricate problems. But that is to be expected. No organization of human beings is ever perfect, and no individual infallible. My working card in the Baseball Writers' Association is still a cherished possession. And among my happiest moments today are the moments spent in the press box, reliving old memories and swapping reminiscences with other old dodos, who shared with me the excitement and the thrill of a writing age long since passé.

At this time, too, there came a change in writing styles: a new and more personal approach to the business of writing baseball. I like to think the change was due to the improved writing conditions that came about when the press box, freed of freeloaders, became a business haven where writers could do their daily stint in comfortable privacy. Maybe I'm wrong. Maybe the bylines did it. There's a certain pride that comes in seeing your name in print above the story you have written, and the sports pages were the first to recognize the fact. Baseball writers were privileged to sign their stories long before "bylines" were permitted to reporters in other departments. Or perhaps the change, which came with the formation of the Baseball Writers' Association, was the sheerest coincidence.

It wasn't a drastic or sudden metamorphosis. Just a funny line here, a humerous quip there, as a harbinger of better things to come.

I recall a descriptive line, written by Charley Van Loan, that raised a great furor throughout the Midwest Bible Belt. Describing the winning play of a Chicago Cub game, Van Loan wrote: "Schulte came home with the winning run like Balaam entering Jerusalem." Not very funny, and not startling by present standards, I must admit. But the good church people were up in arms. Letters poured into the editor denouncing the writer as crude and even sacrilegious in his comment. Bible references had no place on the sports pages, the critics claimed, and anyhow it was in bad taste to hide behind a Biblical incident in describing the manner in which the run was scored. Charley was not too upset by the criticism, and other writers profited by his writing example.

A short time later, Charles Dryden commenting on an interview with Connie Mack following the 1910 World Series, wrote:

"Mr. Cornelius McGillicuddy this morning held a press conference to discuss the World Series. Mr. Mack was sleeping in his chair when the writers arrived. An attendant graciously awakened him. His comments were terse and to the point: 'Judas Priest,' he said, 'what a series! I didn't think my boys could do it! Judas Priest!' As we filed out, the excited Mr. McGillicuddy was sleeping in his chair."

Arthur (Bugs) Baer was a master of the one-line, tongue-in-cheek style. Shortly after he arrived in New York from Philadelphia, he was covering a Yankee game. The colorful Ping Bodie was in the New York lineup. Ping was an outfielder of parts and a mighty hitter, but his base running left a lot to be desired. This day Ping singled off the right-field wall. On the next pitch he attempted to steal second, and was thrown out by a country mile. Bugs's wry written comment was, "Ping's mind was filled with larceny, but his legs were honest."

Out in Chicago, during this same decade, a big-eyed serious-faced skinny youngster named Ring Lardner was covering the White Sox. He was a quiet, reserved chap who had little to say, but was an excellent listener and observer. And how he could write! His style was trenchant at times, and sometimes he was sharply critical, but largely he leavened drama with saving humor, and employed gentle satire as a lance to puncture the ego of "stuffed shirts" and "phonies." In Chicago, he developed a great following through a series of "You Know Me, Al" letters—presumably written by a White Sox rookie to his buddy back home. These letters, for the first time, gave fans a picture of the human side of athletes—their hopes and ambitions, their likes and dislikes, their virtues and their shortcomings. They treated players as human beings, with behind-the-scenes glimpses as the ball clubs traveled on a train, stayed at a hotel, sat around the clubhouse. In those letters Lardner used the needle with telling effect, cutting owners and officials down to size, panning officious managers, and exposing the touts and hangers-on who were using the game to their own selfish end.

During the decade from 1910 to 1920, the whole complexion of baseball writing changed for the better. Lardner, Baer, and the others were largely responsible. They were the human catalysts who brought humor and fun into the baseball picture. Their writing established the fact that wrongs can be righted, "phonies" exposed, and evils corrected, without tearing down public faith in the virtues of the game itself.

At the end of the First World War, the writing style they originated was firmly established. During the so-called golden age of sports it was used effectively by such men as Bill McGeehan, and Westbrook Pegler, and Warren Brown, and Dan Parker, and John Kieran to battle the crazy antics of a nonsensical era. In later generations, it has been effectively employed by such dedicated writers as Bill Corum, Joe Williams, John Carmichael, Tom Meany, and Red Smith to mention only a few.

Tongue-in-cheek writing is still in vogue today. Dick Young uses it from time to time. So does Gene Ward, and Bob Addie, Jerry Holtzman, Joe Falls, and Arthur Daley. And that's good for baseball.

Maybe Messrs. Lardner, Baer, et al. really gave baseball writing a new dimension.

Though there are many similarities in the job of today's baseball writer and the writers who covered the beat with me, there is also one glaring difference. It just has to add up to the fact that today's writers face a tougher task every day than we did. That difference is, quite simply, that we were writing for an audience that quite likely didn't even know who had won the game we covered. Today's writer works to an audience who is not only aware of the score, probably knows how the runs were scored, and has a good chance of having seen the game himself. That makes for a pretty demanding audience.

Sometimes baseball people get upset at writers who seem to be more concerned with the so-called offbeat stories. On occasion, I have been among those baseball people, but maybe I'm mellowing. In any case, I'm becoming more tolerant of the problems that writers today have to face.

One offbeat baseball story that I remember quite fondly was written by Bob Broeg, a good friend, and a fine reporter and sports editor for the St. Louis *Post-Dispatch*. It was during my first term in the commissioner's office, and part of my duty was the administration of the players pension fund. Broeg, armed with a financial report of the plan, turned it over to an independent actuary for an opinion of the commissioner's administration. The reply was that, in the actuary's opinion, the commissioner was paying off the back-service obligations too quickly. (When the plan was started, there were a lot of players who became members, and almost immediately retired. They made one payment and that was it. Obviously, money had to be put into the plan to pay for this service, and it was the contention of the actuary that I was doing it too quickly.)

When Broeg called me to report his findings, and that he was going to write it, I think he expected me to be upset. I wasn't. I'm not trying to be especially noble. I just recognized that Broeg had come up with a good, legitimate story—one I would have loved to get if I was a newspaperman. Also, I knew that Broeg was treating it as just what it was, a story. He was not trying to make a whipping boy of the commissioner.

I still think my reasons for handling the back-service payments the way I did was the correct one. Briefly, since almost all the money came from television, I was always concerned about what would happen if we ran into a television strike at World Series time. With no telecasts, there would be no money coming in. At that point, with the principal and the interest being carried for a year with no payments, it could have been a calamity.

For those of you who think my worries were groundless, I can tell you that we woke up on the morning of a first game of a World Series one year, in just that position. Fortunately, the matter was settled about 10 A.M.

I know I'm a prejudiced witness, but sentimentally I have always felt the heyday of baseball writing occurred in the decade following the end of the First World War—a period that Joe Williams always referred to as "the era of wonderful nonsense." It was a fun period—fun for the writers, fun for the players, and fun for the fans. It was an era when the Frenchman Coué gained fame and world headlines with his "Day by day, in every way, I am getting better and better"; an era when Arthur Brisbane pontificated to the world that "one gorilla can lick a dozen Dempseys."

I had my first contact with big-time sportswriters in late 1921, when I reported to the old New York *American*, fresh out of Colorado Springs, a callow, wide-eyed, bushy-tailed kid, paying my first visit to the city. The first three writers I met were Damon Runyon, who was my guide and mentor, and Grantland Rice and Sid Mercer.

Runyon, in my youthful mind was the greatest reporter of all time, and Rice the greatest descriptive sportswriter in the country. I have never had occasion to change my opinion about either of them. Mercer, of course, was the dean of New York baseball writers at the time. It was Mercer who, single-handed, challenged John McGraw's bullying treatment of one of the sportswriters. Sid made his charges stick, too, and McGraw made public apology—the only time in his whole career, so far as I know, that the Little Napoleon ever deigned to apologize for anything. A few years later Mercer rushed to McGraw's aid, when he thought John was being unfairly castigated. Sid Mercer was that kind of man.

Later that afternoon at the Yankee office I was introduced to Heywood Broun and Bill McGeehan, and Ring Lardner, and at the Giant office we ran into Bozeman Bulger, John Kieran, Frank Graham, and Freddy Lieb. Quite an array of baseball writing talent for that or any era.

John Kieran, to my mind, was the most erudite baseball writer I ever met. He read Latin and Greek fluently, spoke French with a real Parisian accent, and was an authority on Shakespeare. One of his close friends was Harry M. Stevens, the concessionaire, and the two spent many winter afternoons discussing the Bard, and trying to stump each other with little known quotations from minor Shakespearian plays. Once in a while Stevens would miss out, Kieran never.

John was a recognized naturalist too and always carried high-powered binoculars, even on the golf course, where he spent more time watching birds than he did on his game. I recall a game at the old Jungle Club in St. Petersburg when John was paired with Babe Ruth in a foursome. Babe was a long hitter and on a par-four hole he hit a long second shot that hit just short of the green and rolled into the cup for an eagle two.

Babe did a bit of a victory dance, and looked up expectantly for a word of approbation from his partner. John wasn't even there. Babe spotted him far down the fairway, peering intently through his field glasses at a blue heron fishing in a nearby mangrove swamp.

"Look at that *!*!* so-and-so," he roared. "I make the best blankety-blank shot of the season and that dumb so-and-so's looking at some crazy bird and didn't even see it!"

Babe never got over that one. He told the story many times, and never left out a single adjective.

Frank Graham was probably the most loved writer of his time. He was always the gentleman, kindly and considerate, ever generous of his time and strength. I roomed with Frank for two seasons and in that time I never heard him repeat a nasty rumor or make an unkind remark about an associate. Frank could write, too, and during the years developed an intimate interview style that was strictly his own. Many of his associates have tried to copy Frank's style, but to date no one has been able to match it.

To list all the old-timers would be impossible. Each major league city had its favorites—and their names are still recalled whenever craftsmen meet and wherever writers get together. If I have concentrated too much on New York writers I apologize. But my writing career was spent in New York. Those were the men I knew best—in the best days I ever knew.

Today the whole philosophy of baseball has changed and baseball writing has changed with it. New problems have arisen, old problems have become intensified. Gone, possibly forever, are the laughing, carefree fun-days of a carefree fun era. The baseball writer of today must, of course, retain his interest and enthusiasm for the game and the men who play. He must also be expert in his knowledge of the changing rules and nuances of play. Fans demand that. But that is only the beginning. The modern writer must be a bit of an economist as well, interpreting to the reading sports fans the national economic trends that more and more affect our daily sports as they affect our daily lives. He has to have legal knowledge, for we are living in a legal age, and he must understand the legal verbosity of contracts, and court rulings and counter-rulings if he is to present his readers with a factual story that they can understand. He must have the accounting knowledge of a CPA in order to ferret out the salient facts on a corporate balance sheet, or understand the complicated financial setup of the average major league club. He must familiarize himself with actuarial practice if he is to make reasonable explanation of pension plans and the intricacies of health and medical contracts and accumulated fringe benefits.

Quite an assignment, that. But it's only the beginning.

The advent of television has made it necessary for writers to "angle" their stories with "off-field" happenings and player personality yarns that will give a new slant to a secondhand account of a game.

Nor has the increasing number of night games and the switch from leisurely train travel to speedy jet planes, in order to meet schedule commitments, made the job any easier.

Let's illustrate with an average day in the life of a traveling baseball writer. It's the final game of a series, and the club is scheduled to take a plane from the airport (twenty miles from the ball park) one hour after the end of the game. The game is being played in a city located in a time zone with a one-hour differential. That means that when the game starts at 8:30 local time, it is already 9:30 in the city where the writer's paper is located, and to make the deadline it's necessary to have copy in type by 12:30.

The game drags on while the writer fidgets. Finally it's over. The scoreboard clock shows 10:45. That's 11:45 at home. Forty-five minutes to make the deadline—a little less than that to make the bus to the airport or blow the plane. The writer makes it!

But his job is not yet finished. There still are odds and ends to be covered—rumors of a trade to be run down, a disgruntled player to be interviewed for a follow-up story. In the old days of train travel it would have been easy. A leisurely dinner, a long evening for conversation, an opportunity to fraternize with players and other writers— and a comfortable night's sleep to top off the day. But plane travel is different. The manager has his own problems. He's sleepy, and his coaches demand his time and attention. The players are tired, and hungry, and sleepy. They don't want to be bothered. They have little to say—and what they do say cannot be printed in a family newspaper!

Such is an average day in the life of today's baseball writer— with the same routine to look forward to tomorrow, and tomorrow, and a season of tomorrows.

I cannot but wonder how the greats of the past—the Runyons and the Rices and the Lardners—would have handled the complicated situations under today's pressures, and faced all the extracurricular problems that are so much a part of the sports picture today. Certainly I can understand why old-timers who still carry typewriters to the baseball wars look with longing to those bygone days of fun and laughter when sports pages were devoted to sports without thought of laws or lawyers; days when financial dealings were handled on the financial pages and baseball writers wrote without the constant pressure of time, and with ample white space available for their use in painting word pictures of heroic achievement and dramatic success.

It is not my purpose here to attempt any analysis of individual modern writers. There are too many. Suffice to say they are upholding nobly the standards set by their predecessors of other generations, despite the pressures and complexities of modern living.

One observation: Baseball writers have had a closer relationship to their game than any other sportswriting group I can name. Through the years many writers have been brought into positions of importance in the management structure. And, almost without exception, they have performed with credit to baseball and the writing profession.

Ban Johnson left the writing profession to organize the American League, and become a dominant factor in the baseball operations of his period.

Henry Edwards, for many years a writer of note in the Cleveland area, established the American League service bureau to the great benefit of the game. And he was followed by Earl Hilligan of the AP, who carried on the job Edwards started.

In Chicago, Jimmy Gallagher moved from sportswriting to become general manager of the Cubs, moving from there to the Phillies, and into the commissioner's office, where today he is in charge of a sandlot development and scouting program that has been tremendously successful; Eddie Short left his press-box typewriter to become general manager of the Chicago White Sox.

The Philadelphia writers' chapter sent Bill Dooley to the Phillies office to organize a badly needed public relations department and followed with Bill Brandt who, for many years, headed the service bureau in the National League office.

The Hall of Fame in Cooperstown owes much to the baseball writers too. Sid Keener, of the St. Louis *Times,* came in as curator of that institution and served for years in that demanding job. When he retired he was succeeded by Kenny Smith of the now-defunct New York *Daily Mirror.* Kenny is still active. And, to handle historical research, Lee Allen, of Cincinnati, came in to start a research department, which today is the most complete, most documented, and most detailed bureau of its kind in all sports history. Unfortunately Lee Allen didn't live to see the job completed. But another writer, Cliff Kachline of *The Sporting News*, succeeded him, and is carrying on admirably the job to which Lee Allen dedicated his talent and his life.

The baseball writers have made other contributions to the Hall of Fame. Since its inception the writers, by annual vote, have elected modern players to the Hall of Fame shrine of greatness and veteran writers like Warren Brown, and Mel Webb, and Fred Lieb, and Dan Daniel, and Roy Stockton and Bob Broeg have served on the Veterans Committee charged with the responsibility of electing to the shrine these veterans who are deserving but may have been overlooked.

The New York–Brooklyn chapter, too, has made its contribution of talent. Arthur (Red) Patterson, for many years a baseball writer with the *Herald-Tribune*, left his seat in the press box to become service manager for the National League. He was drafted by the Yankees to head their public relations department, and went from the Yankees to the Dodgers. He is presently a working vice-president with the Los Angeles Dodgers—and doing very well, thank you! So is Harold Parrott, former Brooklyn scribe, now with the California Angels. Garry Schumacher, a born baseball fan and proud of it, deserted his typewriter years ago to join the staff of his beloved Giants. He is still with them, a bit grayer and slowed up by encroaching years, but still devoted to the game and the players, to the National League and especially to Horace Stoneham and the Giants.

Finally there's Charley Segar, my devoted friend and associate. Charley came into baseball as director of the National League Service Bureau. He moved from there into the commissioner's office where he served for some seventeen years as secretary-treasurer of baseball. Charley was a quiet workman who hated headlines and publicity. He had a tough job. During his years of service he made many friends. He also made enemies. But that didn't bother him. He supervised the player pension plan and got it off on the right foot. He handled player relations and arguments firmly but sympathetically. Through the years, he settled quietly, via telephone and personal visit, many problems that today would bring columns of newspaper controversy. Like most writers his loyalty was to the game, not to clubs or individuals.

Probably I have overlooked other writers who through the

years have moved from the press box into the baseball management. I mention these few because they come within my own memory and experience. The purpose in mentioning them at all is to call attention to the close relationship between the press and baseball, and to point up the contribution writers have made, and are still making, to the game.

I do not, for one moment, question the craftsmanship or the ability of present day scribes. They have better tools, better equipment, and better facilities than the old-timers. They also have more problems and more responsibilities. Today's baseball writers are broadly better educated, better trained, and more adaptable than their predecessors. Like other fields of endeavor, baseball writing has become more effective through the years. Today it is tops in efficiency and effectiveness. I only hope that it continues. Writers have contributed much to the game, in this age of skepticism. If public confidence is destroyed, if fan interest is diverted, if baseball loses its position as a national institution—the fault will lie in the selfishness and the arrogance of the players and owners, not with the baseball writers.

7

BREAKING THE COLOR LINE

"Though I've belted you an' flayed you,
By the livin' Gawd that made you,
You're a better man that I am, Gunga Din!"

—RUDYARD KIPLING

In the spring of 1947, Branch Rickey, president of the Brooklyn Dodgers, announced that Jackie Robinson, following a sensational season with the Montreal farm club, was being signed to a major league contract, and would start the season with his team.

"Mr. Robinson," Rickey said later, "was a player of undoubted major league caliber. Brooklyn was looking for good, young players. True, Robinson was black—but he could run, he could hit, he was an excellent glove man, and he had the flaming competitive spirit of a champion. Baseball must face facts. Ethnic prejudice has no place in sports, and baseball must recognize that truth if it is to maintain stature as a national game."

Rickey's action was not unexpected. The first long step had been taken the year before when Robinson had been signed by Montreal. Jackie's outstanding performance in that Triple-A league had served advance notice of the inevitable. Even so, no decision in baseball history ever created more furor, or attracted as many headlines or as much editorial comment. Rickey was lauded by the free-thinkers, condemned by the standpatters. Fans were vociferous in their opinions. Some hailed him as the "New Emancipator"; others

93

labeled him "a Judas selling out baseball for a few pieces of silver."

But the die was cast! Even the baseball people who publicly condemned the action as "premature" and "revolutionary" quietly set their scouts to the task of searching the "black field" for competing talent. After three-quarters of a century of heel-dragging, a social wrong had been righted. The color line had been broken.

Most fans today believe that Rickey, by one inspired act, alone and single-handed, broke down traditional barriers and revolutionized the game. That is not true. What he did—for which he deserves eternal credit—was to put an end to delay and vacillation, and force his baseball peers to accept, publicly, an action that for years they had recognized as inevitable. To understand the full impact of the Rickey move, one must delve into the "behind-the-scenes" archives of baseball history.

Contrary to common belief, baseball never had any rule prohibiting the employment of black players. What baseball operators had done, through the years, was bow abjectly to what they thought was overwhelming public opinion. They were afraid to make a move. They were afraid of upsetting the status quo, afraid of alienating the white clientele that largely supported the professional game. Through the years that fear crystallized into accepted tradition—and traditions, at times, can be more stultifying than law or statute.

As a matter of record, some baseball men were toying with the idea of employing colored players long years before Rickey made his move. Even before World War I, John McGraw, of the Giants, believing that performance was more important in pennant races than any question of color, tried to accomplish by gentle chicanery what he had failed to put over by argument and persuasion. John signed two players whom he represented as Cubans. When it was discovered that their skins were several shades darker than accepted Spanish standards, other owners became frightened and McGraw was pressured into abandoning the project as "detrimental to baseball."

In the mid-thirties (a tough financial period for all clubs) John Shibe, of the Philadelphia Athletics, and Sam Breadon, of the St. Louis Cardinals, encouraged a committee of prominent Negro citizens to appear before a joint-league meeting. The committee, headed by Paul Robeson, raised the question of alleged racial discrimination, and urged that black players be admitted to the baseball family.

Some of the owners were sympathetic to the idea and suggested open discussion. But Judge Landis, the then Commissioner, declared that public opinion would be against such a move. He ruled out any discussion on the ground that the question had not been properly noticed on the agenda, as required under the rules. Formal effort to bring the subject before the meeting was stopped by the judge's ruling—but the idea persisted in the minds of some of the officials.

A few years later, a special interleague committee was appointed, with Larry MacPhail as chairman, to "make an intensive study of major league operations and submit a program for modernizing the rules and procedure of the game." MacPhail, after conferring with a couple of other committee members, himself wrote a strong paragraph pointing out that colored players were being discriminated against, and urging baseball to move into the twentieth century by breaking once and for all with its longtime fear-ridden practice. The report was then typed for submission to the owners.

Fear of public reaction again prevailed. After rather pointed discussion, the MacPhail paragraph was deleted on a basis of expediency and timing. By tacit consent, the "colored question" was tabled. But, deep in their hearts, the majority of owners realized that delay and stalling was not the answer. Within the near future they would have to face up to the problem. Try as they might to turn their backs, it was one issue that refused to "go away."

Many fans today still hold the belief that Rickey's move was spontaneous, unpremeditated, and wholly altruistic—a sort of "angel in the night miracle" for the betterment of mankind. That is not true, either. Anyone who knew Mr. Rickey knew he never acted on impulse. Every move he made was well planned. He weighed every pro and con before he acted.

True, there was back of the move a certain sense of altruism. He believed the move was morally right. He also believed that it might be an answer to his own, and baseball's, shortage-of-manpower problem. He knew, too, that he was dealing with an inflammable public question, and he was prepared for opposition. A petition signed by several veteran Dodger players, urging that he not bring Robinson up to the parent club, already was in his hands. It was given careful consideration before it was denied.

The possibility of adverse public reaction was carefully

weighed. The Brooklyn Club's Board of Directors were informed of the contemplated action, and gave their unqualified approval. Most important of all, Rickey selected Robinson himself and he personally handled the careful schooling Robinson was given as to the problems he might face and the personal discipline he would be expected to exert at all times.

Despite some rumor and speculation, the general public and a large segment of the press outside New York seemed surprised at the suddenness of the Rickey action. I don't know how many baseball men, outside the Brooklyn organization, may have been consulted, but I do know the then president of the National League had full knowledge. A few days before the signing was announced, Rickey phoned the league office to explain the contemplated action.

"I know I am morally right," he said, "and I think the timing is good. Do you think I have any obligation to notify Mr. Harridge and the American League?"

"No. No one can guarantee what reaction or criticism there may be—but that is your business. Certainly any club has the right under baseball rules to move players in their own organization as they see fit. This office could not and would not consider any complaints on that score."

"That's all I want to know. Goodbye."

A few days later the decision was announced. Jackie Robinson would start the season with the Dodgers. Baseball's greatest injustice had finally come to an end.

Not that it was easy sailing. There were many problems, little and big, but to baseball's eternal credit they were handled quietly and efficiently, with a minimum of publicity and argument. For instance, there was the question of hotel accommodations on the road. Many of the hotels around the major league circuits still operated under archaic segregation rules and objected to any black clientele. Others, though willing to furnish a room to a Negro player, were unwilling to extend meal facilities in their public dining rooms. The Brooklyn club found a quick answer. They quietly arranged outside accommodations for Robinson and the black players who followed him. The plan worked to perfection. In fact, shortly afterward, when the recalcitrant hotels decided to extend the welcome mat without reservation, some of the black players themselves were reluctant to make any changes.

Spring training created some problems, too. Most of the clubs, major and minor league, conducted their spring training camps in the heart of the Old South, where racial barriers were a longtime heritage. The Brooklyn club was not affected. They had their own private facilities in Vero Beach, and could do as they pleased. But some of the other clubs, who in the meantime had signed black players, were on a spot. Quietly, they went to work. One or two owners were able to talk the hotels into changing their policy. Others rented homes where the black players could live with their families. One club moved its entire team from a recalcitrant hotel into a waterfront motel where they still make their headquarters.

There were minor problems involving some of the veteran players, too. The petition signed by a coterie of Brooklyn players asking Rickey not to bring Jackie Robinson up to the major league club was only the starter. Rumblings of discontent among players were prevalent in several clubs. Yet, only one minor incident ever attracted nationwide attention, and that by the sheerest accident. It is perhaps worthy of comment, if only for the purpose of keeping the record straight.

In the early part of the 1947 season, Sam Breadon, owner of the Cardinals, called at the National League office. A few of his veteran players, he said, were upset by the fact that the Dodgers were using a colored player, and had threatened not to play in any game against Brooklyn so long as Robinson was in the lineup. "I don't know how far they'll go," Breadon explained, "but I've got to do something now. They're talking on the bench and in the clubhouse, and if it continues we might have some serious trouble. What do you think I should tell them?"

"Tell them this is America," he was told, "and baseball is America's game. Tell them that if they go on strike, for racial reasons, or refuse to play a scheduled game they will be barred from baseball even though it means the disruption of a club or a whole league."

I don't know how Sam delivered the message, or to whom he talked. I do know that he called the league office a day or two later to report that the whole matter was settled, and everything was under control. "It was just a tempest in a teapot," he said. "A few of the players were upset and were popping off a bit, but they really didn't mean it. Just letting off a little steam."

Six weeks later, a New York newspaperman attended a private dinner at the home of a Cardinal official. In the course of the dinner conversation, the incident was casually mentioned. The newspaperman called his office and relayed what he had heard. The next morning the incident, enlarged and embellished, was headlined across the sports page of a New York morning paper. The implication was that a widespread rebellion of National League players had been headed off at the last minute by the iron-fisted threat of drastic action by the league office. The story forgot to mention that the headlined incident had occurred six weeks earlier, and by the time the story had been published the three or four players who had said they would never play against black players had already done so.

Because of that ill-timed publicity the Cardinals were unfortunately marked publicly as the great dissenters when, in reality, their players adjusted more quickly than many of the other players who were more vocally vehement in their clubhouse condemnations. But it wasn't really serious. After all, the players were "pros," who were out to win ball games. They were a lot more concerned with performance than with skin pigmentation. As one prominent player remarked: "We're out to win the championship. As long as a guy can run and field and throw and carry his weight with the bat, I'm for him whether his skin is white, or black, or green, or yellow."

Fan reaction was Rickey's greatest concern—and it was Jackie Robinson, as the guinea pig in the great experiment, who had to bear the brunt of the abuse that was shouted from the stands game after game, and day after day, through that first long season. It wasn't easy. Jackie Robinson was a man of great personal pride and dignity. He was a born fighter. How he managed in those first dark days to hold his temper, to maintain his self-respect, and by the brilliance of his performance on the field win the respect of his various critics and change vituperation and vicious vilification into cheers of acceptance, I will never understand. But he did it.

With all due respect to Rickey, I cannot but feel that the one man, above all others, who deserves the eternal thanks of his own race, and all thinking people, for bringing about baseball's greatest reform, is Jackie Robinson himself. I never knew Jackie as intimately as I knew the players of an older generation, but by his conduct under the most trying circumstances, he won my undying respect and admiration. Certainly baseball people should be eternally grateful for the contribution he made to his own people, and to the game.

For one long season, Robinson carried the burden alone. But other owners saw the handwriting on the wall—and went quietly about the business of scouting Negro talent, not only within the continental United States but in the Caribbean area as well. The public and the press have frequently criticized club owners and officials for their dilatory tactics, their failure to accept and adopt modern methods, and their bumbling efforts to maintain a timeworn status quo. Too often these criticisms have been justified.

But, in the acceptance of black players, baseball showed a strength of purpose that will redound to the game's eternal credit. Once they had recovered from the original shock, owners and players alike took up cudgels in defense of the move, not from any altruistic motive but because they recognized the playing potentials and the competitive value of this new source of manpower.

Never were free agents more carefully selected. Never before or since have scouts and general managers investigated so thoroughly the off-field habits, the social thinking, and the personalities of potential signees. Perhaps they may have had some private doubts as to the wisdom of Rickey's motive. But the challenge had been laid down. It was up to baseball to make it work. They met the challenge head on.

Brooklyn brought up Roy Campanella and Don Newcombe, both gentlemen off the field as on, as foils to the flaming competitiveness of Robinson. Second only to Robinson, these two were responsible for breaking down the phoney social problem that, in those early days, constituted the greatest barrier to fan acceptance of black players. Robinson was a man of stern principle and fiery spirit. He hated compromise, and he sought no quarter. It was not easy for him to turn the other cheek; to accept insult in grim-lipped silence, to listen to scurrilous blasphemies from the stands (and often from the opposing bench) and not answer in kind.

But he did it—and the coming of Campanella and Newcombe made the task infinitely easier. For the first time, in the great experiment, Robinson was relieved by some of the burden. For the first time he was not waging a one-man crusade.

I do not mean to imply that Campanella and Newcombe were brought up as window trimming. Rickey was far too astute for such a ploy. They were selected primarily because they were excellent players, who could add strength to the Dodger team. Secondly, and equally important, they had the personality that made them perfect foils for the fiery, crusading spirit of Robinson.

Campanella, especially, made a great commonsense contribution to the solution of the racial problems. On the field, he was great—one of the finest catchers baseball has ever known. Off the field, he was even greater—for he displayed a humanness and understanding that is rarely found in these days. Extremists, white or black, would, it seems to me, profit by his example. After all, the wrongs of a disturbed world, history proves, are solved by common sense, sympathy, and dedication, and understanding.

Campy made another contribution, albeit involuntary and without meditation. At the height of his professional career he was the victim of a cruel accident that left him hopelessly crippled and physically helpless. Most men, under such circumstances, would either give up entirely or look to the world for help and sympathy. Not Campy.

He knew he faced almost hopeless odds, but he never gave up. He worked long hours at therapy; he struggled to maintain his business interests. He never lost his smile, his faith, or his optimism. Today, he is physically barred from playing the game he loved, but he has never lost his interest in the game, or the youngsters who play it. Through the years, from his wheelchair, he has counseled, advised, and coached thousands of underprivileged kids; he has appeared at public functions; he has made speeches; he has been the life of the party at baseball get-togethers.

Baseball, and the world, would be better for a few million like Roy Campanella. And his accident, tragic as it was, brought quick and lasting appreciation of the fact that heart and courage and soul are more important yardsticks in judging values than ethnic difference or skin coloration.

Branch Rickey, throughout his baseball life, made many contributions to the game, but his courage in breaking the color line must be listed as the most important and far-reaching of all—not only for baseball itself but as an example to all the world that courage and faith

are unbeatable weapons, more potent than armies and guns and bloodshed, in solving the problems of a world at sixes and sevens.

Aside from the ethical and moral impact, the signing of black
players contributed a more material benefit to baseball. It provided a
new source of playing strength at a time when it was badly needed. It
was not a temporary harvest, but a whole new field. The black population of this country constitutes between 10 and 15 percent of the nation's total. The black player—either Latin or native-born—has become
an integral part of the game.

A few well-meaning fans even today are expressing alarm over
the increasing number of black players on big league rosters. "Some
regulations should be established soon," they moan, "or the blacks will
be taking over the game." To me, that argument is utter bunk. People
who insist on taking their competitive sports as if it were some sort of
homeopathic elixir bottled in decorative vials neatly labeled "lily
white," or "ebony black," or "daffodil yellow," or whatever are simply
not in tune with the times.

Whether you have one or twenty-one black players on a major
league roster is irrelevant. The one question that baseball and all sports
must face up to is simply this: "Is the selected player the best available
for the position?" If he is, no apologies are necessary. If he is not, if he
has simply been chosen for political reasons to establish numerical
equality or to meet the pressure of racial groups, white or black, then
that decision is morally, socially, and historically wrong, and not to be
tolerated in a progressive human society.

There are those who argue that baseball was behind the times
in its move to bring in black players, pointing out that football and
basketball were well ahead in their acceptance of black players. That
criticism is factually true.

Professional baseball was started at the end of the Civil War,
and a few years later the first professional leagues were formed. Many
rules were laid down for the conduct of the game and the behavior of
players, but no rule for or against the use of black players. Public
opinion was such that no thought was given to a problem then unrecognized. (I have no doubt in my mind that had the question been
raised, baseball rules of that day would have provided for all-white
rosters.) But it wasn't even considered.

Competitive sports, in the final analysis, developed as a product of public desire. They reflect public opinion, but they do not mold public action. They fulfill a public recreational need and through the years have attained a high degree of public affection. But in the field of broad social reform, the onus of leadership, in the final analysis, falls squarely on the shoulders of government.

Baseball may have been dilatory in opening its ranks to black players. That is a matter of opinion. Timing was important, and Branch Rickey's timing was effective. So far as baseball is concerned, the problem is solved forever, and to the great benefit of the game.

Without black players, baseball would have been in great difficulty. Without black players we would have been faced with a growing shortage of playing strength. Without black players there would have been no expansion; there would have been no Caribbean and other international play. Without black players, baseball would never have been able to break its provincial, nineteenth-century boundaries, and become truly national in scope and interest.

A bow to Mr. Rickey. During his lifetime he contributed much to the game he loved. But in my book, the signing of Jackie Robinson was his greatest accomplishment, his finest hour.

8

GOLDEN VOICES

Most of the important changes in baseball through the years have occurred with explosive suddenness and to the accompaniment of blaring headlines and noisy fans. In 1935, for instance, when the effervescent Larry MacPhail introduced night baseball to Cincinnati, he was roundly castigated by owners and fans alike. Vitriolic editorials were written; veteran sportswriters fulminated in righteous indignation; and rival owners accused the redheaded genius of turning a beloved national game into a nighttime extravaganza for the sake of a few more box office dollars.

A decade later when Branch Rickey signed Jackie Robinson to a major league contract, history repeated itself. Rickey, too, was the subject of bitter attacks for destroying the revered traditions of a national institution.

The advent of radio was different. Like Carl Sandburg's fog, radio sneaked in on "little cat feet" before baseball owners and fans realized what was going on. Yet radio and its buxom offspring, television, have had greater and more revolutionary impact on baseball than any other development in more than a century of the game's history.

In 1919, at war's end, radio was still in the experimental stage. Old-timers, I am sure, will recall the old crystal sets and the ham operators who sat up night after night, fiddling with the dials, in an effort to "bring in" some outland signal, or catch the foreign call letters of a station in faraway Europe or South America.

Out in Colorado Springs, I recall staid businessmen traipsing to the police station each noon to get the Arlington time signal on the police shortwave set. They would sit quietly while the police sergeant adjusted the dial. At exactly noon would come the single long beep signifying the hour. Watches would be carefully set, the dial turned off, and the listeners would head back to business, satisfied that all was right with the world for another twenty-four hours.

To those men, radio was an interesting scientific phenomenon, a gadget that intrigued public imagination but lacked the feel of reality. Fooling with a crystal set was fun all right, but not to be taken too seriously—a sort of science-fiction adventure with the entertainment features of a Tarzan story or an imaginary journey to Mars. Only a few dedicated scientists recognized the potential of the new medium as a revolutionary factor in world communication, and were working to that end.

In the 1920s, however, new names were beginning to creep into the public consciousness. Crystal sets were being replaced by modern new creations that offered clearer reception and a broad selectivity of home programs. Floyd Gibbons and Lowell Thomas attained national recognition through their network news programs. In the entertainment field Amos 'n' Andy, and Jones and Hare became overnight favorites. In the field of music, Guy Lombardo, Benny Goodman, and Paul Whiteman became names to conjure with. So, too, did singers like Rudy Vallee, Lanny Ross, Russ Columbo, and the mysterious Silver Masked Tenor. That baseball should follow the trend was inevitable.

In the fall of 1921, Commissioner Landis authorized the broadcasting of the World Series. It was announced as an experimental broadcast, on a one-year basis only. It turned into the longest experiment in sports history. Fifty years later, it's still going strong. The whole future of baseball, in fact of all sports, was changed forever that sunny October afternoon.

The voice that fans heard bringing that play-by-play report

was that of Major Andrew White, a member of the announcing staff of New York's WEAF. Few fans today will recall his name. He was not a baseball fan. He had little interest in sports, and even less technical knowledge. He was selected to do the job simpy because of his mellifluous voice and perfect enunciation—a common standard for selecting announcers in those days, a practice that continued for some years to the utter amazement of everyone except the broadcasting people themselves.

Even as late as 1933, when Chesterfield was sponsoring the André Kostelanetz musical show, there were similar problems. The show had a classical orchestra and operatic soloists Rosa Ponselle, Lily Pons, and Nino Martini. Yet they overlooked all the announcers who had musical training and picked me to MC the show. I had no knowledge of music. I had a voice range of four notes, all flat, and couldn't carry a tune in a handbasket. I couldn't even pronounce the names of most of the composers, but that made no difference. If there ever was a miscarriage of justice in the selection of an announcer, that show was it. But, it paid $100 a broadcast, which was big money in those days, and I wasn't about to pass it up.

I've wondered many times what the reaction of Ponselle, et al., must have been when they learned of my utter ineptness. I'm sure André must have sworn under his breath many times as he coached me in the pronunciation of composers' names, or wasted untold minutes furnishing educational background on numbers I was scheduled to announce on the program. I'm sure they all heaved a sigh of relief when I finally left broadcasting to go with the National League.

Following Andy White on the World Series broadcast was Graham McNamee, and his partner, Phillips Carlin. Like White, they were without sports background or knowledge. In fact, during the 1922 Series, McNamee was the butt of one of Ring Lardner's funniest lines. Ring wrote: "They played two World Series games at the Polo Grounds this afternoon—the one I watched and the one broadcast by Graham McNamee." Along with the humor, there was some truth there, too. McNamee wasn't a baseball expert, and didn't pretend to be. But he brought to his broadcast a personal warmth and sincerity that more than compensated for technical errors. The fans liked him! He was one of them in approach and feeling. He has been gone these many years, but the name of Graham McNamee is still remembered.

The first sports expert to enter the radio field was a young New Yorker named Ted Husing. Ted spoke with the authority of a man who knew his subject. He was arrogant beyond reason. He was jealous of his competitors and resentful of any criticism. He lacked the warmth and enthusiasm of McNamee, but he did know the game and gave to his listeners the sort of unblemished reportorial coverage that fans had come to expect from newspaper accounts.

Unfortunately, Husing's baseball broadcasting was to be of short duration. He ran afoul of Judge Landis over certain remarks he had made on one of his broadcasts. Ted tried to argue with the Judge, but it was no match. The Judge barred Husing from further baseball broadcasts.

Thereafter Ted concentrated on football, and during the 1930s won fame as the outstanding broadcaster in the field of college football. Whatever else he may have accomplished, he will remain in the records as the first trained and qualified sports reporter to do an authentic sports description of a nationally broadcast sports event. That success opened the door for the many others who have followed the Husing pattern to national fame and recognition.

However, it was the day-by-day broadcasts of local games to local audiences that established radio as a real sports factor, and that was no easy conquest. Baseball owners, and promoters generally, were extremely fearful of the effect of local broadcasts on daily attendance and admission dollars. Most owners subscribed to the theory that it was silly to give away the very product they were trying to sell.

The World Series, they argued, was a guaranteed box office sellout, and could be broadcast to good effect in cities outside the market area in which the games were played. But the daily broadcast of games to home audiences was a different kettle of fish altogether. The baseball meetings of those days frequently developed into real Donnybrooks, with the battle lines closely drawn between the advocates of radio and the old-line conservatives who saw red whenever the new medium was mentioned.

Among the owners who saw in radio a great promotional weapon was Philip K. Wrigley, owner of the Chicago Cubs. Wrigley didn't wait for local stations to bid on exclusive rights to broadcast. Instead he issued a blanket invitation to all Chicago area stations to carry all Cub home games without cost and without restriction. It was a daring move, but it paid off. Attendance at home games soared; public interest in the Cubs spread beyond Chicago into Indiana, Wisconsin, Iowa, southern Michigan, and lower Illinois. These new fans were not at all academic in their approach. They were fanatical Cub admirers, who soon began organizing special weekend expeditions to see their favorites in person. In fact, one of the first indications of the power of radio in those early days was the increase in out-of-town patrons, and the number of out-of-state license plates in the ball park parking lots on weekends.

Overnight, Chicago became the baseball radio center of the nation. Hal Totten, Bob Elson, and Pat Flanagan were names to conjure with in fan circles—pioneers in a new and startling industry that would, in less than a decade, draw hundreds of millions of listeners to the parlor sets of a nation, and revolutionize the entire American sports industry.

The success of Wrigley's bold move had a twofold effect on the sports picture. Club owners were convinced that radio was a boon to baseball, not a cannibalistic ogre growing fat on the lifeblood of the game they fostered. Radio stations had proof, at the same time, that the daily afternoon baseball broadcast offered an entertainment buy that sponsors could not resist. Stations in other cities began bidding for baseball broadcasting rights, offering goodly sums for exclusive privileges. The universal language of dollars was one that all owners understood. They may not have been convinced that broadcasting could increase interest and attendance among fans; but they couldn't turn a deaf ear to the clink of those dollars in the club treasury.

Sam Breadon, of the St. Louis Cardinals, was quick to climb aboard the radio bandwagon, with Francis Laux handling the microphone. Laux, like the other pioneers in club broadcasting, was an ardent fan and made no effort to conceal his partisan Cardinal feelings. Neither did Harry Carey, who took over the Cardinal job when Laux was moved up to an executive position with the radio station.

Whether or not broadcasters should permit their emotions to show in their daily baseball stint has ever been a moot question. It still is. Personally, I like it. On the daily local broadcasts, some 90 percent of the listeners are home club fans, who enjoy a bit of partisanship in their game descriptions. They like announcer enthusiasm when the home club is winning, or a bit of sympathetic disappointment in hours of defeat. When it comes to a network broadcast with national coverage, neutrality is demanded. But on the local level, it seems to me, rooting interest is an important part of the descriptive picture.

At any rate, those early pioneers took their rooting privileges seriously, and their example was largely followed by their successors. In Pittsburgh, Rosey Rosewell, the original "voice of the Pirates," established a style that combined fan enthusiasm with expert baseball knowledge. The same thing happened in other major league cities as well.

In Cincinnati, the progressive Larry MacPhail, laboring to breathe life into a moribund franchise, made a real ten-strike. He reached down to put the finger on a slight, sandy-haired young man from the University of Florida. The young fellow's assets including an ingratiating grin, a broad Southern drawl, a refreshing sense of humor, and a deep dedication to baseball. His name was "Red" Barber, and he was destined to become one of the real "greats" of broadcasting and telecasting history.

Red Barber introduced a new element of humanness and understanding in his daily broadcasts. He leavened the dramatic with a saving pinch of humor, and tempered criticism with a wisecrack that gave his audience a chuckle. Back in the twenties, a Brooklyn writer, Garry Schumacher, used the word "rhubarb" to describe a player-umpire argument on the field. Red liked the word, and adopted it for radio use.

It became one of his trademarks, and Barber listeners were quick to take it up. Today it has a definite place in the lexicon of sports, even appearing as an honored and accepted term in the staid columns of Mr. Webster's unabridged dictionary. Now, I don't mean to imply that Barber was a plagiarist. He was not. But he did have a fine ear for an apt phrase, and a great sense of timing. Red's "cat-bird seat" is still used by broadcasters and fans today to describe a fortunate strategic situation. His remark, "the bases are F.O.B."—"full of Brooklyns," shows his gift for spontaneous oral description.

Strangely, the New York area was the last to succumb to the lure of radio. Since New York was the largest fan market in the nation, much pressure was brought to bear on the three metropolitan clubs. But they mutually agreed that they would ban the new media from their parks, and for several years they stuck to their agreement. The galvanizing force that finally broke them down was a young man named Sid Loberfeld, then a member of the WMCA staff, and now a successful New York attorney. Sid was an ardent fan as well as sportscaster, and spent many long hours in the Yankee, Giant, and Dodger offices trying to sell a bill of goods.

Finally, Sid persuaded a reluctant Brooklyn management to give the medium a one-game trial run, and in midseason 1931 fans in the New York area enjoyed their first local broadcast. Four stations were invited into Ebbets Field—WEAF, WABC, WMCA, and WOR. Graham McNamee was at the WEAF microphone, Ted Husing for WABC, Sid Loberfeld for WMCA, and I did the job for WOR. Sid must be credited with first bringing baseball into the homes of hundreds of thousands of grateful New Yorkers.

Measured by modern standards, it was not much of a broadcast. We sat together in a box back of the plate. We talked into old carbon microphones, which were hooked up by telephone lines to the station sending apparatus. We were strictly on our own, without benefit of observer or statistician. The only technician was a telephone employee, whose function was to keep the line open from ball park to radio station. But it was New York's first broadcast, and brought a flood of fan mail that caused the baseball people to sit up and take notice.

Later I broadcast the final series of the year between the Dodgers and the Cardinals, a series that decided the pennant race. (The Cardinals won, and went on to the world championship.) That broadcast, too, was a hit-or-miss production that entirely lacked the professional touch of today's presentations. But it did attract a record listening audience, and produced a dramatic climax that fans still remember and talk about.

In the finale of the three-game series, Dazzy Vance, the leading Dodger pitcher and a favorite of the bleacherites, was on the mound. In the ninth inning, with the score tied, the Cardinals put two runners on base. Vance, in trouble, reached back for that little bit extra, and retired the next two batters. That brought Andy High to the plate. Andy had been traded to the Cardinals by the Dodgers only a few months earlier, after a long and honorable Brooklyn career. During most of those years he had been Vance's roommate and closest friend. Now they faced each other with a National League pennant, and World Series spot, hanging on each pitch.

Vance put over two quick strikes, then wasted a curve ball on the outside. He then came back with another fast ball, and Andy High was ready. He slapped the ball over second base and into center field. It batted in the winning run, and gave the Cardinals the pennant. In his long career, this was the closest Dazzy had ever come to a World Series. And his dream had been shattered by his longtime roommate and best friend. The defeat, Dazzy was to admit later, was the toughest of his long career. (Several years later, Vance finally made it into a World Series as a member of the Cardinals, the same team that had deprived him of his biggest moment.)

By the 1930s, radio's place in baseball was definitely established. All sixteen major league clubs were broadcasting their games, many of them for sizable fees that enabled them to survive the economic rigors of a national depression.

However, it was the advent of television that really turned the economics of the game topsy-turvy. True, radio had opened up an unexpected source of income that added hundreds of thousands of dollars to major league income. But television doubled and quadrupled that mark literally overnight.

In 1950, Commissioner A. B. Chandler signed a three-year World Series contract with NBC that guaranteed baseball $1 million a year, regardless of the length of the series. It was the first million-dollar television contract ever signed for any sports event. In 1953, a new three-year contract was signed that guaranteed $2.5 million a year for World Series television rights. In 1958, the price rose to a cool $6 million a season.

In 1965, the last year of my commissionership, a new type contract was drawn to include a televised game of the week, along with the World Series and the All-Star Game. This brought to baseball, and the twenty-four major league clubs some $13 million annual radio and television income, exclusive of amounts paid to clubs on individual contracts for daily local broadcasts and telecasts. I have no knowledge of the contracts signed since my retirement, but *Broadcasting Magazine* estimates the total income to baseball from radio and television, including both local and network deals, at approximately $43 million a year.

However, the true impact of television on baseball cannot be measured entirely by a dollar sign in front of six or more digits, however appealing that symbol might be to most clubowners. By carrying the game into the villages and farmhouses of the vast hinterland, television has nationalized baseball to a degree unknown and undreamed of by earlier generations. It has developed fan interest and created public idols in areas hitherto isolated. It has personalized the game for fans in Arizona, and Utah, and Medicine Hat.

In a little over two decades of television exposure, baseball attendance has more than tripled. Maybe that is sheer coincidence. It is true that the average American today has more money in his pocket, and more leisure time in which to spend it. Transportation improvements have brought the nation's stadiums and arenas into greater proximity to most of the potential fans, and customers.

Which is cause, and which is effect? Certainly debatable, but one fact is self-evident. Sports participation has never been so widespread; game interest has never been so intense. All this has happened since television first brought the thrills of stadium performance into focus on family screens in American homes.

Television has been a great boon to baseball and other sports, and vice versa. For the owners the bonanza is reflected in bright new stadiums, and the almost monthly increase in franchise values. For the players, the fees paid to baseball by radio and television are reflected in the fabulous salaries paid today. The baseball pension plan—far and away the best ever written in sports history—has been made possible through television fees. Without that income baseball could not possibly meet the cost of such protection. Without that income there could be no six-figure salaries for star performers; no $14,000 minimum for inexperienced beginners.

The old axiom "A workman is worthy of his hire" still holds true. Ballplayers are certainly entitled to salaries commensurate with performance and drawing power. However, there are other axioms equally applicable in these crazy times. The ones about "the straw that broke the camel's back" and "killing the goose that lays the golden egg" also fit this picture. Maybe if all three were posted side by side on every locker in every baseball clubhouse, and above every desk in every baseball front office, someone might get the idea that all is not beer and skittles.

Radio and television have worked unexpected miracles in baseball and all sports. Attendance has tripled and quadrupled over a ten-year period. The millions of dollars poured into sport coffers in the frenzied competition for exclusive broadcasting rights have opened new financial horizons for players and management alike. But there's a limit to all largesse.

Television is a commercial enterprise, and its profit-and-loss statements make no allowance for altruistic philosophy or "pie-in-the-sky" dreams. Owners who figure they can count on increased millions with each succeeding contract are riding for a fall. Players who feel they are aboard an unlimited gravy train on an endless track are only speeding the game toward inevitable trouble. Neither owners nor players will like the idea, but unless there is a leveling off in the economic dreams of both sides, baseball and all sports will eventually face critical, even insurmountable, problems. Too many future commitments are being made on the doubtful prospect of tomorrow's increased dollar income; too many debts are being incurred, backed only by optimistic dreams of pots of gold waiting at the end of tomorrow's rainbow.

Some time, some place, there's a limit to the increasing millions that television can pour into sports coffers. Maybe that time is a long way off, maybe it's just around the corner. Suppose that television bubble suddenly bursts, as bubbles have been known to do? Suppose sponsors should suddenly decide that they can no longer pay the constantly increasing price of television and radio advertising? Suppose constantly rising prices (tickets, transportation, hot dogs, beer, and peanuts) reach a point where Mr. Average Fan elects to stay away from professional games, and go fishing with his son instead?

What then happens to multimillion-dollar pension plans? Who then pays the annual premium to keep the pension in force; who puts up the cash on back-service contracts, or makes up the annual deficit of millions? What then happens to $150,000 salaries and to $20 million franchise investments? I'm no expert economist, but I do know that in this competitive world contracts must be fulfilled and promises honored, if the game is to prosper.

Only government can wink at deficits. Only government can assess taxes, and then withhold salaries to guarantee their payments; only government can print paper money and declare it legal tender; only government can, by congressional action, blithely lift the debt limit by billions, without guarantee of reduction payment, or thought to reduce spending.

Don't misunderstand me. I'm not a prophet of doom, preaching a gospel of sports destruction. But from where I'm sitting, it does seem that the time has come for a little common sense on the part of both employer and employee. Supersalaries may bolster the ego, but they mean nothing without dollars available to pay them, and all the health programs and fringe benefit promises are merely idle gestures if the premiums go by default.

As for present-day franchises—well, the average fan will agree that an investor is entitled to some return on his money. The going major league franchise price is from $15 million to $20 million. Most fans, I think, would also agree that a 6 percent annual return on investment is a minimum expectation in any business. That means the average major league club should show its stockholders an annual profit of $1 million. To my knowledge, there is not a single major league club that can show that sort of profit over a five-year period. Some clubs show huge deficits instead. Many clubs are happy if they can break even after taxes. Really, the only way to make any money in baseball today is to find an enthusiastic group, interested in headlines, and sell them your franchise at inflated prices. Such people, incidentally, are becoming, to use an Alice-in-Wonderland phrase, "scarcerer and scarcerer."

But this is a story of the impact of radio and television on baseball, not a financial report. Certainly, radio and television have revolutionized the game. They have also created their own stars.

It is not the intent here to go into any personal study of the individuals who cover the game locally or on networks. Their day-by-day stints speak for them in terms loud and clear. The broadcasting and telecasting of baseball is better organized and better handled than ever before in history. Today's microphone crews are truly professional in both knowledge and technique. They have developed a personal popularity and a fan recognition, far greater than the acclaim accorded even the greatest of baseball writers. Constant photographic and vocal exposures are potent twin attributes of public acclaim, regardless of which side of the camera and microphone you happen to be working. The fact was forcibly demonstrated by an incident at a recent Old-Timers' game in Shea Stadium.

The Old-Timers were introduced individually to the capacity crowd of over 50,000. As each Old-Timer was announced, and trotted from the dugout to home plate, he was given a heartwarming round of applause. With such popular heroes as Joe DiMaggio, Mickey Mantle, Frankie Frisch, Whitey Ford, Yogi Berra, and Casey Stengel, the fan appreciation developed into a series of standing ovations.

Then, when all the Old-Timers had been warmly greeted, the master-of-ceremonies called on Mel Allen to take a bow. Mel had been away from his Yankees for a number of years, but, at the mention of his name, a thunderous roar of welcome shook the Shea Stadium rafters. It rose to a shrill crescendo as Mel walked from the dugout to the playing field.

Baseball is a game of drama, and emotion, and frenzy. Most fans wear their hearts on their sleeves, and are quick to respond to personal popularity or the tense drama of a climactic play. Like most writers and officials I have witnessed many ovations and demonstrations in my day. I sat in Yankee Stadium that memorable afternoon when a dying Babe Ruth whispered his farewell to baseball, and, with bowed head, accepted the homage of his fans. I was present, too, when a stricken Lou Gehrig summed up his whole sensational career with dramatic simplicity, in a single sentence: "I am the luckiest man on the face of this earth."

I will never forget the October afternoon at old Forbes Field in Pittsburgh when Bill Mazeroski turned a whole city upside down with one swing of the bat. Leading off the ninth inning of the seventh game, with the score tied, Mazeroski hit the second pitch over the left-field fence. It gave Pittsburgh its first world championship in thirty-five years, and the frustration and waiting were all made apparent by the nature of the celebration.

As for ovations, I hold a special memory of one that took place on October 8, 1956. Again, the scene was Yankee Stadium. The occasion was the fifth game of the World Series. From the sixth inning on, though, there was only one story for everyone in that crowd. Don

Larsen was flirting with history. He was pitching a perfect game. The end of each inning was greeted, not with applause, but with a sigh of relief.

Finally, came the ninth inning. Larsen retired Carl Furillo, and then Roy Campanella. Only one man stood between him and immortality, pinch hitter Dale Mitchell. With a count of one ball and two strikes, Larsen pitched. *Strike three.*

Then pandemonium! The crowd let loose in what was probably the greatest ovation ever accorded an individual player in all baseball history. A unique ovation, too, for it was completely nonpartisan. For a few moments there were no Brooklyn fans, no Yankee fans; no National Leaguers, no American Leaguers. It was all Larsen, with rivalries and allegiances forgotten as a baseball world paid ear-shattering tribute to one man's perfection. Baseball had never seen anything like that ovation, which was fitting. It had never seen anything like what Larsen had done, either.

But these are, after all, the memoirs of a fan, and as such I must mention a very personal recollection of fans' reaction. It was the day that Bobby Thomson hit his unforgettable ninth-inning home run against the Brooklyn Dodgers that sent the New York Giants into the 1951 World Series.

I had been elected commissioner a few days before that game was played. For seventeen years, I had served as president of the National League. I loved that job, and cherished the friendships I had made through the years. I reveled, too, in the rooting privileges. Now, I knew I would have to avoid close friendships with owners and players alike.

So, when the committee called me from Chicago to tell me of my election, I accepted with a proviso: that I be permitted to finish the league season as president, and that I be permitted rooting privileges in the coming World Series. When I went to the Polo Grounds that third playoff day, I knew it would be the last game I would ever watch as a league executive. It would be the last game in which I would have close association with the players and umpires I had worked with for almost two decades.

I was hoping for a game I would remember. I certainly got it. That game is still so fresh in fan memory, and has been reenacted so often through the replay of Russ Hodges's broadcast, that it would be foolish for me to recount the details leading up to the famous home run. As a matter of fact, it all happened so fast and dramatically that my own memory is hazy.

I do recall watching the ball head toward the stand, and wondering whether it had enough altitude to clear the wall. I remember, too, the look of utter dejection on Ralph Branca's face as he stepped off the mound. I remember Thomson fighting his way through a mob of frenzied fans, and wondering whether they would pull him to the ground before he could touch home plate and make his run official. All around me fans were on their feet, yelling, jumping over seats, and rushing on the field to join the growing mob around the plate and on the infield. My inclination was to join them in one last hurrah. But I restrained myself and watched the fun from my seat on the first base line.

I recall vividly the scene around home plate. Players and fans alike were mixed together in a wild potpourri of jubilation. In the very center of all the excitement was a figure I couldn't mistake. It was my friend, Toots Shor, ardent sportsman, and one of the most rabid Giants fans in New York history. Tears were running down Toots's face as he embraced player after player, until finally he was swept out toward the pitching mound and disappeared in the swirling mob of jubilant fans.

The next day I met Shor at lunch.

"That was quite a show you put on yesterday," I remarked. "Tell me, how did you get to home plate so fast? You were down that line even before Durocher."

Toots looked at me in amazement. "Are you nuts? I never left my seat. Sure I was shook up, but I didn't move until the excitement was over and the players were going up the steps to the clubhouse!"

An AP photographer, fortunately, had snapped a picture of the home plate turmoil, which was printed in various papers. I pulled out the picture. There was Toots in the very middle of the mob, big as life. You couldn't mistake him.

"What about this picture?" I asked.

Toots took a long look, then shook his head. "I don't believe it," he said, "I just don't believe it."

I'm not sure that Toots has ever really been convinced, despite the photographic evidence. But that isn't really important. It is an example of the drama and excitement that is part of baseball at its best. Ovations and demonstrations are an adjunct of the game. If sometimes the fans lose their cool, if now and then grown men and women forget that they are adults and let their emotions show through, that's all to the good. Letting off steam is important in these hectic days, and the nation's sports stadiums are great places for it.

But to get back to Shea Stadium, and the Mel Allen ovation. It must have been a warming experience for Mel. It was certainly a deserved tribute. To me, it was important for still another reason. Mel Allen never played baseball, nor was he in any sense an athletic hero. He was a broadcaster. His job was simply to describe the deeds of others, to bring the fans at home the drama and excitement of play on the field, just as baseball writers had been doing for more than a half century.

But there was one big difference. In doing his job, Mel Allen's picture was flashed daily on millions of screens; the timbre and warmth of his voice registered in the ears of millions of fans. They knew him intimately, just as in coming years they will know the younger announcers who are working today. That is the power of television, and sports cannot overlook it.

If baseball has a future problem, it is to make sure that the tail does not wag the dog, that television does not (gradually and probably unintentionally) take over the scheduling, and rules, and time of play, to the point where competition is affected and the game becomes programed entertainment rather than a contest. A few pessimists already are predicting a dark future when baseball and other sports will be played in a central arena. Then the games will be taped and distributed to member stations to be shown on prime time at an hour selected by the sponsors on the basis of selling pull. I don't think that will ever happen.

I do think that prices will have to be adjusted. Television networks cannot afford to price themselves out of business by pouring additional millions of dollars into baseball's coffers every time a new television contract is agreed upon. Nor can baseball owners afford to sacrifice their firm control of the game in exchange for "sweetening the kitty" beyond legitimate limits.

Television and sports make a fine partnership. But they need each other. I'm the sort of cockeyed optimist who believes that within the foreseeable future answers will be found. Agreements will be reached, and rules established, which will clear the financial atmosphere and pave the way for decades of sane and honest operation for all concerned (including players). After all, television is operated by sound businessmen, and baseball men are neither as selfish nor ruthless as some critics delight in painting them. Also, players will learn that they have a public obligation that extends beyond the personal battle for salary increase and fringe pension benefits. Maybe they will have to learn the hard way, but they will learn! It's in the cards, and the fans will do the dealing.

9

EXPANSION

Probably no single program in baseball history created more controversy, aroused stronger fan feeling, or brought more vituperative discussion, pro and con, than the movement of clubs and the expansion of the major leagues. For nearly half a century the game had maintained a territorial status quo—ten metropolitan areas in an area generally bounded by the Potomac River on the south, the Mississippi on the west, and the Atlantic Ocean on the east.

In 1903, when the two circuits were stabilized, the setup was sound. Most of the big commercial centers, the big-money interests, predominant political power, and two-thirds of our national population came within the artificial boundaries set for major league baseball. Clubs were privately owned by local sportsmen who built their own parks, ran their own businesses, and took their losses or their profits with a shrug or a grin, as the situation dictated. So far as the rest of the country was concerned, a strong minor league setup ensured competition, and local rivalries begat fan enthusiasm, even though they didn't guarantee performance of major league caliber.

By the end of World War I, the situation began to change. Improved transportation and communication facilities changed the picture. Radio began to grow, and so did speedy long-distance telephone service. Better highways were built, and better cars to ride on those highways. Cross-country trains and commercial flying became factors in the change. The trek from the Eastern Seaboard into the hinterland of the South and the West moved from a bare trickle to flood stage almost overnight.

Cow towns became thriving cities, mining camps grew into industrial centers, and wasteland hamlets became industrial metropoli through the discovery of oil. It was a whole new ball game. Small-town rivalry couldn't hold its own with big-time thinking, and baseball was faced with a problem that couldn't be ignored. Two-thirds of the nation's population was without major league representation.

Unfortunately, there were no rules and no procedures to provide a guideline for any expansion program. Also, there was no apparent willingness on the part of the major league hierarchy to consider any changes. The policy in those days seemed to be one of self-preservation and complete commitment to the status quo.

Then came the stock-market collapse of 1929, and the subsequent depression. Historically, it's a fact that short terms of unemployment and depression have benefited the amusement world. Persons temporarily out of employment have plenty of leisure, and sometimes enough savings to enable them to go to a theater or a ball park during the time they are out of work.

Baseball in 1929 and through 1930 showed increased attendance and increased income. But by 1932, the pinch had come. In 1933, major league attendance was down drastically, with the greatest percentage falloff in the game's history. Two-club cities were particularly hard hit, and drastic action was indicated. Sam Breadon, owner of the St. Louis Cardinals, wanted to transfer his franchise from St. Louis to Detroit. He took the matter up with Judge Landis, then baseball commissioner, requesting a rule as to rights and procedure.

Rules at that time provided that a major league club could be moved into the territory of another major league, only after three conditions had been met. First, the unanimous consent of both leagues. Second, the consent of the club whose territory was being invaded, and third, the payment of a mutually agreed upon indemnity to the invaded club. In the case of a major league club invading minor league territory, only the consent of the invading club's own league was required, with a mutually agreed upon indemnity to both the invaded club and league. Judge Landis ruled, and wisely, that Breadon's request was strictly a league and club matter, and did not come under the jurisdiction of the commissioner except as concerned proper indemnity.

Breadon was unable to make a satisfactory agreement with Frank Navin, president of the Detroit club, and the project was dropped. In 1941, Don Barnes, then president of the St. Louis Browns, undertook to move his club out of St. Louis and into the territory of the Pacific Coast League's Los Angeles club. Judge Landis again held that the transfer was a club and league matter, with the Commissioner assuming jurisdiction only in the question of indemnity judication.

Barnes proceeded with his plans, got the consent of the American League, and had reached tentative agreement as to indemnities, when the attack came on Pearl Harbor. America was suddenly plunged into war, and all bets were off. I felt then, and still feel, that but for the Pearl Harbor attack, the first major league move into new territory would have been consummated then, and a lot of subsequent bitter argument and politicking would have been avoided.

At war's end there came a spectacular increase in baseball interest, and the pressure for expansion was renewed, with the Triple-A Pacific Coast League leading the parade. They argued that they were ready for major league representation and requested that the league, in toto, be raised to major league status. Happy Chandler, the then Commissioner, was fully aware of the problem and the need for some sort of expansion program, if baseball was to retain its standing as a national game. Chandler also recognized the difficulties facing any group that attempted major league status under such circumstances. He accorded the Pacific Coast League a most sympathetic hearing, but insisted that before the matter be submitted for major league action, there first be a full and comprehensive study of the financial responsibilities involved in such a move.

A special committee of the two leagues, headed by the commissioner, made an extended tour of all Pacific Coast League cities. It ended with an executive session at which all PCL representatives were present. At this meeting, the PCL was furnished with full and detailed figures on the costs of a major league operation. The potential drawing power of each suggested club was studied. A profit-and-loss statement of each of the sixteen major league clubs was provided, with full disclosure of every detail of operation.

At the end of the meeting, the PCL went into executive session. Their decision was unanimous. To attempt to turn the Pacific Coast League, in toto, into a third major league would be completely impractical. After a study of major league operations they were convinced that only two of their clubs had the clientele and financial potential for major league operation. San Francisco and Los Angeles, they believed, were ready. Seattle was willing to give it a try. The others wanted no part of the risk. The idea of a ready-made "third league" was abandoned, not because of major league discouragement, but because of the PCL owners themselves were convinced that the plan had no chance of success and could only result in the disruption of a prideful and traditional minor league operation.

The decision of the Pacific Coast League encouraged renewed activity by a group that was convinced there was an easy solution to the expansion problem. Their plan was to advance individual cities to major league status by moving one club from the two-club areas into new territory. They would thereby expand the geographic area, but still maintain the traditional two-league eight-club structure. It looked, for a time, like an easy answer.

In 1953, the Boston Braves, with National League consent, moved their franchise to Milwaukee. There was some grumbling on the part of partisan fans. (Boston fans have ever been articulate, and though they were notoriously short on financial support, they were long on pride and tradition.) But the move was generally accepted in good spirit, and with a modicum of opposition. The Braves, in effect, were trading an antiquated, down-at-the-heel ball park, and a sizable annual deficit, for a modern new park and a million-and-a-half attendance bonanza. They were happy, and Boston fans still had baseball, and their favorite Red Sox.

The following year, the American League stepped into the picture. The Mack family sold their longtime interest in the Philadelphia Athletics to a newly formed Middle Western syndicate that moved the franchise to Kansas City. The St. Louis Browns franchise was transferred to Baltimore. In two seasons, the major leagues had expanded from 10 to 13 cities, while still retaining their original 16 club setup. So far, so good.

Then, in 1957, the two National League clubs in the New York metropolitan area announced they were moving—the Giants to San Francisco, and the Dodgers to Los Angeles. That did it! New York fans, blasé to other moves, reacted with explosive violence to this one. Dodgers president Walter O'Malley was figuratively "tarred and feathered" by fans throughout the five boroughs. Horace Stoneham was labeled "traitor" and "ingrate."

City Hall issued condemnatory statements. The City Council passed resolutions. Politicians got into the act. So did some businessmen, forgetting, I guess, that they had been guilty of the same traitorism in moving their own businesses out of the city to more lucrative and less expensive fields. Fans blew their collective tops, swearing they had been "sold down the river," and vowing they would never attend another ball game. They kept that vow religiously throughout the long, dismal winter. Not until the coming of spring, when the Yankees played their opening game of a new season, did they forget their rancor, swallow their pride, and renew their interest in two base hits and box scores. I'm speaking here of the majority. Some, of course, nursed their bitterness much longer.

I can't say I blame them. Fans are always emotional, and too often they are unaware of the real facts in cases that arouse their honest ire over an unpopular action. Maybe that's the highest tribute they can pay to baseball, and all sports. Certainly, they react violently to any questionable actions affecting sports, and at the same time are slow to respond to equally questionable maneuvering on the part of politicians and big business.

Don't misunderstand me. This is in no way intended as a defense of Mr. O'Malley or Mr. Stoneham or baseball. What is done is done, and most fans, I am sure, realize that baseball is better off today because these moves were made. Maybe the methods were wrong. Maybe the motives of the persons involved were selfish, and inspired by personal gain and profit, but the results were beneficial. Now that it's over I am attempting to tell, for the records, the factual story of those hectic times as viewed through the eyes of a dyed-in-the-wool fan who was fortunate (or unfortunate) enough to be privy to the events leading up to and following the explosion.

First, I suppose, in the consideration of the move should be the question of legality, and the right of clubs under existing statutes.

As concerns baseball's own rules, the record is clear. The Major–Minor League Agreement specifies that "no territory in which a minor league franchise is being operated . . . shall be included in any Major League until such Minor League and Minor League Club shall be paid such sum as shall be mutually agreed upon as just and reasonable compensation for such action."

Both the Giants and the Dodgers met that regulation to the letter.

As concerns federal or state statutes, there was no law, and never has been a law, denying or limiting the right of any individual to move his place of business from one city or community to another, as business judgment might dictate, except as private contracts, mutually agreed upon, might otherwise specify. In a government of free enterprise, General Motors or IBM or any other commercial organization is legally free to move headquarters, plants, factories, or distributing centers from city to city or state to state, as conditions may dictate. The same is true of baseball clubs. Fans, emotionally upset by the move, might clamor for legal action. But under the law, there was no way any judge or any official in baseball could either by edict or injunction stop such a move, however much he might desire to do so. That is a matter of record.

Aside from the legality of the issue, there also arose the questions of moral obligation, of loyalty, of tradition, and community pride. Whether such a move was justifiable, considering ethics alone, depends on many outside factors that fans, in their enthusiasm, are prone to discount. Here are the facts, as I know them.

First, the Giants and Horace Stoneham. For many years, the Giants had held a long-term lease, and had played their games in the Polo Grounds. Through the years, they—the Giants, the Polo Grounds and baseball—had become an integral part of New York life. In their way, they had become as much traditional landmarks as Grant's Tomb, or the Public Library, or the subway system.

But the picture had changed. The famous old park had deteriorated. Transportation facilities, once adequate, no longer met the demands of a growing population. Ninety percent of the available parking space, never adequate, had been taken over for public projects—the center-field area by a highway and a public school; the left-field area by high-rise, low-income apartments. Even more critical, the whole neighborhood had become so run-down that fans were afraid to walk even a block or two to see a night game, and equally reluctant to park their cars in the area, for fear of robbery, or mugging, or even worse. To cap it all, Stoneham was given official notice that his lease, about to expire, would not be renewed. The park was to be razed, and the land taken over for public housing.

Stoneham took his problem to the city fathers. They were sympathetic but could offer no encouragement, either as to playing space, parking facilities, or assured police protection in a run-down neighborhood. The Giants, the pride of New York for three-quarters of a century, were out in the cold with no place to go. It was then that the first conversations looking toward movement of the club to another city were opened—not with San Francisco, but with Minneapolis, where the Giants already operated a minor league franchise.

Over in Brooklyn, meantime, a similar situation developed. It was not as critical as the Giants' situation, but serious nonetheless. The Dodgers owned their park, and were not faced with immediate eviction, but like the Polo Grounds, Ebbets Field was old and antiquated. The playing field was cramped, seating space was entirely inadequate, and public transportation left much to be desired. Like the Polo Grounds, too, the neighborhood around Ebbets Field had deteriorated over the years.

Brooklyn management had long been aware of the situation, and had made sporadic efforts to get the city to help in getting real estate releases for adequate parking and a more modern stadium. In fact, during the regime of Mayor Jimmy Walker, it looked for a time that a satisfactory solution would be reached. The proposal was that the street outside the left-field wall be closed off for two blocks. That would create additional playing area and increase the seating capacity to 50,000. At the same time it was proposed that the city legislate to clear a square block of buildings across Bedford Avenue and sell the real estate to the club for additional parking space. Mayor Walker favored the idea, but no action was taken.

From time to time other proposals and counterproposals were bandied back and forth, but no serious consideration was forthcoming until the mid-fifties. By that time the postwar boom was well under way, expansion pressures were increasing, and Brooklyn's problem became something more than a passing headache. Something had to be done.

Walter O'Malley, then the club president, and board member George V. McLaughlin got their heads together to come up with a plan. They formed an unusual twosome. O'Malley was a practicing attorney, well versed in all legal procedures. He also held an engineering degree, and knew the whys and wherefores of heavy construction. McLaughlin was not only an outstanding banker and financial man but a New York political power as well. Both men were from Brooklyn. Both men were interested in keeping the club in Brooklyn, but, at the same time, insistent that any action had to be financially sound.

Their proposal to the city authorities was concise and definite. The Brooklyn club would guarantee to underwrite and build a modern baseball and sports stadium with a capacity of 55,000, provided the city could clear title to adequate real estate for such a venture. Two provisos were included. The proposed site should be in the Borough of Brooklyn. Also, it should be so located, and of sufficient acreage, to afford proper transportation facilities and adequate parking space to meet foreseen demand.

A series of meetings were held with various city officials, including Mayor Wagner. Civic groups were consulted. The city said they were unable to come up with any guarantee of adequate and acceptable real estate in Brooklyn. They proposed instead that consideration be given to the use of city-owned acreage in the Flushing Park area of Queens. After much discussion and endless surveys, O'Malley and his board rejected the proposal.

His reasons, as publicly announced, were twofold. First, Flushing Park was in Queens, not in Brooklyn. To move the club there would jeopardize the Brooklyn loyalty and support that had been developed through the years. Second, and more important, the proposed site was filled marshland. To build the type stadium desired would require a foundation of piles that would be prohibitive in cost, would possibly require unplanned expenditure through water and seepage damage, and would necessitate a capital expenditure far exceeding any known standard for such a private enterprise.

The story was widely publicized, along with the crisis facing the Giants. Los Angeles and San Francisco, long in the market for major league baseball, got busy. They contacted the two clubs, and a deal was soon made. O'Malley would move to Los Angeles and would build his own park, with private capital. It would be on Chavez Ravine land, furnished by the city in exchange for Wrigley Field, which had come to the Dodgers as part of the Pacific Coast League settlement. While the new park was being constructed, the Dodgers would play their games at the Los Angeles Coliseum.

As for the Giants, the city of San Francisco agreed to build and maintain a new and modern stadium, which the Giants would occupy on a long-term lease. Meantime, Seals Stadium, in the heart of downtown San Francisco, would be available for Giants games until Candlestick Park was completed. The National League, as required by baseball rules, gave unanimous consent to the move. Major league baseball, at long last, had reached the Pacific coast. The old Giants-Dodgers rivalry was still intact, but in a new setting.

And those are the facts as I know them. As to what they prove, you can draw your own conclusions. However, from time to time, friends have asked me whether or not the move was justified. The answer, in my opinion, is easy. As a fan, I was upset by the action. As commissioner, if I had the final decision, and knowing the facts in the case, I would have approved the move with no reservations or qualms of conscience.

Baseball has always been slow to accept change. Only through dire pressure can any radical change be accomplished. The move of the Giants and the Dodgers from New York to California brought that pressure in abundance. The same city fathers who had listened to the pleas of Messrs. Stoneham and O'Malley with amused and tolerant skepticism suddenly realized that these gentlemen hadn't been kidding. Overnight, New York had become a one-club city, and they didn't like it. Somehow, somewhere, they had to find a replacement.

The city enlisted the services of Bill Shea—a move that proved to be a lifesaver. Shea, a gentleman of pleasing personality, was soft-spoken and smiling, but had the tenacity of a pit bulldog when the chips were down. He went into violent action. His first move was to bring Branch Rickey into the picture, and in baseball Rickey had always been a power to reckon with. Between them they came up with the idea of a third major league—the Continental League—with Rickey as president.

It wasn't a very strong league, but it did include cities like New York, Houston, Dallas, and Toronto, cities that had real major league potential. It was backed with strong financial support in every key city. In New York there was Mrs. Joan Whitney Payson. In Houston, a strong syndicate. In Dallas, the Lamar Hunt millions. In Toronto, Jack Kent Cooke, who was later to build an empire involving many sports (but not baseball) in Los Angeles.

A meeting was arranged in New York between representatives of the sixteen major league clubs and the "third league rebels," with Shea and Rickey carrying the ball for the newcomers. "We are prepared to start tomorrow if necessary," Mr. Rickey explained. "We are not looking for war. We much prefer to come in as friendly members of Organized Baseball. I think that every man in this room recognizes that expansion is necessary. All we request is that you gentlemen grant us major league membership as a third league. We believe in baseball, and we want to operate as a part of an established and traditional baseball organization. We are ready to assume all proper obligations. We pledge ourselves to abide by all the rules and take all the risks. All we ask is that you gentleman give us a chance."

Mr. Rickey sat down, and Mr. Shea took the floor. "Mr. Rickey has covered the situation well," he said. "I am in accord with everything he has said. One thing, however, I think should be understood. The Continental League is not a fly-by-night organization. The cities holding membership are pledged to mutual action. As individuals we cannot, any of us, go our own way or make our own decisions. As Mr. Rickey has said, we do not want a baseball war.

"Personally, as you know, my primary interest is to bring a National League club to New York to fill the vacancy left by the move of the Dodgers to California. But I am a member of the proposed new league. In good conscience, I must tell you that until my colleagues in the Continental, by their own decision, release me, I am honor-bound to stand with them to the finish, even though it leads to independent operation outside the existing baseball structure."

Whether or not Mr. Shea was bluffing no one will ever know. Baseball was scared. The nightmare of the Federal League war was common knowledge. Pressure was being applied by the press and public opinion. The structure of baseball was under scrutiny by Congress. With postwar attendance booming to new records, a baseball war would be a calamity beyond comprehension. Compromise was in order, and it came quickly.

The major leagues agreed to expand to ten clubs each immediately. The National League selected New York and Houston as its expansion cities. The American League selected Minneapolis and Los Angeles. It was further agreed that in a reasonable time the two leagues would go to twelve clubs, with four more Continental League cities granted major league status. In return, the Continental League agreed to disband.

It looked like an easy solution. It proved otherwise.

By going into New York and Los Angeles, each league was invading the territory of the other. There were other difficulties, too. Neither of the new clubs had parks ready for occupancy. The Dodgers held a lease on the Los Angeles Coliseum, pending completion of their new Chavez Ravine Stadium. The new American League club in Los Angeles proposed to play their games at Wrigley Field. The New York club, pending the completion of their new park, planned to utilize the abandoned Polo Grounds.

Both the Polo Grounds and Wrigley Field were within the five-mile limit, and consequently in violation of baseball's territorial rule. Unless and until Rule 1 was rewritten, no move could be made, and a revision of the rule required a majority vote of each league. In case of a tie in the voting, the commissioner would cast the deciding vote. As commissioner, I had already quietly informed the league leaders that I would reluctantly vote "no," unless some agreement was reached establishing property rules and values, and unless there was included in the new rule such provisions as would spell out procedure, not only for the immediate change, but for future expansion action as well.

A major league meeting was called in St. Louis. For a day and a night informal argument was hot and heavy. The two leagues were at loggerheads. The formal meeting got under way, and there were two hours of mutual charges and recrimination, with no break in the deadlock. Finally, when it looked as though the whole program would go down the drain, a fifteen-minute recess was called. The three attorneys—Louis Carroll, of the National League; Ben Fiery, of the American League; and Paul Porter, of the commissioner's office— went into conference. Within ten minutes, a compromise proposal was agreed upon.

The meeting went back into session, and Mr. Fiery proposed a new rule providing that no second major league club could be established in any major league city with a population of less than 4 million people. That cleared the way for New York and Los Angeles, while protecting other clubs from expansion.

It was agreed that the new Los Angeles club would be permitted to use Wrigley Field temporarily, and that they would be given rental privileges at Chavez Ravine, when completed, until such time as their own stadium was ready. In New York, the Yankees temporarily waived the five-mile rule to permit the new club to use the Polo Grounds until Shea Stadium was completed. In each instance, property rights were established by the payment of mutually agreed upon damages to the invaded club.

At the same time, another sore point was removed when the American League voted to accept new ownership to operate an expansion club in Washington. This was necessary because Mr. Griffith had moved the Washington club to Minnesota, thereby bringing in two new cities as per agreement with the Continental League and at the same time preserving baseball in the nation's capital.

The proposal, once details were agreed upon, was unanimously adopted. The expansion train was on the track and ready to roll. Many critics still fault baseball for being dilatory in meeting the expansion problem. They may be right. Certainly things would have been easier if they had changed the rules before they were faced with a crisis. Other critics label the owners as "compromisers." The eventual solution was undoubtedly a compromise. Most group decisions are.

But sometimes compromises are necessary. In that connection, I always think of Colonel Alex McGillivray. McGillivray was, as students of early American history know, a Scotsman who headed the great Creek nation during and after the Revolution. At that time, the Creek tribes controlled a vast territory covering western Georgia, Alabama, most of Mississippi and southern Tennessee. Three nations— Spain, England, and the young United States—were battling for Creek trading privileges, and the canny colonel was frequently faced with critical decisions.

"I've discovered," he wrote, "that if you delay a bit to permit the contending parties to let off steam, the problem is either forgotten or it becomes so pressing that the two parties are forced to swallow some of their anger and pride, and become practical. When they have settled the matter themselves, as they always do, I step in and tell them they've been very wise. And instead of making one enemy, I've flattered two friends."

Baseball, I guess, was born with a McGillivrayan complex, and somehow it worked.

10

HIZZONOR, THE UMP

Razzed by the crowds with a comment that's searing,
Cursed and maligned, if he's wrong or he's right;
Constantly subject to hazing and jeering,
Object of panning from morning to night,
Butt for the wit of the bleacherite jokers,
Haled as a robber, a thief, and a chump;
Scoffed at by millionaires, lawyers, and stokers—
This is the lot of Hizzonor, the Ump.

He must have eyes that reveal all that's doing,
Legs that will carry him mile after mile;
Courage to face trouble constantly brewing,
Turning each insult away with a smile.
His life is friendless, tormented, and baited,
Pestered, insulted, and scorned by the mob—
All this is part of his work, as we've stated—
These things aside, it's a peach of a job.

All of the knowledge that's come down the ages,
All of the patience of Job at his best;
All of the wisdom of prophets and sages—
Solomon, Socrates, Saul and the rest—

All of these together would scarcely suffice him,
Or save him from insult, or turmoil, or strife;
Fans still will scorn him, and razz him, and haze him—
Believe me an ump has an 'elluva life!

The story of umpiring is largely a story of personality and individual accomplishment. In no other profession is a man as alone in time of crisis, or so open to personal attack on every decision.

There have been many great umpires in the long history of baseball. The greatest, in the opinion of most critics, was William J. (Bill) Klem. His record speaks for itself. He came into baseball when the one-umpire system was in vogue. For sixteen straight seasons he worked "behind the plate." He umpired more games, over more seasons, than any other major league umpire in history. He officiated in eighteen World Series—a record no other umpire has approached.

He had great personal pride in his profession. He led a long and bitter fight to establish public acceptance of umpiring honesty and integrity. By his own efforts he changed "grudging tolerance" into public respect, and forced official and fan support of umpirical authority on the playing field. Klem was the first umpire to use hand signals for "ball" or "strike" and "safe" or "out." His explanation was simple. "That guy in a twenty-five-cent bleacher seat is as much entitled to know a call as the guy in the boxes. He can see my arm signal even if he can't hear my voice."

Klem was not a public speaker, nor was he given to fine lines or unforgettable adages. Yet, two of his remarks have become legendary. "Your job is to umpire for the ball and not the player," he advised every young umpire. "Remember that, and you won't have any trouble. There is no need for guessing. A decision is called for only when the ball smacks into the glove."

Klem's other great line was voiced in an argument with a few cronies following a game: "Baseball is more than a game to me—it's a religion." That line, too, has become a part of the growing Klem legend.

Bill wasn't interested in high-sounding titles. He picked his own. He always referred to himself as "the old Arbitrator." That, too, was a misnomer. Whatever else he may have been, he certainly was not an arbitrator. On the playing field he was a czar—at times even a tyrant. He ran the game with complete assurance, without regard to public, players, owners, or other umpires. He was totally autocratic. To him there were only two parties to a Klem decision—himself and the baseball—and the ball never talked back.

But, enough of records and cold statistics. What is the story of umpires as human beings? Here are some offbeat incidents that spectators seldom know about, likes and dislikes, repartees and human frailties that are a part of the umpire's job.

Bill Klem was a small man, or a giant. It all depends upon the measuring device. If it's the common yardstick, you have to list him as small. If the gauge is his stature in the eye of fans, players, and baseball people generally, then he's a giant. There were none greater.

Years ago some critic remarked that Klem looked like a catfish. Bill hated that description. In fact, any player who even referred to him as "Catfish" was certain to draw an immediate one-way ticket to the showers. One of the hottest umpire-player feuds in baseball history was launched by that unmentionable word. Jimmy Wilson, one of the more capable catchers, joined the Phillies and was assigned to catch his first major league game with Klem behind the plate.

Art Fletcher, a great practical joker, was the Phil manager. Before the game started he called Wilson aside. "You've got Bill Klem behind the plate and he's a great umpire," Fletcher explained, "but you've got to show him some guts. He likes a fighter. Call him 'Catfish' if he gets tough. That will show him."

Jim followed instructions. In the second inning Klem called a fourth ball on the hitter.

"That ball had the corner," Wilson protested. "It was a strike and you know it."

Klem never moved. "Listen, young man," he said, "you better learn one thing early. When I'm back of the plate I do the umpiring. You do the catching. That way we both do our jobs."

"But, Catfish . . . ," Jimmy retorted.

He never got further. Off came the umpirical mask. Up went the right arm. "Get out," Klem roared. "You're out of the game. No fresh rookie is going to insult me. Get out right now."

Jimmy got. The feud was on. Later Wilson apologized, but

Klem was unforgiving. For the remainder of the season Klem refused to speak to the young catcher, and more than a year went by before they established friendly relations.

Wilson later made a pertinent observation. "That old son-of-a-gun wouldn't even say 'hello' for more than a year. He wouldn't even look at me. But in all of the games he worked behind the plate he never missed a call. What an umpire!"

Klem was not the only umpire with a hate fetish.

George Magerkurth, a National League veteran, saw red when anyone referred to him as "meathead." He could take a lot of abuse and cursing and keep his cool, but he couldn't stand that one term. Players could gesture and curse within reason, and get away with it. But "meathead"—even whispered—was taboo. The guilty player was on his way to the showers before he knew what had happened.

For years Magerkurth and Beans Reardon were at odds to the point that they never worked on the same umpiring team. I never knew the reason until one day when George dropped into the office to report a player eviction.

"Boss," he said, "I'm not a violent man. I don't mind being cussed, or being called a blind so-and-so or a stubborn this-and-that. But that guy I put out yesterday called me 'meathead' so I chased him. I'm not going to stand for that personal stuff."

This probably explains the Reardon feud. Beans was a bit of a wag and, according to other umpires, would occasionally hide behind a door and shout "meathead" at Magerkurth as he passed. Unfortunately, hiding wasn't the answer. Beans's voice was a dead giveaway. George may have been a bit tone-deaf, but Beans's voice wasn't on key, either. Maybe that was the original cause of the feud. At least it seems reasonable.

Billy Evans, for years an outstanding American League umpire, was another who had a "sore spot" for certain comments. Billy was a sports columnist for NEA as a sideline to his umpiring. (Rather, I should say, sportswriting was his avocation.) He was a good writer and never used personal field arguments as a basis for reportorial comment. His pet peeve was the suggestion of an irate player that he would or would not "put that in your column." Not having access to American League umpire reports, I cannot say how many players

Billy put out of the game for such reference. I do know that Babe Ruth was once a victim—one of the very few times Babe was ever ejected from a game. Babe was taken completely by surprise. He laughed about it later and commented that he knew a way of getting a rest whenever Evans was umpiring. I noticed, however, that he never pulled the line again.

One of an umpire's greatest attributes is a sense of humor, which enables him to ease a threatening situation with a bit of light repartee. Tommy Connolly, veteran American League umpire, and second only to Bill Klem in years of major league service, offers a case in point.

Tommy was a slight, quiet, little man in an era when most umpires were big, brawny, and boisterous. He was British born, with all of the reticence and reserve of an English gentleman. He was an extremely religious man, too, in an age of violent argument and colorful profanity. He never raised his voice in anger and considered any phrase stronger than "my gracious" beyond the pale of civilized conversation. But he had a ready wit and a quiet sense of humor that usually quelled the most serious detractors.

He was behind the plate in a Sunday game in Detroit, which was played as usual before a large crowd of avid Tiger fans. The score was tied at 1–1 with the Tigers at bat in the seventh inning. A runner was on second and Bobby Veach was at bat.

Veach hit the first pitch for a line drive down the third base line. Obviously, the outfielder couldn't reach the ball, so the base runner was off and running. Tommy stood at the plate watching the flight of the ball as it curved toward the foul line. It was one of those nip-and-tuck decisions. From the press box it looked like the ball was foul by not more than an inch or two at most, but the fans didn't see it that way, nor did the Tiger bench. Tommy waved the ball "foul" and quietly stepped forward to brush off the plate.

Immediately there was pandemonium. Fans started booing. The Tiger third base coach rushed madly to the plate, yelling and waving his arms. "That ball was fair," he shrieked. "It hit the foul line. I saw the dirt fly. You can see the mark."

Tommy continued to sweep the plate. As the irate coach approached, he looked up and made some comment. The coach listened and dropped his hands. His face reflected utter frustration as he shrugged his shoulders. Then he grinned as he went back to his post. The runner returned to second. What looked like a serious rhubarb died aborning.

That night I cornered Tommy in the hotel dining room.

"What did you say to that coach?" I asked.

"Oh, nothing much. He was yelling that the ball hit the foul line and was fair. All I really said to him was, 'I watched the ball and I'm sure it was foul by a couple of inches. But, I don't want to be stubborn. Tell you what, you trot out there and bring me the foul line. I'll look at it and we'll both be happy.' "

Clarence Rowland, former White Sox manager, and a longtime American League umpire, was another who used a sense of humor and a ready quip to avoid argument. I recall a story Babe Ruth told years ago. Rowland was umpiring at second base when the Babe blooped one over the second baseman's head. The baseman, leaping high in the air in an attempt to stop the ball, missed and fell to the ground. The Babe, rounding first, saw the second baseman prostrate, and decided to try for a double.

But the right fielder retrieved the ball and rifled it into the covering shortstop as Babe slid into second. Rowland, on top of the play, waved Ruth out. But, let's hear Babe's comment:

"As I hooked the bag I was sure I had beaten the tag, but when I looked up, there was Rowland waving me out and all the time he was grinning and saying, 'It's a shame to have to call that close one after that slide. You're out, Babe, but I never saw a better hook-slide. It was perfect.'

"Jeez," Babe added, "I was mad enough to tear the blankety-blank apart."

"But," he added with a sheepish grin, "you can't argue with a guy who's sympathizing with you."

It's too bad that fans and spectators can't enjoy the repartee that goes on during a game. A lot of the language is, of course, not fit for repetition. Not all remarks are funny, nor are umpires always masters of repartee. It's just as well that players and umpires are not wired for sound and that microphones are not installed on benches and in bullpens. But now and then, tense situations do produce some gems that can turn a potentially bad situation into a "laugh-off." That, in my book, is a mark of distinction that unfortunately escapes the fan in the stands.

There was the incident in which an irate batman called out on a questionable strike showed his displeasure by throwing his bat high into the air. Beans Reardon was umpiring behind the plate, and his reaction was positive and instantaneous.

"If that bat comes down you're out of the game," he shouted. The player's jaw dropped. Then he shrugged and started for the runway. No argument, no stormy protest, no profanity. As they say in stage scripts: "Exit, laughing."

Bill Klem had a similar experience with Frank Frisch, then manager of the Pirates, as his victim. Frank was one of my favorite "bad boys." He was a fiery performer who delighted in ribbing umpires. He was a master actor as well. When he had a squawk he wanted the whole audience to know about it. His gestures, at times, were even more expressive than his language, which, in turn included a lot of words not to be found in an unabridged dictionary.

On this particular occasion Frank was in rare form. Throughout the early innings he had given Klem a bad time, but Bill had ignored him. Frank was coaching at third base and by mid-game he had the fans completely hypnotized by his antics. In the seventh inning a Pittsburgh player was called on strikes. Frank let out a yell of anguish that could be heard in Hoboken, clutched his chest, and toppled over to the ground like a man suffering from a fatal heart attack. Tremors raced up and down his legs, his torso shook, and then he stiffened out, his eyes fixed on the sky and his arms extended at right angles to his body.

That was too much for Klem who whipped off his mask and rushed down the third base line.

"I've had it," he yelled. "If you're not dead when I get there, you're out of the game!"

The crowd applauded. Frisch leaped to his feet, doffed his hat to Klem and headed for the clubhouse. Klem returned to the plate and donned his mask. "Come on, let's play ball," he growled. The crowd cheered. Whether their applause was for Klem's forensics or for Frisch's action, I'll never know. Maybe, neither. Maybe they were just happy to have some relief from the tedium of a dull game.

Certainly it was not the first time that Frisch had staged his un-scheduled bit of vaudeville, nor was it the last. I'll never forget a game in Boston when Frank was managing the Cardinals. The Cardinals had a one-run lead going into the seventh inning. It was a rainy day and as the Braves were retired in the sixth the skies really opened. Time was taken, with Frisch arguing vehemently that the game be officially called. He lost that argument. After a half-hour delay, the teams were ordered back to the diamond. As the Braves took the field, Frisch strolled out to the coaching box. The crowd took one look at him and roared. He was wearing rubber boots, a nor'wester hat, carrying an umbrella, and carefully nursing a lighted candle.

Where he got his props I never knew. But, he certainly made his point. He was thrown out of the game, of course. But, that didn't bother him, nor the crowd.

Frisch had his other side, too. As I said before, he was a fighting player. He loved to win. He loved to rib his opponents. On the field, umpires were enemies. But he was as quick to defend them as he was to cause them trouble.

A certain National League club (nameless here) had developed a growing feud with "Uncle Charley" Moran, then approaching the end of his umpiring career. This particular club was playing a series in Pittsburgh against Frisch's Pirates. Charley Moran's team was assigned to umpire the series.

It was a tough assignment. From the first pitch the club was "on Charley" and they never let up. Finally Moran was forced to expel several players from the game. The upshot was that charges were filed against Moran and a hearing was requested. The hearing was called in the league office on the first available off-day.

The morning of the hearing Frisch phoned the league president.

"Do you mind if I come to the hearing," Frank asked. "Maybe I can clear up a few points."

He was invited to attend.

The morning of the hearing some half dozen of the complain-ing club, including the manager and the coaches, appeared. Each of them was invited to speak. They outlined their charges in detail, citing incidents and corroborating one another's testimony in more than an hour of questions and answers. Through it all Frisch sat by silently.

When the complainants had finished their case the league president turned to Frisch. "You asked to be present at this hearing and you have listened to all the testimony. Do you have anything to say?"

"Only this," Frisch replied. "I've had many battles with 'Uncle Charley' in the past and I'll probably have more. I don't think he's the greatest umpire in the world and I've told him so. But I'm not going to sit by and see him crucified. These men here (gesturing toward the complainants) are my friends. But this thing has been framed. You guys are out to get Charley and you're making a big issue out of nothing. You're trying to ruin a guy's whole life because you're sore at him. You're wrong and you're imagining a lot of things that are not true. That's all I've got to say. Good day, gentlemen."

With that, Frisch left the meeting. The others followed. Later that afternoon the charges were withdrawn.

Uncle Charley Moran retired a few years later, with full dignity and, I hope, happy memories.

A so-called bad boy had proved his mettle when it counted most.

Years ago, an unknown writer commented, with some amazement, that "in the whole history of the major leagues there has never been a single case of umpire dishonesty!" So far as I can ascertain, that is still true. Certainly no umpire has ever faced public trial on a charge of dishonesty, and no umpire has ever graduated from the diamond to the penitentiary. That's a record the men of no other profession can match—not politicians, lawyers, doctors, financiers, or even clergymen.

As a matter of fact, in seventeen years as a league president, I had only one case in which I thought an umpire was trying to alibi his conduct on the field. That umpire was given his immediate release, not for any charge of dishonesty but because he withheld certain facts in his report. Usually the tendency of the umpire is to protect the player even at the expense of his own standing.

As all baseball people know, an umpire is required to submit a written report to the league office on any untoward incident in connection with a game. This, of course, includes any serious arguments, brawling, and expulsion of players. Some of these reports made truly fascinating reading. All the words were spelled out to the last letter, and it became an unwritten law with the female secretaries that all umpire reports were to go to the league president unopened. I might mention in passing that even though the educational standards of umpires and players have been vastly improved through the years, the cuss words haven't changed.

One day I received a report from Lee Ballanfant, a young umpire who had come up from the Texas League. Lee, a former player, was a skinny little guy who probably weighed less than a hundred and fifty pounds dripping wet. Lee spoke with a soft Texas drawl, had a good sense of humor, and never looked for trouble. But he could be as tough as nails when the situation demanded.

On this particular day, he reported a run-in with a young infielder named Gene Mauch, who was later to make quite a name for himself as a manager. Ballanfant's report quoted Mauch as having called Lee a lot of names (all spelled out) and of generally bad behavior. The report closed, as so many of them did, with a request for strong action from the league office.

Then Ballanfant added a P.S., and here's what he wrote:

"Boss, if you take this kid's money, and I think you should, then you better take some of mine, too. I gave him as good as he gave me."

That, in my book, is honest reporting. It is also typical of Lee Ballanfant.

I recall, too, a case involving George Magerkurth. Mage was umpiring a game at the Polo Grounds. A rhubarb developed, with a dozen or so players involved. It wound up in an eyeball-to-eyeball confrontation between Mage and infielder Billy Jurges, which included an exchange of language that made up in forcefulness for what it may have lacked in grammar.

Mage delivered his report in person. It was a two-page affair that told of some shoving, an attempted exchange of blows (all wide of the mark), and a lot of lurid language. At the end of the report was a line underscored in red ink. It said: "When he [Jurges] swung at me, I spit in his face. I know I was wrong, but I did it."

The result: Jurges was fined and suspended for ten days. So was Magerkurth. The first and only time, I guess, when player and umpire were adjudged equally guilty and given equal penalties. It seemed the proper thing to do at the time. I still think so.

These two incidents always come to mind when umpire

honesty is mentioned. There were many others. Larry Goetz always included his own actions and language in a "rhubarb" report. So did Beans Reardon, often I fear more pridefully than repentant. In fact, with the one exception already noted, I never knew an umpire to alibi his own conduct either in his written report or in a verbal report to the league president. I always had great respect for umpires. It was a respect that they created by their own conduct. They never gave me reason to doubt.

A lot of fans still cling to the old-fashioned idea that to be successful major league umpires have to be Goliaths in stature, and Samsons in physical strength and endurance. That may have been true in the old "might-is-right" days, when umpires, lacking both official backing and rules of conduct for players, ruled by fear and ran the game by physical threat. But those days are over. Thanks to the pressure of the Klems, the Connollys, and the others, and the wisdom of the rules makers, umpiring today is an honored and honorable profession. Umpires today are better trained, better disciplined, better paid, and more respected than ever before in baseball history.

We have had men like "Silk" O'Loughlin, "Cy" Rigler, "Hank" O'Day, Billy Evans, George Moriarity, Bill Dineen, and Barry McCormick. All of them were big of stature, all were proficient performers through trying eras of umpire development. In later years, there have been big men like Cal Hubbard, George Pipgras, and George Magerkurth to carry on the "Goliath" tradition.

Tall, skinny "beanpoles," like Lon Warneke, Larry Goetz, Eddie Rommell, and Harry Geisel, have also played a part in upholding the tradition of umpiring. And there have been many "little guys" too. Both Bill Klem and Tommy Connolly were small men compared to the "behemoths" who were their contemporaries. Both worked in the days when umpires worked either alone or with one partner, and little guys were supposedly taboo. Yet no two men have contributed more to the umpiring profession, and to baseball, than these two. As proof of that, I pointed to the fact that as of today, only two umpires are among those elected to Baseball's Hall of Fame—Bill Klem and Tommy Connolly.

Through the years there have been many other little guys— George Hildebrand, Babe Pinelli, Lee Ballanfant, Jocko Conlan, Augie

Donatelli, Cy Pfirman, Bill Stewart, and many more. The point is that size is no yardstick for measuring the ability of an umpire. Desire, agility, judgment, and personality—those are the important factors.

Bill Klem, after he retired from active duty to become the league's Supervisor of Umpires, held meetings with every umpire team when they came into New York. He always expounded on the same theme.

"The best umpired game is the game in which the fans cannot recall the umpires who worked it," Bill would declare. "If they don't recognize you, you can enjoy your dinner knowing you did a perfect job." That sounds a bit funny coming from Bill. If ever there was an umpire who made his presence known as soon as he stepped on the field, Klem was that man.

But his theory was sound. Umpires do not look for trouble. If trouble comes, they handle it in their own way, sometimes well, sometimes not so well. When trouble came to Bill Klem, he stepped out to meet it, and a lot more than halfway. So far as he was concerned, there was never even a thought of hiding his light under a bushel. Klem's point was that umpiring a perfect game is its own reward.

Let me ask a couple of questions.

Who was the umpire behind the plate when Don Larsen pitched his perfect World Series game?

Who was the umpire behind the plate when Bobby Thomson hit his famous home run?

If you can answer those two questions correctly, without recourse to the record books, you are eligible for the leather medal designating you as one of the world's great baseball authorities.

The answer to the first question is Babe Pinelli. That one is a little easier than the other question, because the last pitch of Larsen's perfect game was a call third strike, and there was some interest in who had called the pitch a strike. But the second question, well, therein lies a story.

Just before we left the commissioner's office, Frank Slocum, one of my assistants, conducted a private little survey. He submitted the "name the umpire" question to Bobby Thomson; Ralph Branca, who was pitching; to Rube Walker, who was the catcher; and to Dodger infielders Gil Hodges and Jackie Robinson. There was no question that this was the most memorable game of their careers. Yet not one of them could identify the plate umpire in that game.

For your information, the man behind the plate that day was the late Lou Jorda. A lot of kindly people might feel that Jorda, had he lived long enough to know of the survey, might have been disappointed by the findings. I don't agree. Jorda was a quiet workman. He never sought headlines or publicity. Like Klem, he believed that the knowledge of a job well done spoke for itself, that the greatest applause an umpire could receive was silence. That survey, in Jorda's eyes, would have been a great compliment.

Larry Goetz was the quiet type of umpire. So, too, was Al Barlick, despite his foghorn voice and positive manner. Both were dedicated men, who took their job seriously. They commanded the respect of the players the moment they walked on the field. They did share a common umpiring fault. It was their inability to relax once a game was over. Both Goetz and Barlick were brooders who took their problems too much to heart. I used to urge them to worry less and laugh more. They were not politicians. They were not a ready source of material for writers and broadcasters. Nor were they public speakers, with a ready wit and a flood of funny stories to keep an audience constantly amused. But they were *umpires*, among the best in baseball's long history.

Most umpires fall into one of two categories. Either they are of the Klem school, czars who run the game with despotic assurance that brooks no argument, or they are the Connolly type, quiet, diplomatic, and judicious. Ninety-nine percent of them are easy to classify. The remaining one percent are the mavericks who defy classification.

Two of the mavericks come immediately to mind: Beans Reardon and Bill McGowan. Both were personality boys, unpredictable, brash, and flamboyant, with no respect for tradition and no time for the stodgy rules of procedure.

McGowan, who served the American League so well for many years, was more than a good umpire; he was a great one. He followed no rules of procedure, laughed uproariously when solemnity was indicated, kidded players when others would have been angry, was unexpectedly serious when levity seemed in order. I think Cal Hubbard, another great umpire, described McGowan's genius perfectly when he said: "Bill is seldom challenged, because, well, because he's McGowan. He has established a reputation, and that keeps the beefs to a minimum. But I hope he never gets in an argument about a rule. I don't think Bill McGowan owns a rule book. I'm not sure that he has even read one. He umpires by instinct, and his instincts are great."

Beans Reardon, too, was a law unto himself. He was down to earth in his treatment of both friends and enemies. If a player cursed him, Beans replied in kind, and with a vocabulary that left the person dazed and gasping. If a player threw a bat or a glove, Beans would throw his mask higher and further; if a wisecrack was offered, Beans would top it, "in spades." He stopped the garrulous Frank Frisch cold on one occasion when Frank was being particularly obstreperous. It took place in the Polo Grounds, not far from Frisch's New Rochelle, New York, home, where Frank loved to spend his time.

"All right, Dutchman," said Beans, as Frisch advanced to the plate with a squawk, "come on and we'll argue. But get this straight. You're staying in this game to the finish. I know it's a lousy, hot day, and you'd like to be sitting around up in New Rochelle. But I've got to stay out here all day, and you're going to stick around with me."

That did it. Frisch doffed his cap, bowed in mock obeisance, and returned to the bench. It was definitely Reardon's round.

On another occasion Beans used a different approach. The third-base coach left his post to argue a point. Beans stopped him with an imperious gesture. "Stay where you are," he yelled. "I'm tired, and I don't feel like arguing with any dumb, blankety-blank coach. If you come in here, you might as well keep right on going. You'll be out of the game."

That one worked, too. There was no argument.

The long feud between Reardon and Klem is a matter of history. They didn't really hate each other; rather it was a clash of personalities and procedures. To Klem, umpiring was a religion, to be treated with formal respect and utter solemnity. To Reardon, it was a job, like selling beer or painting houses. It was a challenge that had to be met if you hoped to hold your job. Methods were of less moment than results.

Strangely enough, each recognized the ability of the other. I remember a conversation I had with Klem, in which Reardon was discussed. The Old Arbitrator shook his head in puzzlement.

"That crazy Reardon," he said. "I don't see how he gets away with it. But, boss, he's a good umpire, and a great asset to baseball."

Later, discussing Klem, Reardon expressed the same sentiment in almost the same words.

Baseball, like politics, makes strange bedfellows.

Earlier I mentioned the "bad boys" of baseball, using Frankie Frisch as an example. Frank was not alone. In the old National League days, he had plenty of company—men like Casey Stengel, Charley Grimm, Leo Durocher, Jimmy Wilson, among others. They presented plenty of problems, but they added a lot of color, too. They gave me a few headaches, but they provided a lot of entertainment as well. Two-thirds of my happy memories today center on them. Baseball, of course, has changed. A lot of the raucous behavior, the brawling, and the gang revolts against umpire authority have disappeared. And that's good. But as an oldtime fan, reliving memories of the past, I must admit that I miss the free-and-easy zaniness of those days and the swashbuckling personalities.

One story in particular that I feel must be told, involves the colorful Casey Stengel.

Some years ago when Stengel was managing Brooklyn, the Dodgers were engaged in a Sunday double header with their arch rivals, the Giants. Though the Dodgers weren't going too well, a capacity crowd of some 30,000 faithful fans filled Ebbets Field.

In the first inning, with two out and a man on second, Mel Ott was called out on a low-outside pitch. Ott addressed a few words to plate umpire "Ziggy" Sears, and just that quickly, Ottie was thrown out of the game. His eviction proved to be the only cheering opportunity the Brooklyn fans had. The Giants won by a lopsided score.

In the second game, umpire Sears moved to third base, and Stengel took his position in the third base coaching box. The Giants scored five runs in the first two innings. The Dodgers finally got a runner to third base in the fifth inning, with two out. Then the Giant catcher (I think it was Harry Danning) caught the base runner flat-footed with a throw to third. It was close, but Sears was in a perfect position to call the play, and signaled "Out."

Casey immediately went into action. He gestured wildly with both arms. He kicked the bag, and the dirt alongside. He jumped in the air. He went down on his knees, as if in prayer. Meantime, his jaw was waggling like an unhinged shutter in a strong wind. I couldn't hear what he was saying, but he was saying plenty. I've seen a lot of Stengel demonstrations over the years, but this one was a masterpiece, worthy of Barrymore at his best.

And Sears? Ziggy just stood there, arms folded—and laughing! Finally, Casey finished his routine, shrugged his shoulders, and slouched to the dugout. No action by the umpire, no eviction, nothing.

At game's end I went to the umpire's dressing room, and found my umpire still chuckling.

"What in heaven's name was wrong with you out there, Ziggy?" I asked him. "You put Ottie out of the game before he could say a dozen words. Then Stengel does everything but undress you, and you stand out there grinning like a damned Cheshire cat! What's the idea?"

Again, Sears started to laugh.

"He wasn't arguing or calling me names, Boss. All the time he was waving his arms and kicking the dirt he was saying, 'Don't pay any attention to me, Ziggy. We've got a big crowd, and these guys are kicking hell out of us. I've got to give the people something to cheer about. You know how it is.' "

Maybe there's a moral in that story. Maybe it is that bad boys do have their good points; or maybe it's support for the old adage "Don't believe anything you hear, and only half of what you see."

Oh, yes, I nearly forgot. The episode cost Sears fifty dollars. Probably the fine was unfair. But he did give me a headache and spoiled my afternoon.

It is difficult to sum up in a chapter, or in a volume, my thoughts about umpires and umpiring. They are very special people doing a very special job. My long acquaintance with a great many of them during my years as league president and as commissioner brought home two very salient points.

The first is that good umpires are tougher to find than good ballplayers. The major league baseball player is a specialist, and replacing him is often a difficult job. The same thing is true of umpires. They are specialists, too, even harder to replace.

Baseball has recently inaugurated a program to develop umpires in an organized way. It is needed, and needed badly. Umpires are dedicated people, who start out working under tough conditions for short money. They have to love baseball, and baseball owes it to its future to encourage that love in a material way.

The second lesson that I learned about umpires is that a league president can make a lot of problems for himself, if he isn't careful in his dealings with umpires. The secret of good relations with umpires is very simple. The key word is truth. The league president's dealing with his umpires can be handled most simply by adopting one standard operating procedure: "Believe them or fire them." If you have an umpire, and you don't believe his reports, get rid of him. If you do believe his reports, then take action.

Because if you're convinced that the umpire is truthful, and that his judgment is good, then you take the necessary action against the offending player or manager. If you don't take that action, your problem is easy to locate. Just look in the mirror.

I owe a lot to umpires. Their dedication, their friendship, their ability, all helped to make my job easier. I salute them. I toast them. I thank them.

11

RECORDS, ASTERISKS, AND PEOPLE

Baseball fans have great curiosity—largely about people.

The average fan is not concerned with operational problems of management, or the laws and rules that govern the game. His interest, like the kid at the circus, centers on the performers—their feats on the playing field, the records they set, their personal life off the diamond, their hopes and their disappointments, their triumphs and disasters.

In fifty years of close contact with the game I have appeared at father-and-son banquets, at adult smokers, in veterans' hospitals and army camps, at school and Little League affairs, even at formal government hearings and church and business gatherings. When it comes to baseball they are all alike. They all want stories of performers and the questions they ask follow a standard pattern, whether the questioner is a Little Leaguer or his doting grandfather, a laborer or financial wizard, a millionaire or pauper.

Is the modern ballplayer better than the old-timer?

Will so-and-so break the record for home runs, or shutouts, or stolen bases, or whatever?

Was Babe Ruth as great as they say? Do you think he would

151

hit as well against modern pitchers under present-day rules and conditions?

Are black players better athletes than their white counterparts?

And—most frequently asked of all questions: What are they really like, these heroes we watch and read about in the sports pages every day?

That question is easily answered. Professional ballplayers as a group are a perfect cross-section of the America of their time, no better or no worse than the same number of men picked from all sections of the nation. There are good and bad ballplayers, just as there are good and bad lawyers, or ministers, or politicians. Some are educated, some are not; some are conservative, some are radical. They come from farmlands and from cities, from Bible Belt areas and from teeming ghettos. Each bears the mark of his environment; each reflects the training received from parents, and the broad philosophy of his home community. Baseball is only the melting pot into which they are drawn by a unique, common talent. All profit to a degree from this exposure. Some acquire a whole new outlook that will influence their lives forever; others pick up a social veneer that is only skin-deep and ends when their playing days are over.

Baseball is not, nor does not profess to be, a builder of human character or a champion of moral uplift. It is a game—and a good one! It furnishes participant as well as a spectator entertainment. Whatever may be its impact as a social or moral influence is incidental. But this I do believe. In the whole history of baseball there have been few professional players who haven't emerged better citizens and better Americans because of their baseball experience.

But enough of philosophizing!

Another common question at fan gatherings is the matter of records, old and new. Will this mark stand forever? Will that one be surpassed? It's an old axiom of baseball, and all sports, that "records are made to be broken" and that is true. Records have been a traditional part of baseball for nearly a century. Much of the thrill of the game for fans is witnessing an old record wiped out and a new one established, particularly if the old record was of real importance and long standing. I make that statement tongue in cheek as concerns some present-day marks. The record book today is cluttered up with a lot of minor records that mean nothing. Even the most rabid fan can hardly become ecstatic over the fact that on July 22, 1876, John Ryan of the Cardinals loosed 9 wild pitches in a single game. Certainly no world-shaking reaction can come from a notation in the book that nine pitchers are tied for the doubtful honor of "most hit batsmen in a single inning." Any mark on single-inning performance is historically unimportant and when it is followed by the notation "tied by many pitchers in both leagues" it would seem to me the word "record" might well be dropped in favor of "frequent performance." However, it does give statisticians something to do and telecasters something to talk about. That's probably the answer.

To attempt to guess what records will be broken and what new mark will be set in the years ahead would be foolhardy. It is a truism that in baseball anything can happen, and usually does. Yet there are some records that probably will stand for all time: some of them already have stood for generations; others are comparatively recent. These are ten marks that I believe will never be bettered:

1. Denton (Cy) Young's pitching record of 511 games won during his lifetime career.
2. Charles Radbourne's record of 60 pitching victories in a single season. Set with Providence in 1884.
3. Charles (Kid) Nichols's feat of winning 30 or more games per season through seven consecutive seasons.
4. Walter Johnson's lifetime record of 3,508 strikeouts.
5. Lou Gehrig's record of 2,164 consecutive games.
6. The record of 100 or more RBIs for 13 consecutive seasons, also held by Lou Gehrig.
7. Ty Cobb's record of 4,191 lifetime hits.
8. Joe DiMaggio's record of hitting safely in 56 consecutive games.
9. Babe Ruth's lifetime record of 2,056 bases on balls.
10. Don Larsen's perfect World Series game. This one may be matched some day, but it will never be beaten. You can't beat perfection.

There's another mark that might be listed here too. It is presently held jointly by two men. In 1932 Alvin (General) Crowder of Washington went through the season without hitting a single batsman.

He pitched 327 innings. Sandy Koufax of Los Angeles tied that record in 1956. Sandy pitched 323 innings.

Another record that most fans thought would stand forever is now being threatened. That is Babe Ruth's mark of 714 lifetime home runs. Whether Hank Aaron can better that mark before he hangs up his spikes is a moot question. As this is written he needs 42 more homers to do it. Hank is a great hitter, and he is in great physical shape. Maybe he can make it. If he does he will deserve the plaudits of sportsmen everywhere for a miraculous accomplishment. If he fails I have a hunch the Babe's record is forever safe. As the game is played today, with night ball games, all-night plane rides, tight schedules, and the stress of modern living, I just can't conceive of any modern player, other than Aaron, having a real chance of coming close to the mark.

Speaking of Ruth's records, maybe this would be the time and place to set the record straight as concerns the Roger Maris mark of 61 homers in the 1961 season. A lot of my newspaper friends have enjoyed kidding me about the "Asterisk" incident. As a matter of fact no asterisk has ever appeared in the official record in connection with the Maris feat. Roger hit 61 home runs that season to set an all-time record and he is given full recognition for that accomplishment. But his record was set in a 162 game season. The Ruth record of 60 home runs was set in 1927 in a 154 game schedule.

Late in the 1961 season when it became apparent that Maris had a great chance either to tie or better the Ruth mark, newspapermen raised a question as to how any new record would be handled. The commissioner was asked to make a ruling. That ruling was a simple one. In case the record was broken in 154 games the Maris mark would be recognized, and the Ruth record dropped. If the Ruth mark still stood at the end of 154 games but was subsequently broken in the eight additional games of the 1960 season, then both records would be recognized as official and given equal billing in the record book.

That is what happened. At the end of 154 games Maris had 59 home runs to 60 for the Babe. During the additional eight games of the 1961 season Maris hit two homers to bring his total to 61. The 1962 official Red Book carried two notations.

Most home runs in a season, 162 game schedule, Roger Maris, 61.

Most home runs in a season, 154 game schedule, George Ruth, 60.

Detailed information on each record was carried side by side. They still are. Page 311 of the 1972 Red Book carries a complete record of the 61 home runs hit by Roger Maris. Page 312 carries the same full report of the 60 home runs hit by Babe Ruth. No asterisks! No apologies! Just two official records of two great baseball accomplishments that fans will never forget. I still think it was the right decision.

Oh, yes, during the conference the word "asterisk" was mentioned; not by the commissioner but by Dick Young, one of the outstanding baseball writers of his time. Dick remarked kiddingly, "Maybe you should use an asterisk on the new record. Everybody does that when there's a difference of opinion."

Dick and other writers have had a lot of fun with "asterisk" stories through the years. But the honor is not mine. To Dick a low obeisance for a clever line, with or without an asterisk.

But to get back to fan questions.

Whatever the occasion, and wherever the meeting, one question was sure to be asked: "Do you think modern ballplayers are better than their counterparts of a past generation?"

My answer has got to be a qualified "yes!"

Old-timers, I know, will argue that point till the cows come home. They have great pride in their own accomplishments. They have lasting respect for the men who played with and against them in the days that were; and with justification. There were giants in the old days, men whose accomplishments still stand unchallenged in the record books, men whose performance will remain forever green in the memories of the fans who thrilled to their play. However, my answer to the fans is based on the game as an entity, not on a comparison of individuals.

All sports have improved. It was only a few years ago that the world's pole-vaulting record stood at 14 feet, and the four-minute mile was but a figment of an optimist's imagination. Remember the days when the forward pass was a scatter-gun operation to be used only in sheerest desperation? Or the not-far-distant past when the most astute quarterback's repertoire consisted of a few power plays and end sweeps, and the Statue-of-Liberty play was the acme of strategic deception? Remember baseball in the days of the dead ball, when ten home runs a season was a great accomplishment for even the greatest slugger?

Times have changed, and so has baseball.

I hope fans will continue to argue and battle for their heroes. If they ever lose that interest baseball will suffer. The old-timer talks pridefully today of the swashbuckling tactics of a Cobb or a Ruth or a Frisch or a Wagner; he boasts of the pitching prowess of Johnson and Alexander; of Hubbell and Grove and Walsh and Feller—and rightfully so. But he conveniently forgets that those heroes were exceptions; that along with these superstars were some 400 unsung, mine-run players who are never mentioned once the argument gets under way. I suppose the same thing will be repeated in that future time when today's youngsters become old-timers who will recall the Mays, the Mantles, the Koufaxes, the Aarons, and the Brooks Robinsons as rebuttal to the arguments of yet unborn fans of a future generation. I hope they do. If so it will mean that baseball's banner still flies high in the sports skies. But that is only matching memory against reality, and memory is a conveniently tricky witness.

To me there's no question. Baseball is an improved game today. It's better played, it's speedier, and it's more scientific. Modern ballplayers, as a group, are bigger, stronger, and better conditioned than their precedessors. They are better educated and better coached; they have better equipment and better tools. They operate on truer infields and smoother, better-manicured outfields. Clubhouses are more comfortable and better equipped; training quarters compare favorably with the best hospital emergency rooms, and are supervised by trainers versed in the latest therapy procedures and have the last word in theraputic equipment with which to work.

All these things are good. All these things favor the players. Off the field conditions are better today too. Salaries have reached phenomenal heights. Bonuses to youngsters for signing their first contract, minimum salary guarantees, and a pension plan that carries with it a family health plan and guaranteed insurance up to the time the pension starts, alleviate the financial worries that beset the old-timers. Never before have players and operators had more reason to take pride in their profession. Never before have youngsters of ability faced greater opportunity for a glamorous and worthwhile baseball career than is offered today.

Players have changed too, and not all the changes are good. That the modern players have every physical advantage, both as to individual training and working conditions, is self-evident. Whether or not they are making full use of those advantages is a moot question. Maybe I'm a prejudiced witness, swayed by sentiment and memory, but it seems to me that modern players lack the enthusiasm and zest for the game that marked the performance of the old-timers. To the old-timer every game was a battle, with no holds barred. Every play was a challenge, every rookie a potential enemy trying for the job that the veteran cherished and defended.

I'm not a bloodthirsty person looking for murder and mayhem as part of my daily baseball diet. But I do recall with nostalgic pleasure those days when base runners went into each base with spikes high and infielders responded with swinging tags that left a calling card of bruises as warning that they were on the job. I remember, too, the infield play of the Frisches and the Martins and their ilk, making scrambling stops with their chests or jaws to cut off base hits and get their man. The "dust-off" of hitters was common practice too, an accepted part of the game. Hitters expected to "hit the dirt" frequently and were seldom disappointed. Today's players, protected by helmets and ear covers, squawk loudly at any inside pitch and call an umpirical council of war every time a batsman is hit above the waist or is forced to hit the dirt to avoid a high fast one.

The change that bothers me most, however, is the attitude of players toward the game itself. Old-timers played the game because they loved it. They talked, and read, and dreamed baseball twenty-four hours a day and 365 days a year. "If they want me to quit, they'll have to cut the uniform off me" was a common expression, even for superstars like Cobb and Ruth and Wagner, for to those old-timers baseball was a way of life. They asked for nothing more.

Today the attitude is different. Modern players are more blasé. Their interests are broader and more cosmopolitan. They play the game and play it exceedingly well, but without any particular dedication. I do not imply that they do not try to win, or that victory is less sweet or the rewards of victory less appealing to them than to their predecessors. I do think their concept of the game is different. To the modern player baseball no longer is the alpha and omega of existence, as it was to the old-timer. "Cutting off the uniform" is no longer a necessary requisite to ending a career. Qualifying for a pension to ensure future security is—and that's the way they play the game.

Don't misunderstand me. I still stand by my original statement. Modern baseball and modern players are basically better than their predecessors of a past generation. Nor do I intend to criticize or be-little today's performance. What I am trying to point out is that we are living in a different age, with different economic and social pres-sures. Today's ballplayer is the product of that new environment. If it were possible, through some magic alchemy, to transpose the genera-tions I am convinced the net result would be the same. The modern players would, under such circumstances, perform according to the rules, the mores, and the attitudes of that bygone period. And the old-timers, translated to the modern era, would follow the pattern of today and profit by it. For that is the story of time and human progress, and baseball and all sports are simply mirrors reflecting the spirit of the times in which they operate.

But to get back to the questions fans commonly ask.

Babe Ruth has been gone more than a quarter of a century, but his memory is still green and many of his records still stand in the golden book of baseball accomplishment. Which I guess really answers the question, even before it is asked.

Anyhow, here is the question inevitably asked by youngsters who know him only as a legendary figure out of the past: "Was Babe Ruth as great as my Dad claims? Do you think he would hit as well against modern pitchers and under present-day rules and conditions?

The answer is a loud and unqualified "*yes.*"

I have seen most of the great baseball figures in action. And in my opinion the Babe was the greatest player of all time. He could do everything. He was, as everyone knows, a great hitter. He also was the best left-handed pitcher in the American League during his pitching days. He had one of the strongest and most accurate throwing arms in baseball, and, in his prime, he had enough speed to be a threat on the bases.

He was a born hitter, and born hitters are not affected by rules or conditions. To be a great hitter you have to have keen eyes, quick reflexes, perfect timing, power and confidence. Babe had them all, and with that equipment, opposing pitching becomes a minor factor. Whether Babe could hit more home runs, if he were playing today, than he hit in his real career, I would not attempt to say. He hit 714 during his career, and most of those against a deader ball, over a shorter season. No one has yet tied that record, and there have been some great challengers through the years. As hitters, men like Cobb, and Hornsby, and Williams, and Foxx and Greenberg, and Mantle and Di-Maggio rated among the best, past and present. All had their chance; none came close.

If he were playing today Babe would lead the pack, as he did before. In his day he hit home runs off Johnson, and Grove, and Alexander. With all due respect to modern pitchers, I think he would perform equally well against the Seavers, the McNallys, the Lolichs and the Blues of the present generation.

Are black players better athletes than their white counterparts?

My answer is that I do not believe athletic prowess is measurable by any ethnic yardstick. In recent years the performance of black players has been phenomenal, both as a group and as individuals. The percentage of black players in the major leagues today is far greater than the percentage of black citizens in our national census. But I do not believe that skin pigmentation is the deciding factor. The answer is economic rather than racial.

For many years blacks played baseball in their own leagues but were denied the right to participate with their peers in "organized baseball." Finally the doors were thrown open and they flocked eagerly to baseball's banner, anxious to share in the high salaries, the economic security and the social rewards baseball offered. They were hungry. They were ambitious. They were stirred by incentive almost passionate in its intensity. They visioned a new field of golden opportunity and they were ready! They signed on, and they brought new zest and new enthusiasm into the game. Today we are witnessing the result. Only a year ago eight of nine men in the starting lineup of the champion Pirates in a World Series game were black. Furthermore, any fan who is up on baseball can name at least six black players who are a cinch to be named to the Hall of Fame, once their playing days are over and eligibility established. And that's great.

But through the years the law of averages will prevail. Unfortunately men are inherently lazy. As his financial situation improves and his security is assured, the impelling "crusader" spirit fades and zestful enthusiasm is dissipated. What had earlier been a challenge turns suddenly into a workaday job, and the headlines and applause, once so eagerly fought for, become commonplace and are taken for granted. That has happened thousands of times in the history of mankind and will continue to happen so long as human frailties endure.

I don't mean to imply that black players will eventually lose their athletic incentive or slump away to mediocrity. There will always be black stars as there are white stars. But the yardstick that measures their greatness will be performance alone, not the color of their skin. And that's as it should be in a competitive world.

Whenever fan groups get together, young or old, large or small, discussion eventually centers on the selection of an All-Time team. So far as I am concerned, when that stage is reached I know it's time to go home.

For many years learned historians and military experts have argued the comparative genius of great conquerors. Who was the greatest general? Was it Alexander the Great? Or Julius Caesar? Or Napoleon, or Wellington, or some other figure of world military history? So far the experts have been unable to reach agreement despite research through thousands of documents and records. Who was the greatest philosopher? Was it Aristotle? Or Erasmus? Or Kant? What explorer surpassed all others in his contribution to a growing world? What scientist has accomplished most in his field?

No one, however learned, has ever come up with irrefutable finding, to answer these questions, either, nor ever will.

In baseball and sports the records are too scant, the rules of play are too varied through the years, and, above all, emotions and memories are too deep-seated to select even one man, much less an entire team.

A few years ago, when baseball was celebrating its centennial as a professional game, Commissioner Bowie Kuhn conducted a poll to select the All-Time team. Thousands of ballots were received and tabulated. The results were announced at a huge dinner in Washington preceding the All-Star game. The living selectees were flown into Washington, and were presented with beautiful trophies. It was a great promotional stunt, well staged and well publicized, and baseball's national image benefited tremendously.

But as the commissioner remarked later, the vote was more a popularity contest than a studied selection. There was no real unanimity on any one man. At many positions the vote was so divided that any one of three or four candidates could have been selected.

I have to smile a bit at the naïvete of enthusiastic fans who remark that "after fifty years of close association with the game you should be able to pick an All-Time team that would be official." With ten years of contact I might have had the temerity to try. After fifty years I have had personal acquaintance with so many "greats," have watched them play day after day, and have read of their accomplishments and studied their records to a point where I am completely befogged. For me to attempt such a selection would not only be presumptuous, it would be insulting as well, both to the public, who might take such selections seriously, and to the great players who would have to be passed by.

A few months ago, during a visit to a Veterans Hospital, I did pick a 25-player squad from among the stars I have actually seen in action. No players were picked from present-day rosters, and Mathewson was left off because, though I knew him, I never saw him pitch.

Here's the squad I picked:

Catchers: Mickey Cochrane, Bill Dickey, Gabby Hartnett
Pitchers: Left-handers—Robert Grove, Carl Hubbell, Sandy Koufax
Right-handers—Walter Johnson, Grover Alexander, Bob Feller, Ed Walsh
First Base: Lou Gehrig, Bill Terry
Infielders: Eddie Collins, Rogers Hornsby, Honus Wagner, Harold Traynor, Frank Frisch, Joe Cronin, Charley Gehringer
Outfield: Ty Cobb, Babe Ruth, Joe DiMaggio, Tris Speaker, Mel Ott, Stan Musial

That's the list. I think it's a pretty good team—one that could probably win a pennant without much trouble. It might even win a World Series now and then.

P.S. I nearly forgot the manager. This team doesn't really need one, but the union requires one be named. So I picked Walter Alston. He's the best handler of men in the game today, and this bunch requires a lot of handling.

Any more questions?

12

LORDS OF BASEBALL—AND
OTHER UNFORTUNATES

"If you prick us, do we not bleed? if you tickle us, do we not laugh? if you poison us, do we not die?"

Shylock in *The Merchant of Venice*

Baseball owners are neither gods nor devils.

They are human beings like the rest of us—no better and certainly no worse than their counterparts in less publicized fields.

Trying to convince baseball fans of that fact, however, is a tough assignment. Like trying to sell a youngster on the painlessness of modern dentistry while he's undergoing treatment for a throbbing molar, it is a discouraging exercise in futility.

Baseball fans are sentimentalists. They want their heroes to be Galahads, wearing a toga of greatness without stain or blemish. Such heroes can be created only by performance on the playing field, not in the business office. When an incident occurs to cast discredit on a player, fans are quick to rise in defense of their hero. They don't want their illusions shattered. The easy out is to find some other scapegoat who can be tarred with the onus of guilt. Owners and the Establishment, in such cases, are the perfect targets. That has been true since professional baseball first came into being. It is true today.

That is why I was so completely amazed by the fans' reaction to the recent player strike. For the first time, fan sympathy and support was preponderantly with the management and against the play-

163

ers. For the first time even the most sentimental fans seemed to recognize that "selfishness" and "greed" were not confined solely to the Establishment, and players, as a group, felt the whiplash of fan disapproval and criticism.

Maybe that's good. Maybe not. At least it's an interesting switch. Sentiment is an important attribute in all sports, but sometimes the dividing line between deep-rooted sentiment and maudlin blindness is razor-edge thin.

As concerns the strike, I do not plead the case for management, nor imply that the fault rested entirely with the players. In any area of broad disagreement, both sides must accept part of the blame. I do deplore the public display of pique and childish resentment by both sides. Maybe, under our present laws, some form of legal arbitration serves a useful purpose. Certainly collective bargaining has proved its value in cases involving thousands of employees engaged in similar jobs, where fixed mass salaries are involved, hours of work are to be resolved, and skills, or the lack of them, constitute a common denominator.

Sports, it seems to me, are different. Players are artists, and their individual skills determine their personal status. There is no question of seniority, no question of graduated salaries based on years of service. Every move toward mass standardization is a move away from competitive challenge, and competition is the lifeblood of athletic endeavor.

I have great respect for the intelligence of modern players. I have equal respect for the fairness and the business acumen of baseball executives. If communication lines are kept open, and both sides are willing to suspend personal prejudices in an effort to arrive at a fair solution, I am sure that baseball can come up with a workable plan that will eliminate future strikes and bitter recriminations.

But that, of course, is just one fan's opinion.

There seems no reason for extended discussion of the whys-and-wherefores of that unfortunate incident. The facts have been aired. To rehash them here would only reopen old wounds, and add more fuel to the fires of controversy. In my opinion, the whole episode was a tragic mistake from which both sides can learn a valuable lesson. That the image of baseball has been tarnished, at least temporarily, is self-evident. Any repetition of the strike process would make that damage irreparable. Both sides should recognize that fact.

Baseball is too great a game to be endangered by player greed or management stubbornness.

Sentiment in baseball is not the sole property of fans.

Many owners are sentimental, too. Like little boys making their first date with a girl, they frequently try to hide their feelings behind a shield of sophomoric braggadocio. But sentiment sometimes takes over unexpectedly, and in strange ways.

Such a case came to light in the transfer of Willie Mays from the San Francisco Giants to the New York Mets. That deal started out as an ordinary transaction like dozens of others that are made during the course of a season. Before it was concluded, Mrs. Payson and Horace Stoneham were engaged in a mutual effort to make sure Willie was guaranteed maximum security for the rest of his career and beyond. At the finish, Mays himself was sitting in on the conference— a sort of referee and arbiter of his own destiny.

Some skeptics were quick to charge that the whole business was a public relations gesture deliberately planned to remove some of the heat engendered by the players' strike. I don't buy that. I have known both Mrs. Payson and Mr. Stoneham for many years. Both are baseball sentimentalists and dyed-in-the-wool fans. Willie Mays was a mutual idol. When the chips were down, sentiment carried the day— and baseball profited.

Over the years there have been many other instances of management sentiment and consideration. Some of them have been publicized. Most have not.

Take Clark Griffith, for instance. For many years, Griff was pictured as a pinchpenny owner—canny in all his deals, hard-boiled in his baseball philosophy, and niggardly in his treatment of players. Clark was tough. He had to be. Griff was not a wealthy man, and the financial demands of keeping the Washington franchise alive were enough to challenge the patience of a saint, or cause the most confirmed optimist to cry in his beer.

Yet, Clark Griffith, over the years, "cared for" more old and veteran players than any other owner I know. "Gabby" Street,

Walter Johnson's favorite catcher, was, for some years, a Griffith henchman. "Nick" Altrock remained on the Griffith payroll until his death. "Ossie" Bluege entered the "front office" when his playing days were over. Joe Judge was a constant visitor to old Griffith Stadium, and a pinochle partner of Griff's through many long winter seasons. And there were many others—retired veterans who found sympathy and relaxation and a made-to-order "old-timers' clubhouse" in Griff's office suite. Clark Griffith, the Old Fox, certainly deserves a place among the owner-sentimentalists.

Sam Breadon, late owner of the Cardinals, was another of the baseball "Lords" who carried a wide streak of sentiment hidden beneath a hard-boiled veneer. Sam, like all fans, had his idols. Among them was Grover Cleveland Alexander, one of the great pitchers of all time, who spent his declining years with the Cardinals.

At the end of his career, Alec retired to Nebraska. One day, an Associated Press story informed the nation that Alec had been picked up by police in a Mississippi waterfront dive. He was down-and-out, penniless, and seriously ill from drink and exposure, the story said. On the strength of that story, columnist Dan Parker next morning devoted his entire column in the New York *Daily Mirror* to a castigation of baseball owners in general, and Sam Breadon, in particular, for their "selfish heartlessness" toward a fallen hero. It was quite a column— one that figuratively stripped the Breadon hide inch by inch, then added salt to the exposed wound.

What Dan did not know was that, months before, Breadon had personally arranged for a Nebraska couple to take Alec into their home as a permanent paying guest, and that a sizable amount was being forwarded each month to pay for his care, with a bit extra for what Sam called "cigarette money." Breadon had never mentioned it.

Breadon's first knowledge of Alec's "run-out" came when he received a letter from the Nebraska couple enclosing three of the monthly checks, with the information that Alexander had disappeared three months previously. Sam immediately returned the checks with instructions that they be turned over to Alexander when and if he returned. "He'll probably need the money to get back on his feet," Sam wrote.

But he didn't tell that, either. Alec knew it, and to Sam, that was sufficient. His objective was to help a friend, not court public acclaim. Sam, you see, belonged to the old school. He took pride in his public image as a hard-boiled business nabob. He didn't want that image tarnished by any public display of sentimental kindness or philanthropic weakness.

Not all displays of sentiment involve kindly response to human misfortune. Wrigley Field in Chicago is the only major league park without lights. Many fans wonder why? The answer, once again, is sentiment.

Wrigley Field is located in a desirable residential area of Chicago's North Side. When the site was selected, William Wrigley, Sr., promised residents of the area that he would build a stadium in which the whole community could take pride. Furthermore it would be maintained with all the care and attention that residents gave to private homes in the area. No construction would be undertaken which would detract from the attractiveness of the community, or interfere with the private lives of its residents. Mr. Wrigley kept his word. So, too, has his son, Philip K. Wrigley. Wrigley Field has long been regarded as one of the most beautiful ball parks in the nation.

When night baseball proved successful, Phil Wrigley was under great pressure to install lights. He recognized the financial benefits of night play. He consulted with many engineers in an effort to develop an underground lighting system that would eliminate unsightly light towers, and avoid any annoying glare that might reflect in the windows of private homes near the park.

That plan proved impractical. But, still, Phil Wrigley remembered his father's promise. That's why there are no lights in Wrigley Field. Just another example, I guess, of the "greed" of some owners.

There have been many examples of owner kindnesses and generosity through the years. To list them all would require a good-sized volume. The ones I have cited here are sufficient to prove the point. Sentiment in baseball is not dead. It still lives in the hearts of fans, and in the hearts of the Establishment, as well. And that's good!

In the beginning, a baseball club, like a country grocery store, was a one-man operation. Each owner ran his business with all the arrogance of a medieval lord of the manor. He signed his own players, sold his own tickets, policed his own grounds, and set up his own laws—all with little regard for the rights of his associates and no fear of legal difficulties.

The early owners were rugged individualists who shaped baseball to their own image. They conducted their business with casual informality, whether across an office desk, or over the bar of a convenient taproom. They operated largely on a cash basis and had little patience with formal bookkeeping or financial records (this was in the days when there was no income tax). Their word was their bond, and a handshake sufficed to seal a deal or consumate an agreement. They were in truth "Lords of Baseball," monarchs of all they surveyed. But the picture soon changed.

By the turn of the past century, the American League had come into being, and the two-league operation brought competitive problems that the old paternalistic setup couldn't handle. New policies had to be established, new procedures set up, and new rules formulated to meet the increasing problems of management. For the first time, owners, faced with endless meetings and discussion, and long hours of wrangling debate, found it necessary to delegate some of their authority to others. No longer could they enjoy the luxury of carefree hours at the ball park. The close give-and-take association with fans had to be sacrificed, and with it the public image of owner warmth and understanding. The owner-player relationship was weakened and the longtime owner-fan contacts disappeared.

Fans were not interested in new rules or procedure or the complex problems of business and legal change. With owners removed from the field-picture, fans had to look elsewhere for their "goats" and "heroes." For a time, the field managers took over. They gave the interviews, they signed the players, and they got the headlines. In Chicago, fans and newspapers still referred to "Comiskey's White Sox," in recognition of the club owner, but the rival team across town began more and more to be known as "Chance's Cubs," after the manager. Other managers also enjoyed that kind of fame. In New York, it was "McGraw's Giants," in Philadelphia, "Connie Mack's Athletics," in Detroit, "Hughey Jennings' Tigers." I suppose it could well be referred to as the "field manager era." It lasted well through the First World War. Then the advent of Ruth, Gehrig, Hornsby,

Grove, and the other colorful figures of that era turned fan interest toward performer "heroes" instead. But vestiges of the manager-days still remained. Player-managers like Frank Frisch, Bill Terry, and Mickey Cochrane continued to get headlines throughout their careers. No manager in history was more popular than Casey Stengel during his Yankee and Met days, and of the recent crop such leaders as Walter Alston, Leo Durocher, and Ted Williams always drew the attention of fans everywhere.

Even so, the field manager era was but a passing phase in the development of today's baseball "establishment." The greatest step forward came at the end of the World War I. It was unplanned and inadvertent, but it changed the whole baseball picture. It was largely due to the perspicacity and genius of two men: Branch Rickey of the St. Louis Cardinals, and Ed Barrow of the New York Yankees.

The two men were not friends, and they did not work jointly. They were of different backgrounds, and different temperaments. They faced different problems and employed different methods. Their relations with each other were often stormy, frequently bitter. But both were experienced baseball men dedicated to the game. Their objectives were the same: to build a championship club and a championship executive office to go with it. They did exactly that.

Both men worked under the same title: General Manager. There was nothing unusual about that. There had been many general managers before them, usually glorified flunkies without business experience, content to busy themselves at unimaginative details, without either pride or program. Barrow and Rickey were different.

Before most other clubs realized what was going on, the Cardinals had a stranglehold on player supply, and the Yankees were running roughshod over their American League opponents, making a shambles of the pennant race and the World Series. They had the baseball bit in their teeth. Either the other major league clubs had to meet that challenge or be relegated to the status of perpetual "also-rans."

Promptly, the other clubs followed the Yankee-Cardinal lead. Every club installed the general manager system—*real* general managers this time, with full authority to act, and long experience to guide the acting. Rickey and Barrow, by their individual performances, had forced open the door to a modern era—the age of the General Managers—and the beginning of a new concept of baseball management. It is still with us today, and going strong, thank you.

To attempt to list all the contributions Rickey and Barrow made to baseball during their long careers would serve no purpose. Chiefly, they forced baseball to take action, action that probably should have been taken long before. Suffice to point out that as a result of their examples:
- The present-day farm system was brought into being
- A scientific scouting program was evolved
- A minor league training program was set up
- The draft was adopted, and rules passed to assure young players of advancement as talent warranted
- The Major-Minor League Agreement was changed to ensure continued minor league operation with financial assistance if needed.

Most interesting from an establishment point of view is the increase in baseball personnel traceable to these developments. Branch Rickey, particularly, was a personnel expert, who believed in always having a trained young man ready to take over when a veteran retired. Baseball today is the better for having "Rickey" men who continue to carry on the precepts and the principles of the man who trained them.

George Trautman was one. George was trained by Rickey for a career that eventually led Trautman to the presidency of the National Association, the governing body of the minor leagues. Larry MacPhail, to my mind one of the top executives in baseball history, was another Rickey protégé. Larry not only introduced night baseball to the major leagues but also fostered the player pension plan and headed three major league clubs before he retired. Larry followed the Rickey tradition by training Buzzie Bavasi and Lee MacPhail for baseball careers.

Of all his protégés, the one I think Rickey admired the most was Warren Giles. Warren served an apprenticeship in the Rickey farm system, then went on to head the Cincinnati club. He missed, by one vote, being named commissioner, and went on to serve many years as president of the National League. Warren, in turn, started Gabe Paul, now president of the Cleveland club, and sponsored his own son, Bill Giles, now an executive with the Philadelphia Phillies.

There were others, too. Bill DeWitt, longtime club operator, is a Rickey man. So, too, is Bing Devine, now the general manager of the St. Louis Cardinals. Somehow I have a feeling that some future historian may decide that Rickey's greatest contribution to baseball was not the farm system, or breaking the color line, but the caliber of the men he trained and sponsored for baseball careers.

The "Lords of Baseball" did not create the philosophies or establish the economic rules that governed their operations. Their actions, good or bad, simply reflected the spirit of the times in which they lived. The modern baseball establishment follows the same pattern. The function of baseball, and all sports, is to provide entertainment and pleasure and relaxation. If sports can bring its devotees a little surcease from worry, a few hours of release from the cares of a workaday world; if it can provide a grin here and a thrill there; if sports can bring to youngsters their dreams of greatness, and to oldsters pleasant memories; then it will have fulfilled its destiny.

It is not the intent here to discuss the characters or the personalities of the various owners and officials who make the current baseball establishment. Rickey and Barrow have been mentioned at some length because they set off the explosion that forced baseball out of a Victorian era and into a modern, twentieth-century operation. Others were mentioned as proof of the fact that sentiment can prevail at times, even in the establishment.

Two other owners, Tom Yawkey of the Boston Red Sox and Bob Carpenter of the Philadelphia Phillies, are perfect examples of the "fan" spirit that exists in management ranks. Both men came into baseball at a time when the going was particularly rough. They took over the moribund clubs because they loved the game. Their enthusiasm has never waned. They are neither "front runners" nor "quick-buck artists." They are simply fans, with all the enthusiasm of the most rabid bleacherite, and a faith in baseball that they are willing to back with dollars when the going is rough.

Two other men who deserve passing mention for a different reason are Walter O'Malley of the Los Angeles Dodgers, and Roy Hofheinz of the Houston Astros. Both are shrewd men, with a bit of gambling instinct in their makeup, and no aversion to headlines or public controversy. They had the courage to put their dollars into the construction of privately owned parks at a time when most owners were demanding municipal arenas as a personal franchise right. Today, Houston's Astrodome and Dodger Stadium in Los Angeles stand out as models of stadium construction, a credit to baseball, and a challenge to every stadium-conscious municipality in the nation.

With all due respect to these various owners and officials, however, the real pressure that forced modernization of the baseball management structure came from outside influences.

The advent of radio and television gave the game a new concept. Clubs were forced to organize entire new departments just for the purpose of handling television arrangements.

Expansion, pressured by an insistent Congress, brought not only franchise problems but schedule, travel, and housing problems as well.

Legal questions arose, with accompanying judicial hearings, suits and restrictive statutes, that forced clubs, leagues, and the Commissioner's Office to establish individual legal departments to meet the challenges.

Increasing tax problems required an expanded accounting department, with new accounting systems and vastly larger bookkeeping facilities.

The player pension plan, originally handled by one man in the Commissioner's Office, became so large and so complicated that an expert staff had to be created to handle it.

Formation of the Players' Association brought the National Labor Board into the picture, and necessitated the employment of trained labor arbitrators.

In the operating end of the game, there were complicated growth problems, too.

Ticket departments had to be enlarged, along with concession facilities. Public relations, once a one-man job, grew to departmental size, with specialists to handle the *Yearbook*, club movies, a speakers' bureau, and special promotions such as Old-Timers' Day, Bat Day, Helmet Day, and all the rest.

Don't misunderstand me, I don't mean to imply that these changes were detrimental, or that baseball was being forced into moves it resented. Far from it. Baseball today has greater attendance, larger radio and television audiences (from which both clubs and players benefit), more newspaper headlines, better ball parks, better transportation facilities, and more efficient management than ever before in history.

What I'm attempting to explain is the extent of, and the reason behind, today's establishment. Progress is not accomplished without cost, whether it comes by edict or by evolution. The more complex the operation becomes, the less personal the individual contact, whether it is General Motors, or a grocery chain, or baseball.

Baseball and all professional sports today have become unwilling victims of their own booming popularity. The casual friendly camaraderie that was typical of club management in the old days of one-man operation is now a memory. Fans and writers, being sentimentalists, resent the change. So do many baseball officials and owners. But there is little that can be done about it.

The whole world is in a state of flux. Protesters today raise their voices on every street corner. They fault nations and governments; they condemn public institutions as archaic; they ridicule time-honored moral principles and laugh at the old-fashioned standards of law and order and majority rule. Unfortunately, they offer no solution for the evils they so condemn, no new program to replace the old order, no plan to utilize new scientific knowledge to the benefit of a suffering humanity.

Baseball and all sports have been caught up in that maelstrom. Maybe that's good. Not that sports have particular influence in national affairs or any voice in the settlement of international economic problems. They do not. But baseball and other sports are closer to the hearts of the masses than are government and industry. They speak a universal language that people understand. They offer competition sans hatred, the thrill of conflict without bloodshed; friendship without the quid pro quo of business negotiation. The late Branch Rickey often referred to baseball as "the moral equivalent of war." Lacking Rickey's gift for words, I call it understanding through mutual respect.

An example of baseball's real value can be found in an incident that took place during the tenure of President Eisenhower. His vice-president, Richard Nixon, made a trip to Venezuela. Our relations with Venezuela were not good at the time, and an international incident was created when Mr. Nixon was assaulted and stoned by an angry Caracas mob. A short time later, the State Department called the Commissioner's Office, requesting that a clinic of selected major league players and officials be organized for a Venezuelan tour to encourage and instruct Venezuelan youngsters in playing baseball.

The group was organized, and the first clinic was held at the very spot where the Nixon attack had occurred. The players were a bit fearful about what might happen. They need not have worried. A huge crowd of youngsters and parents turned out, and the party was given a tremendous ovation. For two weeks the party toured Venezuela, holding two or three clinics a day in a dozen cities and towns. It was a happy tour, without a single untoward incident. At the end of the tour, the President of Venezuela expressed his personal thanks to the group, and Walter Donnelly, a former ambassador, commented publicly that "that tour did more to clear the atmosphere than a dozen top-echelon conferences."

Another example of sports influence, of course, was the recent "Ping Pong incident," when an American table tennis team, unheralded and unsung, opened the sealed gates to Red China, thus paving the way for a presidential visit that brought international repercussions throughout the civilized world.

Maybe Mr. Rickey was right. Maybe baseball, and all sports, can, by a folksy let's-have-fun approach, help solve some of the problems that harass the world today.

But back to the baseball establishment.

The new organizational setup is not, in itself, the answer. It simply constitutes the machinery for getting the job done. The procedural strategy must come from the imagination, the loyalty, and the experience of hundreds of unknown employees who make up the establishment. They face a difficult assignment.

Complicated problems will continue to rise in the future as they have in the past. As an example, the major leagues are still in imbalance from expansion. Only an economic miracle can head off some further franchise changes. The establishment must face that possibility and be ready to act promptly. Probably any move will bring down the wrath of fans in the deserted towns. But that is to be expected. It's part of the picture.

In recent years, the Yankees were purchased by the Columbia Broadcasting System, and the St. Louis Cardinals by Anheuser-Busch.

Fans and writers alike were quick to condemn both moves. One fan was quoted as saying: "It's an infringement on the right of free speech. If a star is traded away, or one of our heroes is a holdout, we've got no one we can blame. You feel silly booing a brewery, and you can't take it out on your pal who runs the tavern, just because he happens to serve Budweiser."

As a fan, I can sympathize with that viewpoint. As an erstwhile official, however, I must recognize certain facts. The new type of ownership has worked out successfully, and unless there is an abrupt change in our national economy, the number of such ownerships will increase rather than decrease.

So long as television continues to pour huge amounts of money into baseball's coffers, the industry will attempt more and more to influence the staging of the show. That is natural. Yet baseball must be constantly alert to make sure that the tail doesn't wag the dog. If, on the other hand, television income is curtailed, the player pension plan will be in jeopardy, and the economic structure of the game threatened.

Legal problems are constantly increasing; this will continue until that happy day when laws are simplified so the public can understand them, and courts determine a common interpretation of statutes for all people regardless of lobbying influence or political power.

There are little matters, too, that will give any establishment pause. There are increasing overlaps in football and baseball scheduling that can bring headaches, especially as concerns municipally owned arenas, jointly occupied.

Despite these few examples, I have confidence.

Baseball is in good hands. Today's "establishment" is much better equipped to meet the complexities of operation than were the "Lords" of another generation. True, the fan of tomorrow will be denied some of the warmth and personal contact that old-timers knew. There will be less give-and-take camaraderie between fans and officials. But fans will watch the game in more comfort, and they'll see better play under better conditions that the old-timers ever dreamed.

Management will be chided and criticized, of course. That's part of the game.

But—through it all—baseball will continue to grow.

13

THEY ALSO SERVE

Baseball is probably the world's best documented sport.

Dedicated statisticians have devoted their lives to recording individual accomplishments, team records and averages, unusual feats and historic moments. Scores of books have been published. Hundreds of articles have been written—all of them extolling the game and the outstanding feats of the players.

But cold figures cannot record the breadth of individual devotion, nor statistical tables, however accurate, measure individual loyalty. Memories are ofttimes inaccurate, and perhaps prejudiced as well. That is understandable. For memories are born of the heart rather than the mind, and find their root in sentiment rather than logic, in fancy rather than fact. To most fans, baseball is a world of tinsel and fireworks and excitement, of headlines, and pictures and crowds, of competitive accomplishment and player adulation.

Memories are vagrant—and frequently stray into dark corners and down deserted lanes leading to spider-webbed rooms in ghost-haunted houses, where statistics do not enter and records are of the heart rather than the hand. As I write my personal memories of baseball's greats, I can't help dreaming a bit of the loyalty of those others of lesser stature—the unsung men behind the scenes who labored to make the path smoother for the great stars hurtling their way across the sports firmament.

I thought of the hardworking, unsung club secretaries and the lasting contributions they have made to the game. Most fans know little and care less about the behind-the-scenes labors necessary to assure proper staging for a show of stars. Fans are vaguely aware that somewhere, sometime, someone has to make up travel schedules, and make sure that space is available when and where needed to make those schedules work. Road secretaries handle that job. They make all hotel reservations for every move, whether spring training, regular season, or World Series. Numbers don't faze them. In spring training they play nursemaid for veteran stars and rookie greenhorns alike. Spring training is a time of movement—of constant coming and going. This calls for tickets and accommodations for a half-dozen individuals, headed in as many different directions at as many different times. Or it may require the mass movement of thirty or forty persons with plane and bus transportation to be coordinated, and hotel accommodation and taxi service on arrival. Perhaps it's an All-Star game or World Series, with 150 persons in the party. There are game tickets to be acquired and distributed, limousine service to be provided for officials and honored guests. The club secretary takes it all in stride. He looks after the press; he supervises the press gate; he checks the turnstile and attendance record at home and on the road; he handles seating arrangements for visiting groups and distinguished guests—but why go on? The club secretary certainly is one of the unsung heroes of the game. His name doesn't appear in the record book. He might not be able to hit a curve ball with a bull fiddle or run ninety feet without resting, or throw a ball across the diamond, but without him baseball wouldn't be the same.

That's why, as I write, memory turns to traveling secretaries I have known through the years: Eddie Brannick of the Giants, the dean of them all, who recently retired after more than fifty years of devoted service. Eddie spent his entire baseball career with one club. I venture he knew more transportation and hotel men, was better liked by more newspapermen, traveled more baseball miles, knew more players and witnessed more World Series games than any other member of baseball's official family. Certainly his record of more than fifty years of unstinting service to one club should stand forever—a prideful reminder of the loyalty and devotion of road secretaries of the past, a challenger to performers of the future.

Eddie was but one of many I recall. In the earlier days there was Eddie Eynon, for years the traveling secretary of the Washington Senators; close friend of presidents and senators, bon vivant and alter ego of Clark Griffith. I recall too Sam Watters who, for years, was guardian angel and nursemaid for Pirates big and little, from Fred Clarke and Honus Wagner to Wilbur Cooper, Pie Traynor, and the brothers Waner, Big and Little Waner. There was Willis Johnson, secretary of the Browns when Sisler was in his prime and Urban Shocker was spit-balling his way into baseball history; and Walter McNichols of the Cleveland Indians, who started in the days of Lajoie and Flick, saw Speaker ruin rival hopes by going back to grab a fly off the fence of old League Park, and lived to see the Indians established in their new stadium on the shore of then unpolluted Lake Erie.

Later there was rotund Bob Lewis of the Cubs, court jester, playing straight man to Charley Grimm comedy and making new friends for the Cubs simply by being himself; Leo Ward, a bit grayer of hair and slower of locomotion but still active, though the Gas House gang of his vintage has long closed the record of greatness and a later vintage that included great Musial, have hung up their spikes and settled down to dream of the days that were.

I remember "Duffy" Lewis, member of the great Red Sox outfield of Hooper, Lewis, and Speaker. Duffy won the heart of fans by his play on the field, but I remember him most as road secretary of the Braves, smiling at defeat and never losing his cool, though his lot was the bitterness of team incompetence where once had been championships and public acclaim. Still functioning too is Donald Davis, the pint-sized ball of fire, who joined the Braves when they were dying on the vine in Boston, enjoyed with them the honeymoon in Milwaukee, suffered through the baseball divorce, and still carries the professional torch for Hank Aaron and a new generation of athletes in Braves uniforms but Atlanta background.

The point is that laboring behind the scenes, far from the glamour, excitement, and applause of public acclaim are a group of dedicated men whose loyalty remains unquestioned and whose contributions to baseball have been both gratuitous and immeasurable. To them a deep salaam.

The club secretaries are not the only unsung heroes of baseball's hierarchy. The trainers too have contributed their bit through the years, and are just now beginning to receive some of the credit to which they have long been entitled. The idea of trainers has long prevailed in baseball. Since the turn of the century big league clubs have maintained training rooms in the home clubhouse. Since the early twenties facilities have been available in the visitor clubhouse as well.

But in the early days the term "trainer" was pretty loosely used. For the most part the so-called trainers were, at best, masseurs whose equipment was limited to a few bottles of liniment, a few rolls of soft bandage, a supply of adhesive tape, a bottle of aspirin, a supply of sodium bicarbonate, and a variety of patented pills guaranteed to cure anything from plague to hangover. If a player suffered a sprain he was strapped with adhesive tape and returned to the lineup. A sore arm called for massage and a few pills, and a friendly pat on the back was the standard panacea for any trouble that a bandage couldn't reach or liniment cover.

In his off-time, the trainer acted as the club baggage man in charge of uniform trunks, bat bags, baseballs, and other equipment. He ran errands for the players, shined shoes, and ran the tobacco canteen as a sideline. If necessary, he also handled the players' laundry on the road and during spring training. A few of the wealthier clubs did employ men who had been trained in elementary therapy and first aid. Most clubs, however, were content to ride along with any trainer who had a strong back, was willing to work, and was satisfied with minimum salary.

By the mid-twenties, however, the picture had changed. Specialists like Andy Lotshaw of the Cubs, "Doc" Weaver of the Cardinals, and Jorgenson of the Pirates had demonstrated the value of employing trained and experienced therapists. Today the little hole-in-the-wall training rooms have been transformed into emergency hospital suites, equipped with the most modern instruments and the best facilities medical science can produce. Modern trainers are professionally trained. Some of them are M.D.'s. All of them are expert therapists. And they all have hospital connections with neurologists, orthopedic specialists, and cardiac experts who respond to emergency calls without question or delay.

So far as training and medical know-how is concerned, it's a whole new setup. No corporation in the world has better facilities, more up-to-date equipment or better trained personnel than does baseball today. Everything is of the latest design—modern, efficient, practical. Only in one respect is the modern therapist comparable to his old-fashioned predecessor. He is still taken for granted—an unsung hero toiling in the shadows of obscurity, sharing only vicariously in the plaudits that are so much a part of the game.

Certainly the trainers must be listed in any recital or behind-the-scenes loyalty and devotion. Like the others to whom this chapter is dedicated, they have contributed much. It seems to me it is about time public acknowledgment was made.

Two other groups must also be listed in any compilation of the unsung contributors to baseball's appeal. The bullpen coaches who train and direct the pitchers are, of course, an integral part of the baseball establishment. They appear in uniform, they travel with the team, they listen to the cheers, and they share in the excitement. Yet theirs is a strangely undercover operation conducted on the fringe of greatness and the dying echoes of applause for accomplishment that they have helped create but in which they have no participation.

Old-time ballplayers, past their playing prime, are not really unsung. They have been through the mill. They have been a part of the competitive hurly-burly. They have enjoyed the kudos, the applause, and the laudation. As Warren Brown expressed it: "They have smelled the roses when they were in full bloom." Now they are in baseball because they love it. Maybe, at times, they miss the headlines and the excitement. That is only human. But they are still an important part of the game, doing their job day after day, knowing that the publicity parade has passed them by.

For that they deserve recognition along with the scouts who spend their days seeking for likely prospects, their nights dreaming of stardom not for themselves but for the unknown youngster who that day has impressed them with his God-given throwing speed, or his finesse on the bases, or his ability to drive the ball beyond the frenzied reach of a striving outfielder and into the distant bleachers for a home run. They are a part of the picture, members of the establishment, and, measured by their loyalty and devotion to the game, true lords of baseball.

The other group who must be considered as unsung champions are not officially of the baseball family at all. They are the sports photographers. They have been contributors to baseball popularity since the first cameraman was given the assignment to cover a ball game in the days when baseball was new. The wise Chinese who, centuries ago, observed that "one picture was worth more than ten thousand words" was right. Pictures have been an integral part of sports education since the camera came into being. Without the magic of photography there would be no television of ball games, no illustrated articles and instructions, no movies of important series. Without cameras, sports pages would be without the visual climax of supreme effort or individual achievement.

Yet, strangely enough, the men who contribute these pictures, whose imagination and planning are behind every lens snap, whose dedication to their art and pride in their work has given mankind visual evidence of historic development, are largely unknown and unsung. Sportswriters have had bylines for many years, cartoonists and artists have signed their productions—but photographers remain nameless. Occasionally press associations and individual publications have taken credit to themselves, by crediting a picture "AP photo," "Tribune Staff photographer," or "NEA Service" as the case may be. But only in the past few years has the photographer's name been mentioned.

Some few years ago, the Hearst chain printed a picture and brief obituary of Bill Ironson when he died after long years of outstanding service. Recently, Ernie Sisco retired after fifty years of photographic service with *The New York Times*. Ernie was honored by a personal letter of recognition from Governor Rockefeller. Those are the only two personal tributes I have ever been aware of and I have known scores of photographers over the years. I have watched them work: I know how dedicated they are and the long hours they spend on the job. Like all fans, I appreciate the pleasure they have given to enthusiasts and the contribution they have made to baseball and all sports.

Certainly, when it comes to listing the unsung heroes who have given untold pleasure to unnumbered millions by their unsung contribution to sports—the sports photographers must be high on the list. Baseball owes them a great debt. In return I can only voice one fan's "Thank you."

14

THE RESERVE CLAUSE

"Myself, when young did eagerly frequent
Doctor and Saint, and heard great argument
About it and about: but evermore
Came out by the same door wherein I went."

—OMAR KHAYYAM

No baseball rule or regulation has ever been more widely debated than the so-called reserve clause. Nor has any other rule been so generally misunderstood. To this day, its defendants argue vehemently that the right of reserve is the very backbone of baseball operation, without which the professional game could not exist. Opponents cry "slavery" and "peonage" and argue just as vehemently that the rule is a blot on American justice, and should be eliminated.

In a previous chapter, I discussed the origin of the rule at some length. In the light of recent legal action, it might be well to review some of the facts and conditions involved. It is important to remember that the reserve clause has been in operation for almost a century. Like most rules, it was born of trial and error. In the early days of professional baseball, player pirating and contract jumping were commonplace. Strong clubs raided weaker ones; star players openly listened to overtures from rival clubs and rival owners. The reserve clause was conceived to correct that evil. There were no national antitrust laws at the time; there was no legal question of the right of employers to regulate employment practices as they saw fit.

The rule worked.

Piracy and contract jumping disappeared. Clubs were able to establish continuity of personnel; fans were convinced of the honesty of the competition, and national interest in the professional game soared. Only the players expressed unhappiness—and for an unexpected reason. The original rule provided for the reserve of only two players on each club roster. This, the players argued, was unfair since it set up a player caste system, making stars of the reserved few and "second-class citizens" of the others. At the request of the players, the rule was amended to include the entire roster.

Soon, however, it became apparent that the rule needed further refinement. Owners were quick to take advantage of the total reserve. Players signed to minor league contracts were refused advancement, and major league players were shunted to minor leagues, even though they had the ability to hold a job with one or more opposing major league clubs. The answer was the adoption of two new rules.

The "draft" rule ensured the right of a player to advance to a higher classification as ability justified. The "waiver" rule provided that no player could be outrighted to a club of lower classification, until his contract had first been offered, and waivers obtained, from all clubs of higher classification than the club to which it was proposed to assign his contract. Those two rules have, for more than a half century, been a part of the reserve clause.

Later, an amendment was added providing that no veteran player (ten years in the majors) can be sent down to the minors or have his contract transferred to another major league club without his consent.

Many skeptics today are quick to imply that both the draft and the waiver rules were forced legislative acts passed by "slave-holding Simon Legrees" attempting to justify an unjustifiable reserve clause. I can't accept that. Half the trouble over the reserve clause and the antitrust charges is due to the peculiar make-up of team sports. Clubs and club owners are both competitors and partners in the same business.

Under those principles, I should suppose that the legality of the reserve clause could properly be tested in the light of purpose and effect. Obviously, restraint on bargaining power or the opportunity to negotiate for a job or pursue a calling is not per se illegal.

Every personal service contract restricts the activities of the employee in greater or lesser degree. Labor unions greatly limit the freedom of employment of union members and of nonunion members. The closed shop is an example. Strict apprenticeship rules in many unions limit the opportunity for entering and continuing in a particular trade. Musicians cannot perform in many communities unless they are members of the local, as distinguished from the national, union. Restrictions upon the places where and circumstances under which lawyers and other professional men may pursue their professions are imposed not only by statute but by rules and regulations of bar associations, medical societies, and the like.

Professional baseball entertains the public by the playing of a prearranged schedule of league games between independently owned clubs. The public interest and patronage, upon which players and owners depend for their livelihood, demands first a good contest on the field and good competition among the clubs in a league, and, second, the unquestionable integrity and honesty of the game and its participants. Without such competition and integrity, public patronage would be lost and professional baseball, as a means of livelihood for thousands, would cease to exist.

Baseball clubs, as I have said, are both competitors on the field and partners in business. Ordinary industry does not face the problem of this dual relationship. In baseball, competition is the end in itself. What the public pays for and demands is a competitive contest. To excite interest the contest must be reasonably equal and uncertain as to result. This feature alone distinguishes baseball from ordinary industry.

The motion-picture industry has frequently, but erroneously, been compared with baseball. The only thing they have in common is that they are both furnishing public entertainment. But Paramount is in no way concerned with the business success of Warner Brothers. If Paramount induced Warner Brothers' best actors and actresses to sign up with Paramount, it would benefit Paramount and injure Warner Brothers. But, even if Warner Brothers were ruined, Paramount would have no business concern about it; its position in the movie field would be strengthened. However, in baseball if a club were free to induce Johnny Bench, Henry Aaron, Brooks Robinson,

Tom Seaver, and Mickey Lolich, and other stars to play for it, with the result that its superiority became overwhelming, all other clubs in the league would suffer because they are really partners in baseball. Each league member and each player is damaged by the destruction of competition among teams, with the resulting loss of public support.

As between the American League and the National League, and between teams in the minor leagues, the reserve rule is the foundation of professional baseball. If one league is permitted to raid another league for players without the limitation of the reserve clause, the lower-class minor leagues could not exist. For as they developed players and promoted public interest in them, clubs in larger cities would snatch them away without any compensation, thus depriving the club of its players, its team organization, its public interest and support, and its investment in the development of these players. The unique structure of baseball, with the reserve clause as its keystone, provides a nationwide system of apprenticeship for developing players' skills and experience and, at the same time, protects the player and assures advancement commensurate with his ability, through the draft and waiver rules.

Industry also does not have the problem of public confidences in the loyalty of employees to employers. The public buys a Plymouth without concern as to whether the employees of the Chrysler Corporation are doing their best for that company or are trying to get jobs with General Motors or Ford. But the public demands that each baseball player have full loyalty to and extend his best efforts for his club. How can public confidence in player loyalty and will to win be maintained, if the player, while playing for one club, seeks a job with another club or is pressed with offers from several other clubs, against some of which he is playing?

To preserve competition on the field, the competition for players must be regulated. This is an axiom to which all baseball operators agree and which experience has proved.

The reserve clause cannot be considered apart from this unique nature of baseball. Baseball is a sport—a game. It must have rules as to how it shall be played and who shall play it. The reserve clause is one of the rules dealing with the question as to who shall be eligible to play.

Each club must be out to win. At the same time, some equality of competition must be preserved. The clubs have attempted to achieve this—and by and large they have achieved it—by the baseball rules and regulations of which the reserve rule is one.

There may be some controversy among historians as to the facts of baseball's origin, but there is no argument as to when the first eligibility rule became necessary. That occurred on the day and the hour when the first two baseball teams played their first competitive game. From the very beginning, such rules were necessary to provide a common basis for competition.

The first real test of baseball's legal status came at the end of the Federal League battle just before World War I. The Baltimore Federal League club filed suit against the National and American leagues, charging violation of the newly passed antitrust laws. The Baltimore club did not mention the reserve clause per se in their complaint, but based their claim on alleged "combination in restraint of trade."

The suit was carried to the Supreme Court for decision. The court, after listening to long legal arguments, made its decision. Mr. Justice Holmes, speaking for the court, ruled, in the now-famous Holmes decision that baseball was basically a sport, conducted in local parks before local spectators, and was not subject to prosecution under the Anti-Trust Law.

Later, Mr. Justice Brandeis, in a clarification of the intent and scope of the antitrust ruling, further strengthened the position of baseball and team sports when he said:

> . . . the legality of an agreement or regulation cannot be determined by so simple a test as whether it restrains competition. Every agreement concerning trade, every regulation of trade, restrains. To bind, to restrain, is of their very essence. The true test of legality is whether the restraint imposed is such as merely regulates and perhaps thereby promotes competition, or whether it is such as may suppress or even destroy competition. To determine that question, the court must ordinarily consider the facts peculiar to the business to which the restraint is applied; its condition before and after the restraint was imposed; the nature of the restraint and its effect, actual or probable. The history of the restraint, the evil believed to exist, the reason for adopting the particular remedy, the purpose or end sought to be obtained, are all relevant facts.

With the Holmes decision, baseball appeared to be safe. As other professional sports developed, they assumed that they, too, came under the broad Holmes umbrella. For more than a score of years, the whole question was dormant. Then came the advent of television and radio, involving vast sums of money, and the huge interstate audiences brought new legal doubts.

Was baseball really a sport, or had it developed into big business? Interest was at a new high. Pressure was on for the expansion of major leagues into new cities, in new areas. Minor leagues claimed major league broadcasts and expansion pressures were killing them. When the major leagues attempted to keep their broadcasts out of minor league towns, the Liberty Broadcasting System, which operated a widespread "Game-of-the-Day" program, filed restraint-of-trade suits in Federal Court.

Earlier, a Mexican promoter, Jorge Pasquel, induced several major league stars to jump their contracts with pie-in-the-sky promises that never materialized. That, too, brought the reserve clause into the spotlight. Commissioner A. B. Chandler handled that situation promptly and firmly. Players who jumped their contracts were immediately suspended, and other players were persuaded not to join the hegira.

In fairness to the commissioner, it should also be pointed out that he acted with fairness as well as sternness. Once the jumping players came back, the commissioner reinstated them, with all pension and other privileges, and without penalty. But the fat was in the fire. Minor league owners and radio stations with any sort of grievance, real or imaginary, started legal action. At one time, baseball was faced with more than a dozen different antitrust cases, asking for a total of more than a million dollars in damages.

In 1951, a restive Congress got into the picture. Bills to make baseball subject to the antitrust laws were introduced in both Houses. Exhaustive committee hearings were held, with scores of witnesses appearing, including many of baseball's greatest stars. In that connection, it should be noted that the vast majority of players staunchly defended the reserve clause as necessary and beneficial. There were a few dissenters. But even the most violent critics testified that in their opinion some sort of modified reserve clause was necessary to maintain competition and fan confidence in the integrity of the game. If they were "slaves," most of them admitted, it was a happy sort of slavery, with good salaries, a lot of fringe benefits, public recognition, and social privileges.

Many baseball men and fans were called in before the hearings were over. I don't know how much time they spent there collectively or how they enjoyed themselves. In 1951 and 1952, I appeared as a reluctant witness before seven different congressional hearings, and four Federal Court trials, testing the legality of player contracts and baseball's status under the antitrust laws. It was a great experience, but a tiring one.

In the course of the hearings, I did establish a personal friendship with a lot of well-known public figures. In the House of Representatives there were men like Emanuel Celler, Kenneth Keating, William McCulloch, and Pat Hillings, for instance; on the Senate side there were figures such as Estes Kefauver, Phil Hart, Ed Johnson, and Stu Symington. That was very worthwhile. At the same time I was kept so busy supplying required information, digging up official records, and writing demanded reports, that I was able to attend only a few ball games. For that I will ever hold the Congress of the United States guilty of cruel and unusual punishment.

More than a year passed before the House bill came up for a vote. It was defeated by an overwhelming majority. The Senate bill was locked in committee, and never called up for a vote. Again, it looked like sports were home free. But the rejoicing, if any, was short-lived.

Less than a year later the "Toolson" suit was filed in Federal Court. After a defeat there, the case was appealed to the Supreme Court. With Chief Justice Warren presiding, the court refused to review the case. The Holmes ruling was still in effect, the decision said. If baseball was to come under the antitrust law, Congress should take the action, not the Supreme Court. So far, Congress seems content to let the matter rest.

Later, the Supreme Court again had occasion to rule on the merits of the case. The Curt Flood case was aimed directly at the reserve clause. The "slavery" issue was definitely raised, and the court was importuned to declare baseball's contract rules illegal. Once again the court held that the Holmes decision still applied, and that any change should be brought about by congressional action rather than court decision. At the same time, the decision was so worded as to invite congressional action.

All of which leaves the whole question of legality and future procedure very much up in the air. Even as these lines are written, another congressional hearing is under way, involving basketball, football, and hockey. Congress must decide two questions. First, does the unique competitive character of professional team sports justify broad exemption from the antitrust laws? Second, how can the Congress best provide leeway to permit player development and honest competition and still come within the letter of the law as written? Those are the $64,000 questions.

The conjecture as to what decision may be reached, or what the congressional action may be, would be both presumptuous and silly. Sports people, of course, hope they will be permitted to operate under rules that recognize the problems peculiar to the partner-competitor aspect of team sports. Most important is that a firm decision be forthcoming. Whether favorable or unfavorable, a definite decision will serve good purpose. It will remove the doubt and uncertainty in sports operations. It will set legal guidelines that should remove the worry and expense of constant legal threat, and that is good.

Any congressional act that recognizes the need of restrictive rules to guarantee fair competition to maintain public faith in the honesty of the game would enable baseball to continue to operate under present procedures without fear or worry. A decision that removes the present exemption and makes every phase of baseball operation subject to antitrust litigation would have a much more profound effect on the game.

But baseball will survive, in any event.

Maybe I'm a cockeyed optimist, but I have enough faith in management, in the players, and in the loyalty of the fans, to believe that proper answers will be found. Certainly rules would be changed. Contracts would require revision; new rules controlling player transfers would be required; scouting and development programs presently in effect would have to be altered, and new methods to provide equitable competition and assure public confidence, devised. It is not an easy assignment. Today, it seems to be the fashion to deplore the bumbling tactics of the baseball establishment. But remember this. Most club owners today are businessmen operating complex industrial corporations outside baseball. They know antitrust requirements. They have faced legal adjustments in their business operations, and have solved them. What they have done before, they can do again. They may not like it, but they'll do it. That, the fans can depend on.

One observation: In any elimination of the reserve clause, now or in the future, the prime sufferers will be the players, and indirectly, the fans. Management can protect itself. Players cannot.

First of all, the sizable bonuses paid out to untried players when they sign their first contract will be out the window. No club can afford to make such payments, unless they are assured of the player's services if and when he makes the grade.

Training programs will have to be curtailed. It costs a club thousands of dollars a year to train a young player for the major leagues or class AAA competition. For the average player, that training is a three- or four-year process. No club will happily underwrite such a program, knowing another club can step in and grab the player when the training period is finished.

Scouting will be affected, too. It will become more selective. Many youngsters who today are given a chance for a baseball career will be passed up.

All these programs have been developed as a result of the reserve system—unexpected virtues that offset, to some degree, the possible evil of the alleged peonage contracts that exist today.

Nor is the young untried rookie the only potential victim under a nonreserve system.

Today there are 960 players signed to major league contracts (24 major league clubs, each with a 40-player reserve list). Salaries range from the $14,000 major league minimum to approximately $200,000 in the case of two or three superstars. Probably a couple dozen outstanding players are paid at least $100,000 a season. (The average major league salary is probably between $30,000 and $35,000.) Undoubtedly, the reserve clause giving clubs the assurance of a player's service on a long-term basis has played a big part in bringing salaries up to that level.

I do not mean to imply that those salaries are out of line. In these wild days of inflation, any workman—common laborer or baseball personality—is entitled to all he can get. Nor do I imply that club owners are by nature so generous or so philanthropic that they offer huge contracts as a sympathetic gesture with no thought of financial return, I do point out that the reserve clause, whether legally right or wrong, has given to baseball a continuity of action that has developed better competition, better performance, and better entertainment than would have otherwise been possible.

To eliminate it abruptly, and without some compensating regulation, would affect 90 percent of the players adversely. The superstars would profit. With an open market, their ability and drawing power would set the stage for the wildest bidding baseball has ever seen. Undoubtedly, their salaries would go up. Unless they were signed to long-term contracts, the bidding would be repeated each year, which, from their viewpoint, would be good.

Unfortunately, there are only a handful of superstars to reap the golden reward. Nine hundred others would pay the price in salaries, in loss of opportunity, in proper training, and in their ability to retain what they treasure most—namely, the minimum salary, which is the springboard for salary negotiation each season.

But the problems are not only financial.

I have deliberately avoided any discussion of extraneous problems such as the danger of a rumored scandal destroying fan confidence in the honesty and integrity of the game; the weakening of playing strength of poorer clubs to the benefit of the wealthy clubs; and the possibility of admission-price increases to the point where baseball is no longer a game for the masses and youngsters are denied the right to see their heroes in action. All these things are, after all, mere conjecture.

I repeat, if Congress decides that baseball's rules are illegal, so be it. Baseball will not die. New answers will be found. New legal rules will be established. What those answers will be or what course new rules will take, I do not know, but I have faith in the fairness of the officials who run the game, in the integrity of the men who play it, and in the loyalty of the fans who love it. The answers will be forthcoming.

If, sometime in the distant future, baseball does lose its appeal as a national sport, it will be from corruption, and avarice, and moral breakdown from within—not from congressional action or court decrees.

15

COOPERSTOWN!—
MYTH OR HISTORY?

The "when, where, and why" of modern baseball's origin has long been the subject of conjecture and argument. That argument will continue to rage so long as fans have voices and fathers regale sons with memories of thrills and heroes of a boyhood long past.

Learned antiquarians have produced many tomes dealing with man's eternal interest in sport and recreation. The germ from which our modern game of baseball evolved, they point out, was first planted by some aboriginal man tossing a stone into the air and whacking it with a club torn from some aboriginal tree. That was the beginning of the so-called ball-and-bat games—the baseball, lacrosse, tennis, and golf we know today. By the same token other sports evolved in similar fashion—track-and-field events from prehistoric man's frantic efforts to escape danger by running and climbing to the shelter of a nearby cave; boat racing and other water sports from that moment when man first straddled a fallen log and successfully splashed and paddled himself across a prehistoric stream.

These learned men point out that the ability of primitive man to use the rocks and trees and streams about him to practical purpose, to use his imagination to turn these weapons to self-preservation into tools of pleasure, was the first feeble step in the long struggle from barbarism to what we are pleased to call modern civilization. It is an interesting thought and as plausible as any of the myriad theories that have been advanced in a belated effort to document an undocumentable age.

In this connection, I recall an incident in the Yankee clubhouse. It occurred in the twenties when the opening of King Tut's tomb vied for first-page headlines with other world-shaking events such as the Teapot Dome scandal and the antics of Izzy and Moe, those twin actors in the farce of Prohibition enforcement.

Benny Bengough, youthful Yankee catcher, was reading the King Tut story. It told of the discovery, on the walls of the tomb, of a faded mural depicting ancient Egyptians playing a game involving a ball and a wooden object resembling a modern bat. A few of the Yankee players were in the clubhouse, and Benny read them the article.

"I guess that will hold a lot of those guys who claim we stole the game from the British," he chortled. Then, musingly: "Ancient Egyptians, huh? And a ball and bat. What wo you think of that?"

Over by his locker Herbie Pennock was tying his shoes. Without bothering to look up he remarked drolly: "I'll tell you what I think. I think they ought to examine that bat. If they look carefully they'll probably find Babe Ruth's autograph."

And that was that!

I do not argue with the antiquarians. Certainly sports are as old as written history. People have played games since the beginning of time. The Aztecs played a "ball-and-bat" game before Columbus discovered America. They built great stadiums to accommodate thousands of spectators who watched the contests. The ruins of several such arenas still exist. American Indians played lacrosse—a ball-and-bat game—long before the first white man set foot in the New World.

But the game of baseball that we know and play was born in America—of Americans, for Americans, and by Americans—and ancient Egyptians be durned. That the game is a product of evolution cannot be denied. That various forms of baseball were played in the colonies, and in various areas of the new republic following the Revolution, is also true. Even the most ardent Cooperstown devotees admit it. The committee that finally selected Cooperstown as the birthplace of baseball stressed that their decision involved the "modern diamond game," not the historical background of the various local games from which it sprang.

The Cooperstown story began in 1907 when the National Commission appointed a committee to "consider all available evidence, and determine as accurately as possible the date and the location on which the first game of modern baseball was played."

The committee was most impressive. The task they faced was equally impressive. Heading the group was Colonel A. G. Mills, Civil War veteran, former president of the National League, and himself an enthusiastic amateur player. Other members were:

The Honorable Arthur F. Gorman, U.S. Senator from Maryland

The Honorable Morgan G. Bulkeley, first president of the National League, ex-Governor and U.S. Senator from Connecticut

Nicholas E. Young of Washington, D.C., veteran player, first secretary and later president of the National League

Albert J. Reach of Philadelphia and George Wright of Boston, two of the most famous players of their day

A. G. Spalding, player, founding member of the National League, and founder of the Spalding sports good company

James E. Sullivan of New York, president of the AAU who acted as chairman of the committee

What research methods they used, what volume of evidence they considered, or what logic directed their decision has never been reported. One of the main witnesses in the investigation was Abner Graves, a retired octogenarian mining engineer who lived in Denver. Graves had lived in Cooperstown as a boy. He testified that he and other lads of the village frequently played a "newfangled" game of baseball outlined to them by young Abner Doubleday. Doubleday, according to Graves, had drawn a chart of the proposed playing field, showing four bases laid out in diamond shape, with playing positions indicated for ten players. (The tenth player was an extra shortstop, positioned between first and second bases. The basemen played directly on the bag at first, second, and third. The diamond itself and the rules governing putout and runs scored were very like today's rules.)

Graves's testimony as to dates was a bit vague. The introduction of the Doubleday chart was drawn, he remembered, either in 1838 or

1839. He never wavered in his insistence that Doubleday had sketched out the first diamond, and that the game as later refined by Alexander Cartright, was basically identical with the Doubleday concept.

In 1908 the committee issued its report stating that Abner Doubleday, by laying out the first diamond, had fathered the game of baseball as we know it today. The first diamond, the committee agreed, was laid out in Cooperstown, New York, and the first game of modern baseball was played there in 1839. The little village on the shore of picturesque Lake Otsego suddenly found itself tapped for historic greatness.

As a matter of fact Cooperstown has claim to historic greatness without any recognition by baseball. James Fenimore Cooper had spent his boyhood there. Lake Otsego was the "Glimmerglass" of Cooper's *Deerslayer* and the adjacent rolling hills and valleys were the locale for many of his Leatherstocking tales. For generations the Mohawks and the Iroquois had held their powwows at Council Rock on the edge of the village. And at the source of the Susquehanna River, at the foot of Cooperstown's Main Street, General Clinton of Revolutionary fame pulled the coup that won him permanent renown as one of the great heroes of American history.

Caught in a pincers between hostile Indian and British forces, and threatened with the capture or annihilation of his army, Clinton rose to the challenge. He assigned half of the army to build a dam to shut off the flow of water feeding the Susquehanna. The other half built a fleet of bateaux in the now-dry riverbed. Then, under cover of darkness, he loaded his troops in the bateaux, cut the dam to release the flood, and floated his whole army to safety, while the unsuspecting enemy slept.

Baseball fans were interested in baseball; the charm and history of the village meant nothing. They didn't question Cooperstown's claim to historic fame. They did question the judgment of the committee. For a short time the argument waged hot and heavy. Editorials were written, historians fumed and fretted, but the committee stood fast. And the National Commission backed them. Cooperstown it was, and Cooperstown it stayed.

There was an interesting aftermath to that argument. In 1926 the National League celebrated its fiftieth birthday with a big dinner at the old Astor Hotel. Colonel A. G. Mills was one of the honored guests. The colonel was then in the twilight of his years, but he was still very erect, mentally alert, and very articulate.

It had been some sixteen years since the committee had made its report and the roar of opposition had faded to a whisper. Many of the writers present were not familiar with the report and asked Colonel Mills to fill them in on details. He described the work of the committee, the evidence uncovered, and the Abner Graves's testimony that had weighed so heavily in the final findings.

One of the writers, Joe Vila of the *Sun,* came up with the $64 question. "Colonel, that's an interesting story," Vila observed, "but what conclusive evidence do you have that the first game was actually played in Cooperstown?"

With twinkling eye and a wry smile the colonel replied:

"None at all, young man. None at all, so far as the actual origin of baseball is concerned. The committee reported that the first baseball diamond was laid out in Cooperstown. They were honorable men, and their decision was unanimous. I'm willing to let the matter rest right there. This we do know," he continued. "We know that baseball developed through long processes of evolution. We know that it developed as a rural game for ours was basically a rural nation. We know that once the diamond was devised and the game standardized, it was taken up eagerly by thousands of youngsters, in hundreds of typical American villages and hamlets scattered over thousands of miles of pioneer American country side. I submit to you, gentlemen, that if our search had been for a typical American village, a village that could best stand as a counterpart of all the villages where baseball might have originated and developed—Cooperstown would best fill the bill. Unless and until new evidence is developed, or a more typical spot is discovered, I'll stand with Cooperstown—and the committee."

The committee report, as so often happens, proved a ten-day wonder. Once they had voiced their doubt, the general public lost interest. Baseball folk themselves, ever addicted to a philosophy of letting sleeping dogs lie, went happily back to their seasonal routine and promptly forgot the whole business.

Only in Cooperstown was there any flicker of interest in keeping alive the dream of a national baseball monument, so suddenly aroused and just as quickly bypassed and forgotten. Over a period of years sporadic efforts were made to rebuild the old Phinney pasture (where Graves testified the first game had been played) into an adequate baseball park. But that was a local Cooperstown project, without outside support or interest.

From baseball ranks only two men continued to show interest in augmenting the committee report by positive action. Sam Crane, former player, and baseball writer on the New York *Evening Journal*, maintained pressure on baseball folk to do something about Cooperstown. John Heydler, then president of the National League, also conducted a one-man campaign for baseball action. Heydler's efforts did get some support. John K. Tener and Harry Hempstead made a joint journey to Cooperstown in 1919. In 1920 a benefit game was played between Cooperstown and neighboring Oneonta, with Heydler donning the mask and protector to umpire the first inning. The game netted $3,019 and formed the nucleus of the fund, which, in 1923, was sufficient to allow the village to purchase the Phinney pasture and build Doubleday Field, where today the annual Hall of Fame game is staged as a part of the Induction Day ceremonies. But that too was a local gesture. What was needed was some new idea that would give nationwide impetus to local planning.

That impetus came in 1935.

A descendant of Abner Graves, rummaging around the attic of an abandoned farmhouse, came across a battered old trunk. The trunk contained a blackened, torn old ball and a packet of yellow, ancient letters explaining that the ball had been used by youngsters in games played on the Phinney pasture during the Doubleday era. The misshapen relic attracted the interest of the county historical society. Local people flocked to see it on display in a local shop. One of them, Stephen C. Clark, went into action. He bought the ball for five dollars, had it mounted, then displayed among other memorabilia of the Otsego County Historical Society.

Stephen Clark, resident of Cooperstown, a historian, philanthropist, and enthusiastic collector of early Americana, visualized that old baseball, brown with age, bursting at the seams, as the centerpiece for a display that would keep Cooperstown forever mindful of its baseball heritage. He added his own prized baseball collection of paintings and prints, including a famous drawing showing Union prisoners playing baseball at Salisbury Prison during the Civil War, and the original oil painting of a championship match at Elysian Fields in Hoboken in 1866.

More important, he assigned a member of his management staff, Alexander Cleland, to scour the country for other authentic relics to add to the collection. He couldn't have found a better agent. Cleland, a stocky, red-faced little Scotsman, with the broad burr of the highlands in his speech and the missionary ardor of a John Knox in his soul, adopted the project as a personal challenge.

In the course of a year he visited baseball people from coast to coast and back again. From the National League office we were able to send him the original Temple Cup, emblem of the professional championship in the 1880–1890 period. Clark Griffith sent his collection of pictures from Washington; Judge Branham and Taylor Spink, from their voluminous files, sent documents, pictures, official papers, which formed the nucleus for the library that was to come later. Connie Mack, William M. Wrigley, Mrs. Christy Mathewson, and Mrs. John McGraw made valuable contributions.

Convinced now that his project was worthwhile, Clark took a further step—the real clincher. Quietly, in 1935, he called a meeting of village fathers, historical society officials, and the legal and financial experts who handled the various foundations representing the vast Clark family holdings. He proposed the organization of the National Baseball Museum, Inc., "for the purpose of collecting and preserving pictures and relics reflecting the development of the National Game from the time of its inception, through the ingenuity of major General Abner Doubleday in 1939, to the present."

Furthermore, Clark said, he would personally take the responsibility of erecting in Cooperstown a suitable building to house such collection in perpetuity, and he invited organized baseball to join with him in establishing the first museum in American history to be devoted entirely to a sport—baseball.

That did it.

Baseball folks, like it or not, suddenly found themselves involved up to their collective necks in a new venture that, despite some skepticism and a certain amount of foot-dragging, was destined to do more toward the development and promotion of the game's tradition than anything else in baseball's history.

I'll say this for baseball people. They may be skeptical of

change and slow to act, but once they get involved they go all out. Before the year was out organized baseball had set up a fund of $100,000 to stage a season-long celebration of baseball's centennial, culminating with a Cooperstown Day in which all organized baseball would join to confirm the legend of baseball's birth and send the game roaring happily into its second century.

Meantime Clark had decided that the proper time to dedicate the museum was 1939—the centennial of the year the committee had decided marked the birth of modern baseball. Cleland was charged with arranging a dedication day program. It would be an all-day celebration, Clark decided, culminating with a ball game in the refurbished Doubleday Field as the afternoon feature. Cleland was interested in some sort of publicity gimmick that would guarantee a good attendance for the celebration. He was particularly anxious to enlist the support of organized baseball for the project. He dropped into the National League office to see what could be done.

Cleland said that radio stations in upper New York had already agreed to cooperate, and suggested that they might conduct a radio fan poll to select an All-Star team—the winners to be announced as a part of the ceremonies. The winning candidates, he explained, would be invited to be Clark's guests at the celebration.

By happy chance I had visited the National Hall of Fame at New York University a few days before Cleland's visit. I was much impressed, and had a notion that a Baseball Hall of Fame would be great for the game. Cleland's visit afforded opportunity to try the idea out.

"Why just a local contest, and why an All-Star game?" I countered. "I don't think baseball would go for that. What's needed is some sort of national promotion that will interest fans throughout the nation and can be continued year after year. Why not a Baseball Hall of Fame? We've already got a building to house it. All we need is a sound plan."

Cleland was enthusiastic. So was Clark. My job was to sell baseball people. I immediately called Judge Landis, Will Harridge, William Branham, George Trautman, and Frank Shaughnessey. All of them applauded the idea, except the judge. He couldn't see it. He said his office couldn't become involved in any local promotion. The judge maintained that aloofness throughout the rest of his life. He did attend the dedication celebration, made a fine dedication speech, and entered fully into the spirit of the day—but so far as I know he never again went near Cooperstown.

I could never understand his attitude. He was a great man. His record in and for baseball speaks for itself. Maybe he felt that Cooperstown didn't rate such recognition. Maybe I caught him at a bad time.

Anyhow, it was a small matter. We went ahead with the plans. Within a short time a meeting was held with Alan Gould of the AP, Davis Walsh of INS and Jack Cuddy of UP. The project was outlined to them. They enthusiastically endorsed the idea and suggested that candidates be elected by a vote of sportswriters rather than by a cumbersome fan vote. They agreed they would conduct the first poll. That method still prevails. So does the rule, suggested by Alan Gould, requiring 75 percent vote for election.

Within a few weeks the plan had been accepted by the Baseball Writers Association, and ballots sent out to some 200 active writers. Early in 1936 the ballots were counted. Five men were chosen—Honus Wagner, Ty Cobb, Babe Ruth, Walter Johnson, and Christy Mathewson—five immortals whose names will forever head the list of those whose performance goes unchallenged, and whose memory will remain green so long as baseball endures.

The last lingering doubt of the acceptance of the Hall of Fame idea was answered. The writers accepted their responsibility seriously and gladly. They have continued in that spirit ever since. The first Hall of Fame in the annals of American sport had become a reality.

The Cooperstown celebration and dedication ceremony is too well known to require any extended comment. Twelve thousand fans that day crowded the little village and heard Judge Landis deliver an inspired dedication speech. Never before or since have so many great personages of baseball, players and officials alike, joined together in one place to honor baseball. The President of the United States extended official greeting. Postmaster General James Farley supervised the sale of a special commemorative stamp recognizing baseball's centennial as a national game. It was baseball's finest hour, perhaps never again to be duplicated by any sport, any time, anywhere.

And that's the story of the beginning. Succeeding chapters are being written each year. In twenty-five years more than ten million visitors have been registered—and they're still coming at the rate of more than a quarter-million each year. What started as a single colonial brick building has grown to a huge complex. A new wing has been added to the museum—a wing almost twice as large as the original building. A cathedral-like hall now houses the Hall of Fame, separate and apart from the museum.

A library has been constructed, dedicated to the writers, the artists and cartoonists, the photographers, and the radio and television men who have contributed so much to the growth of the game. A motion-picture theatre providing some 150 spectator seats has been added, with daily showings of films, old and new, depicting the thrill, the excitement, and the personal glory of half a century of baseball performance. That library today is the depository of the greatest array of records, historic documents, pictures, and authentic books and articles ever assembled on a single American sport subject in the history of the nation. It contains the complete record of every man who ever played a major league game, together with the documented histories of leagues and clubs. And new material is added each year to keep information up to date.

Meantime, the Hall of Fame, built as an afterthought, has developed into baseball's greatest monument. At that original installation ceremony in 1939, eleven great stars came, one by one, through the single museum door, to be introduced to the assembled fans. Today more than 150 names have been added to the growing list; more than 150 plaques adorn the walls of the great hall where baseball salutes the memory of those men whose contribution to baseball off the field and on has been outstanding in the judgment of their peers.

Other sports have been quick to follow baseball's lead. Football has its Hall of Fame, too, an imposing structure in Canton, Ohio. That's good. So, too, do basketball, golf, tennis, and boxing. Even horse racing has joined the group. But baseball was the first—the first to dream a dream, and the first to give that dream life and body in workaday brick and mortar and steel.

It hasn't always been easy. There have been serious problems. Policies have frequently been questioned. Elections have on occasion been greeted with less than 100 percent enthusiasm. Some owners have been lukewarm in their support. But baseball has been fortunate, too. There has always been a Clark family to rely on, and a Paul Kerr to take charge when the going was rough. From the ranks of baseball

Tom Yawkey, Joe Cronin, Bob Carpenter, and Warren Giles have never faltered in their support, and the Baseball Writers Association has never turned down a request or failed to meet a responsibility.

Most encouraging of all has been the enthusiasm of the players themselves, both the present generation and the old-timers. They have been through the mill, so to speak, and are as anxious as the most rabid fan to see the traditions, the memories, and the thrills of their game preserved. Bill Terry, Charley Gehringer, Frank Frisch, Joe Cronin, and Waite Hoyt have never missed a meeting of the Old-Timer selection committee, and are regular attendants at the Induction Day ceremonies. There are others, too, but to name them all would require a volume.

One serious problem lies ahead—the problem of transition. The generation that saw the Hall of Fame dream become reality is nearing the end of an active career. Soon a newer, younger generation will take over. It will be up to them to carry on. If, as I believe, they have a real feeling for the traditions and the memories that baseball has engendered, the Hall of Fame will be in good hands. If they permit themselves to be bogged down by the skepticism and doubt and cynicism of this skeptical age then the Hall of Fame will be in real danger—and all baseball with it.

But enough of conjecture.

Baseball had a dream.

Without Stephen Clark, Sr., that dream could never have become reality.

Without Stephen Clark, Jr., and Paul Kerr, and the others there would have been no progress.

The most intriguing thought of all: without a battered trunk, an ancient ball, and a packet of time-stained letters, baseball would have been without its greatest monument.

In the box score of baseball history, a kindly Providence should be credited with at least an assist.

16

THE COMMISSIONER'S OFFICE

ARBITRATION

There's a board of arbitration fixed for labor,
Baseball claims its board of arbitration, too:
Capitalistic agitation
Now is met by arbitration
Every union has its arbitration crew!

Children arbitrate with parents in the morning
Teachers arbitrate with children through the day—
Life itself, and all creation,
Is a board of arbitration,
Till some doctor arbitrates our life away.

Scientific arbitration fixes salaries;
Politicians arbitrate the nation's fate;
Men of high and low positions,
Even lawyers and physicians,
Welcome every chance that comes to arbitrate.

There's a board of arbitration now for fighters;
There's another board to arbitrate for peace;
Up they spring, throughout the nation
Till we ask, in desperation,
"Will the bloomin' arbitration never cease?"

The commissionership of baseball is a very lonely job.

Most fans, I suppose, would question that statement. To them, the commissionership seems a glamorous post; the commissioner a lucky stiff with great power of decision, plus the privilege of close personal contact with the "greats and near greats" who make baseball history.

In answer I can only speak from personal experience. In more than a dozen years as a sportswriter and radio announcer, I was privileged to know great sports figures intimately. I traveled with them, ate with them, played cards with them. I rejoiced in their triumphs, and joined with them frequently in discussions of their off-field problems. In seventeen years as a league president, I was able to maintain most of those friendships, and make new ones in the field of ownership and management.

During those years, I was in the midst of the action and the fun. I had rooting privileges, too. I could build my own personal idols, pull for my favorites, criticize my adversaries, and socialize with my friends. There was no official protocol to say me nay.

The minute I entered the commissioner's office all that changed. Off-the-cuff statements, once accepted as light repartee, became official pronouncements. Friends remained friends, but the warmth and camaraderie of the old days were gone. World Series press parties, where I once spent long hours wining and dining with old cronies, now became brief official calls, with laughter stifled and every comment carefully scanned by "security guards" before I made it.

After joint major league meetings, it was customary to meet with a group of baseball men to discuss the day's happenings over a few drinks and a leisurely dinner. As commissioner I dined alone, or with other officials, or with my staff. Even at fans' and writers' banquets, protocol demanded that the commissioner be seated on the dais, surrounded by dignitaries and honored guests, with no opportunity to mingle with old friends, or cut up a few touches with other fans. It was enough to drive a man to drink—and frequently did.

I'm not complaining. The more authority a man is given, the less private life he is permitted. Every commissioner of baseball faces the same problem. But not every commissioner has behind him the friendship and memories of a quarter century of close contact with writers, players, and officials of the game he is called upon to govern. At least the outsider can start all even, without closets to clean out or fixed habits to overcome.

I still stand by my opening statement.

Being commissioner of baseball is a lonely job.

If the public is interested in the workings of the commissioner's office (which I doubt), it is important to understand the origin of the commissioner idea—the purpose outlined, the objectives sought, the authority conferred, and the changes that have occurred in the half century it has been in existence.

Though the idea of some sort of centralized government had been bandied about for some years, the actual appointment of Judge Landis was made in haste and born of fear. The White Sox scandal, following closely on the heels of the Federal League war, sent baseball into a tizzy. The Federal League fiasco had left a bitter taste in the mouths of fans in cities where the defunct league had operated. The player scandal challenged public faith in the honesty and integrity of players and management alike.

Something had to be done quickly to restore that public image. The Office of Commissioner was set up. Judge Kenesaw M. Landis was induced to resign his post as a United States Federal Court judge to accept appointment as the first commissioner. His duties:

1. To investigate, either upon complaint or upon his own initiative, any act, transaction or practice alleged or suspected to be detrimental to the game of baseball, with full authority to take such preventive remedial or punitive action, or impose such penalties, as are hereinafter provided.

(In the case of a major league, or club, the fine could not exceed $5,000. In the case of a major league employee or player, the penalty might extend to suspension or permanent ineligibility.)

2. To hear and determine finally any dispute between the major leagues that may be certified to him for determination by the president of either major league.

3. To hear and determine finally any dispute to which a player is a party, or any dispute concerning a player, which may be certified to him by either or any of the disputants.

As you can see, the only time the commissioner had authority to instigate an investigation of his own volition was in cases of "conduct detrimental to baseball." In all other cases, he was in the role of a judge, acting only after the case was certified to him by one or the other of the involved parties. Unfortunately, the detrimental-to-baseball clause failed to define scope or reason. Judge Landis himself made the interpretation. "Detrimental to baseball," he said, was to be interpreted as acts of moral turpitude; betting on ball games; throwing games or having knowledge of such action on the part of others, and failing to report such knowledge; knowingly associating with unsavory characters. In fact, it was any act on the part of individuals or clubs that, in his opinion, adversely affected the honesty and integrity of the game, on the field or off.

So far as I can ascertain, in a long and honorable career as commissioner, Judge Landis exerted his authority under the detrimental-to-baseball provision only three times.

1. In the famous White Sox case, he permanently barred seven players from baseball, five of them for conniving to throw games, and two for having guilty knowledge that they failed to disclose.

2. He threw "Cozy" Dolan and Jimmy O'Connell out of baseball for failure to report an attempted bribe.

3. He barred William Cox, owner of the Philadelphia National League club for betting on ball games, and ordered the National League to find a buyer for the club. (This wasn't an easy assignment. The club then was in critical financial trouble. But thanks largely to Herb Pennock's friendship with Bob Carpenter and his father, a deal was made. The judge was happy—and so was the National League. They still are.)

Those three decisions made baseball history, and they set a precedent in "detrimental to baseball" interpretation that still stands.

Judge Landis made many other decisions in the course of his long reign. Most of them had to do with violations of operating rules.

He opposed the growing farm systems, and on two occasions gave free agency to large groups of players on the basis of club "cover-up." Once the St. Louis Cardinals organization was the victim; another time the axe fell on the Detroit Tigers. Both cases attracted a lot of publicity and some vehement arguments. The result was a clarification of the player option rule, eliminating all vagueness and spelling out procedures in terms that a child could understand. The rule was passed at a joint session, and the judge accepted it. There have been no further mass free-agency decisions.

Not that succeeding commissioners have been lax in enforcing the rule, for they haven't. It is still the function of the commissioner to enforce all baseball rules as written, most particularly rules covering players' rights. Commissioner Chandler, I know, always had player interests in mind. I don't know the exact number of players granted free agency during his regime, but there were several. During the years I served as commissioner, more than a score of players were declared "free agents" because of rules violations. In every instance the violating club was barred from reacquiring the player's contract, and in the majority of cases the club was fined. The commissioners who have succeeded me have, I am confident, followed the same procedure.

A lot of fans, and some writers, insist that the commissioner today works under the same agreement, and with the same broad authority granted when the office had its inception. That is not true. After the death of Judge Landis in 1944, a new paragraph was added to the Major League Agreement. It specifies that "No Major League rule, or other joint action of the two Major Leagues, and no act or procedure taken in compliance with such Major League rule or joint action of the two Major Leagues shall be considered or construed to be detrimental to baseball."

In other words, the authority granted to the commissioner under the detrimental-to-baseball clause was restricted, as Landis surmised, to acts that affect the honesty, integrity, and moral standards of the game. Joint rules and actions are exempt.

At the same time, there was stricken from the agreement a final paragraph that provided that all signers of the agreement waived their right to file court action against any ruling the commissioner might make. This paragraph was dropped at the suggestion of lawyers who pointed out that the paragraph was without meaning, because no court would uphold such an agreement. Maybe they were right, but the paragraph, legal or not, did carry a moral obligation that strengthened the commissioner's hand. A few years later an abortive attempt was made to amend the agreement to provide that "no league rule or no procedure or action under such rule shall be considered or construed as detrimental to baseball." The proposal, obviously made in pique, did not find favor with a majority of owners, and when the then commissioner expressed strong opposition, the whole matter was tabled. It has never been revived.

That the operation of the commissioner's office has changed through a half century and five administrations is self-evident. But those changes have, for the most part, come about from outside pressures and not from any deliberate action from baseball operators to curb the authority of the commissioner or alter the original concept of his function.

Let's look for a moment at that original concept.

The primary and immediate function of the commissioner was to police and preserve the honesty and integrity of the game, and its players. His weapon was the detrimental-to-baseball clause, which gave him complete authority not only to investigate, but to take punitive action as well. The subsequent amendment was definitive rather than restrictive. It spelled out certain limitations (already recognized by the first commissioner), but did not change by one iota the authority to act or penalize.

For more than a half century, every man who has occupied that office has taken full advantage of that clause. True, there has been, from time to time, public criticism of this or that commissioner because he was too lax or too stern in his actions. That is to be expected. Regardless of that criticism, the fact remains that the confidence of the fans in the honesty of baseball players, and the integrity of their performance on the field, is equaled by few sports and excelled by none.

As a matter of record, 90 percent of the work of the commissioner's office involves violations by clubs and individuals of the rules that they, themselves, have set up. All transactions of any nature involving leagues, clubs, or players, must be filed immediately with the commissioner. This includes not only major items such as major

The original inductees when the Hall of Fame was dedicated in Cooperstown, June 12, 1939. *Front row:* Eddie Collins, Babe Ruth, Connie Mack, Cy Young. *Back row:* Honus Wagner, Grover Alexander, Tris Speaker, Napoleon Lajoie, George Sisler, Walter Johnson

National Baseball Library, newest building in the Hall of Fame complex

Four generations of Hall of Famers, and a rabid fan at a dinner tossed by Toots Shor as part of the National League Birthday celebration. The big guy, *at far left*, is Toots Shor. *Left to right:* Early-day baseball was represented by Kid Nichols, 1880 to 1904; turn-of-the-century baseball by Cy Young 1890–1911; pre-war baseball by Ed Walsh 1904–1917; and Mickey Cochrane 1925–1937.

Frank Frisch accepts Hall of Fame pin from Commissioner Frick following Frisch's induction in 1947.

Actual Hall of Fame wing, added 1949

Mr. and Mrs. Jackie Robinson chat with Commissioner Frick at a baseball dinner. Mickey Mantle listens in.

Commissioner Frick and manager Eddie Stanky join in admiring Stan Musial's "Big Bertha" with which he won batting titles and membership in the Hall of Fame. St. Petersburg training camp, 1952.

Casey Stengel, *at right*, gets his copy of the new rule changes including the new balk rule. Yanks training camp, St. Petersburg, Florida, 1958.

The old and the young get together at a baseball luncheon to sell war bonds in 1942. Connie Mack of the American League joins Ford Frick, the president of the National League, for the photographers. Over $30 million in bonds were pledged at the Waldorf luncheon.

President Franklin Roosevelt is presented with National and American League passes for the 1940 season.

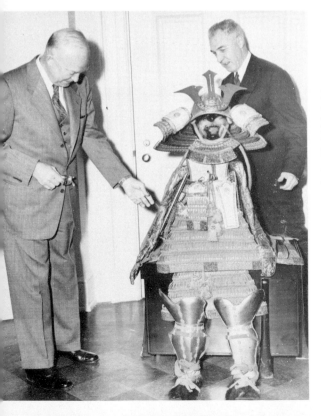

Following the 1953 visit of the Giants to Japan, Commissioner Frick presents President Eisenhower with an antique set of samurai armor—the official gift of the Japanese baseball leagues and the Japanese fans.

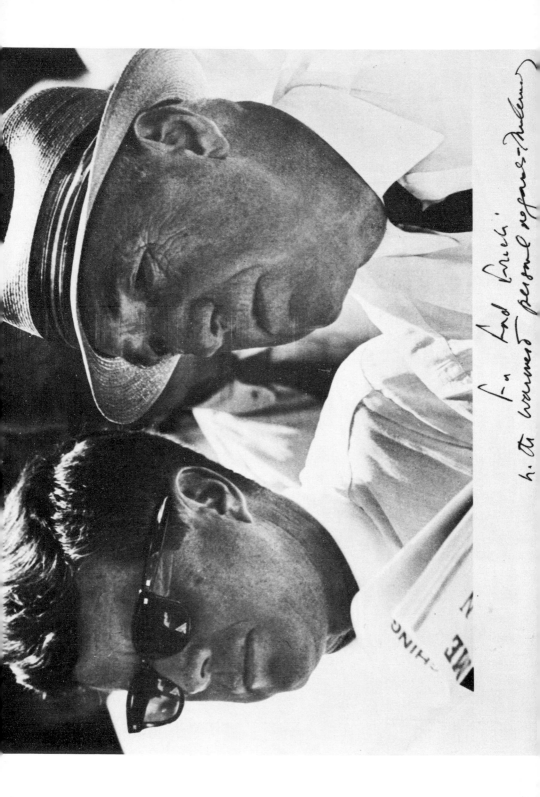

Sometimes it's not easy to be a fan.

Grandfather points out a star player to an interested grandson in a game at Boston's Fenway Park.

league and major-minor league agreements and rules—but full reports on any action under such rules, such as farm agreements, options, contracts signed or transferred. That contract report must include salaries, bonuses, and any extraneous provisions that might lead to future argument or in any way affect player welfare. These documents are carefully read, all special provisions noted, flagged, coded, and filed for ready reference.

These documents and records constitute an effective basis for the "policing" job that is so great a part a commissioner's duty.

In his ruling on violation of operational rules, the detrimental-to-baseball clause cannot now be applied. Many fans and writers feel that the power of the commissioner has been greatly reduced by that amendment. Theoretically, I suppose, they have a basis for argument. Practically that is not true.

The amendment providing that joint rules and agreements or actions taken under such rules could not be deemed "detrimental to baseball" did limit the commissioner in punitive action, particularly because it established a maximum for fining, and eliminated the application of a "permanent ineligibility" penalty in such cases. But so long as a $5,000 fine can be applied to clubs or individuals; so long as the right to cancel a deal, grant players free agency, order suspensions of up to one year, or bar an official from participating or voting in joint or league meetings, the authority of the commissioner is sufficient. Only his pride his hurt.

In fact, the commissioner has two effective weapons that most fans do not consider. First is his indirect control over any proposed changes in, or amendment to, prescribed rules and procedures. All such proposals must be considered and voted on by the two leagues in joint session. At the league meetings preceding the joint session, these proposals are discussed and a league vote taken. In the joint meeting, the vote is by leagues with the president of the league casting his "yes" or "no" vote in accordance with majority opinion in his league. If the two leagues are at variance, the commissioner casts the deciding vote—and his vote is final. There can be no appeal.

If he has strong feelings, pro or con, he can vote his personal opinion and that ends it. If he desires, he can call for a poll of clubs before rendering his decision. If he feels that some rule or action is necessary, but that the proposal as written is unsatisfactory, he can express his opinion and call for further debate, and/or a qualifying amendment. If, after debate, no satisfactory compromise has been reached, he can still vote "no," and thereby quash any change.

That is what happened in the much-publicized St. Louis meeting, when the territorial rights rule was amended to permit an expansion program to which both leagues were definitely committed. I have already discussed that meeting in some detail in the chapter covering expansion. I mention it again because it demonstrates so clearly the power of the commissioner to control and direct controversial legislation. Without the power to demand fair compromise, and without the latent threat to vote "no," thereby delaying the whole expansion program, the St. Louis meeting would have been a complete fiasco. In cases like that the "final and deciding" vote is a more potent weapon than all the detrimental-to-baseball clauses ever written.

Admittedly, the St. Louis incident was a bit out of the ordinary. Because some sort of legislative action was absolutely necessary to get expansion off the ground, it aroused much comment before and after. But it was not uncommon. In more than thirty years of official baseball connection, I can count on the fingers of one hand the number of joint meetings when a tie-breaking vote by the commissioner was not necessary to decide the fate of some proposed rule or action.

At some meetings, he would vote on only one proposal. There have been meetings when the commissioner was called upon to decide the fate of five or six proposed rules. On most occasions, the tie-breaking vote was not publicized. At the press conference, it was common practice to announce the passage or defeat of the various proposals without comment as to the voting margin. Occasionally some writer interested in a particular item on the agenda would ask what the vote was. In those cases, he was always given the information. In my book, that's proper procedure. If the test of great umpiring is the inability of the spectators to recall the name of the man making the decisions, the same yardstick applies to commissioners and other baseball officials.

The other great unwritten power of the commissioner is persuasion. Any commissioner assumes added stature the minute he dons the official robes of office. People in baseball, and the general public, may question his judgment or disagree violently with this or that decision, but they do respect the office. That's where persuasion comes in. A telephone call or a man-to-man conversation frequently will head off a sticky situation before it develops into a reality. Nor is that merely a personal philosophy.

As president of the National League, I served under two commissioners, Judge Landis and A. B. Chandler. They were men of different backgrounds, with different philosophies and different personalities. Judge Landis ran his office as he ran his court, with judicial dignity and positiveness that at times bordered on the arrogant.

He was intolerant of opposition, suspicious of reform and reformers, and skeptical of compromise. To him there was no gray zone of doubt—only the black or white of legal guilt or innocence. He ruled the game as if baseball were a courtroom, and players and officials were culprits awaiting sentence for their misdoings. Yet with it all, he was a kindly man, with a sense of sympathy and compassion that bubbled to the surface at the most unexpected times and places. He had a great sense of humor, too, which he tried unsuccessfully to camouflage behind a jutting chin, a thatch of unruly white hair, and the rumpled old hat he wore with theatrical flair whenever he appeared in public. But those twinkling gray eyes always gave him away. He enjoyed a good laugh, even at his own expense.

The judge had many supporters. He had critics, too. He was the perfect selection for the era in which he ruled. There are critics who argue that he would be lost in the hurly-burly of today's complex operations. Certainly the commissioner's job is different today and the problems vastly more complex than they were a half century ago. Whether or not Judge Landis, or any man of his era, could adjust to today's conditions, I am not prepared to argue. In any case, the question is completely academic. But one thing I do know. The judge laid down the basic rules under which the office operates. He started procedure and practices that have become traditional. And he certainly left baseball a better and stronger game than he found it.

Two Landis stories come immediately to mind. I heard the first when I, as a young newspaperman, dropped into his office one day. Landis was still sitting on the judicial bench when the story took place.

A man, well into his sixties, had been found guilty of murder, and was before Landis for sentencing. The penalty was a mandatory life imprisonment.

"When I pronounced sentence, the old man collapsed," said Landis. "He fell back in a chair, crying and sobbing like a baby. His lawyer tried to quiet him, but he kept moaning, 'I can't stand it! I can't stand it!' Believe me, it was tough. I felt very sorry for him."

"What did you say to him?" I asked Landis.

"What could I say?" the Judge replied. "He was guilty and admitted it. Anyhow, the sentence was fixed by law. I just patted him on the back a bit and said to him 'Now, Daddy, I tell you what. You just go on up there to the prison and do the best you can.' What the hell else could I say?"

I had another experience with the judge a few years later when I was president of the National League. I was sitting in the judge's private office when the phone rang. The judge answered, and after an exchange of amenities, sat for a time listening to the voice at the other end of the wire. Then he interrupted.

"Listen," he exploded, "I'm the commissioner—not a personal nursemaid. You got yourself into the jam. Now get yourself out. There's no baseball rule involved. It's just a case of someone lying— you or him. If you want to file formal charges, put them in writing. Meantime, why don't you call Harridge. He's the president of your league. Goodbye."

As he hung up, the judge turned to me. "Let that be lesson number one on your new job," he said. "Never go looking for trouble. Let 'em come to you. And don't start bothering me with your own league problems. They're your babies. I've got problems of my own."

And that was that. Except that Will Harridge told me later that the judge had called to tell him of the phone call and suggest the way it should be handled.

Sometimes the judge's bark was more frightening than his bite.

The point is that Judge Landis demonstrated early that, despite "big stick" headlines, persuasion was the greatest weapon in the commissioner's arsenal. An incipient crisis, headed off by a telephone call or a quiet face-to-face confrontation, could be more effective than a dozen decisions after the fact.

Commissioner Chandler followed the same precepts. Both men insisted that baseball officials, individually and as a group, operate in compliance with the rules that they themselves had laid down. Both men recognized and insisted that certain responsibilities rested with the individual leagues, and refused to act as whipping boys or nursemaids in such matters. Yet in seventeen years of close contact with the office, I never got the cold shoulder when I asked advice, nor an evasive answer when I sought interpretation of a seeming ambiguity in a rule or action.

Each commissioner, of course, functions differently. It is not the intent here to discuss personalities, or the differences of approach and policy. I can only try, from my personal experience, to give a fleeting picture of the problems a commissioner faces, and the techniques employed by his staff in meeting and solving them.

I was very lucky in having a loyal staff. I was even more fortunate in having Warren Giles as National League president, and Will Harridge, and later Joe Cronin, in charge of the American League. We knew and respected each other. We worked together for many years. We were, in a sense, working together as a board of directors. We met frequently, informally, often at a luncheon table. We met at formally called meetings when some immediate problem arose. It was a happy relationship. In my opinion it was good for baseball, too. Over a period of years, many seemingly irreconcilable differences of opinion were resolved quietly and amicably—problems that otherwise might have become both serious and long lasting.

Every commissioner has a right-hand man in his organization, a man he can trust to relieve him of much of the tiresome detail of operation. Judge Landis had Leslie O'Connor. Commissioner Chandler had Walter Mulbry. I had Charley Segar, a former newspaperman who, through long experience with me in the league office, was thoroughly conversant with every rule in the book. Charley was the official troubleshooter, interpreting procedure and rules. If rules were involved, he had the answer. If it was a matter of policy, he would confer with the commissioner, then call back with an official ruling in short order. I have no idea how many cases were handled in that manner. I do know that for every case publicized through formal penalty, there were at least twenty threatening situations headed off before they became serious. That, too, is part of the commissioner's job.

Since the primary function of the commissioner, as listed in the agreement, is to protect the honesty and integrity of the game, each commissioner must have trained investigative personnel. During my years as commissioner, that job was handled by "Buck" Greene, former federal agent. Buck worked quietly, and without fanfare. His appointment was never publicly announced, though I am sure his identity became known to many officials and players.

Fortunately, there were no serious cases during those years to warrant public attention. There were minor cases aplenty to keep Buck busy. Recently, I ran into Buck at a ball game. From his records, he sent me these figures.

During the fifteen-year period, 839 arrests were made. These included bookmakers picked up in and around local ball parks; gamblers, scalpers, pickpockets, and the like.

During the course of investigations, 430 nightclubs, taverns, scalper hangouts, and other suspicious places were investigated. Two restaurants where alleged unsavory characters assembled were declared out-of-bounds to players and club personnel. In St. Louis, a restaurant-bar directly across the street from the ball-park entrance sheltered an undercover gambling outfit. Evidence was submitted to Cardinal owner Gussie Busch, who solved the problem simply and promptly. He bought the property, threw out the tenants, razed the building, and turned the property into a badly needed parking lot for baseball patrons.

Because of variations in, and lack of, gambling laws in most states, most of the men arrested had to be charged with vagrancy, and got off with light sentences. Several, however, were given jail terms. One man, arrested in Philadelphia for bribery, was given a three-year sentence and fined $10,000.

There are, of course, various routine matters that also go to make up the duties of the commissioner. He is in complete charge of the World Series, including the price and sale of tickets (with the contending clubs acting as agents); he supervises the All-Star games and conducts the poll to select the players; he negotiates contracts for the televising of World Series, All-Star Game, and "Game of the Week" telecasts.

Maybe these facts will serve to answer the frequently asked question: "Just what are the duties of the commissioner's office?"

Over the years, baseball has seen many changes. The problems that Judge Landis faced were much less complex than those facing Commissioner Kuhn today. Today's commissioner must be more a diplomat and less a czar, more an executive and less a rugged individualist. He must be more an arbitrator than a supreme judge.

Today the umbrella created by the Supreme Court decision of 1922 is frayed at the edges, and leaking in spots. As a result, once-dormant laws have been revived. New and restrictive laws are being submitted to the Congress. Unions and union agents have forced their way into the act. Financial responsibilities have doubled and tripled over a ten-year span—and the end is not in sight. Every rule that baseball adopts, and every decision the commissioner decrees, must be tempered to withstand legal challenges and congressional debates.

I think baseball and all sports have been well handled through the years. They have given the public competitive entertainment through honest games, honestly played to honest completion. They have met the policing challenge without flinching. They have made the commissioner system work. Maybe they are now the victims of their own accomplishments. Maybe in their enthusiasm they have built a public image of potency and power that exceed human capacities. I confess I don't know the answer.

But, as concerns baseball, this I do know. The commissioner is in a tough spot. However much the justification, he cannot flaunt national law. His decisions must be tempered to fit the times. He cannot roll in the mud of a labor argument one moment, and the next moment don a clean shirt and assume authority as final judge and arbiter. As a commanding general his job is to develop strategy to win the war, not to man the skirmish lines or lead a scouting patrol. Baseball, and the public, must realize that fact.

No man, however capable, can be all things to all persons. To expect him to be chef, waiter, dishwasher, host, and chief speaker at his own banquet is nonsensical and unfair. I have known all the other men who served as comissioner. Without exception, they were honest, dedicated men intent on rendering the best possible service to baseball. I have known other men, equally capable, who were presidents of great industrial institutions. This thing I noticed. When a phone breaks down, no one calls the president of "Ma Bell" to make repairs; and no one criticizes the president of General Motors when a worker is accidentally killed in an assembly-line accident.

By the same token, I cannot understand why the commissioner of baseball should be expected to inject himself into each petty club argument, or take the rap for every player-owner squabble.

Maybe a false image has been built up through the years. If so, it's time for a change. The image of a demigod czar, wielding a flaming sword in the name of justice, piety, and motherhood has served great purpose. But no longer. Modern times demand modern realities. The sooner the public understands that the commissioner is, after all, human; the sooner they realize he is neither a prophet of doom nor a Daniel-come-to-judgment, but a capable, dedicated man doing the best he can on a difficult assignment, the better it will be for all concerned.

I believe in the commissioner idea. It still works. But the czar image no longer fits. The fact is the commissioner is a hardworking executive trying, as best he can, to weld scores of individual enterprises into a national institution for the purpose of providing honest competitive entertainment for a sports-minded public.

17

NOTES FROM A DIARY

"The time has come," the Walrus said,
"To talk of many things:
Of shoes—and ships—and sealing wax—
Of cabbages—and kings—"

> *—Through the Looking-Glass.*
> *The Walrus and the Carpenter*

A LIVELY CORPSE

Critics today often proclaim that baseball is dying.

They sadly bemoan the passing of minor leagues as indicative of dying interest in moribund sport.

That, to me, is bunk!

Baseball interest among the inarticulate "little people" is greater than ever. The interest simply gallops in a new direction so far as organized baseball is concerned. Today we're inclined to judge baseball interest by the paid-attendance figures of other sports like football, hockey, and basketball, and noting the percentage of yearly increased attendance in those sports as compared to baseball, come to the hasty conclusion that baseball is on the way out.

That, too, is bunk.

We forget that the newer professional sports started from scratch. That they have shown phenomenal growth over a short life is undoubtedly true. And that's good. But percentages are misleading. A rookie ball player, going to bat for the first time, strikes out. His per-

221

centage is .000. The second time at bat he singles. Immediately he became a .500 hitter. Yet a Hank Aaron, with a midseason average of .350, gets two for four in a game, and his average goes a single point. Even the severest critic would hesitate to say that Aaron was slipping or that the rookie was a challenge to the Aaron record.

Baseball has changed. What has happened, it seems to me, is that baseball has followed a national trend. Modern communications, with nationwide sports programs, plus modern transportation, have changed our whole way of life. They have destroyed provincialism and eliminated small-town rivalry. The village baseball team has bowed to progress along with the buckboard and the fringed surrey. But youngsters still play baseball on cow pastures, and in city parks, in summer camps, and on school teams, in numbers undreamed of a generation ago. Furthermore, they have better equipment, they are better coached, they play more games, and they have just as much fun!

Baseball dying? Pooh, as Branch Rickey used to say, three poohs.

Mr. Gallagher Quotes Some Figures

Jim Gallagher, former writer and executive, and for some years a member of the commissioner's staff, is a "figger filbert." Furthermore, he knows the amateur field throughly.

I recently showed Jim a clipping from a column in which the writer claimed that "kid interest" in playing baseball was on the wane. "Kids today," the writer pontificated, "are turning from baseball to other sports. Professional baseball should take warning."

Jim snorted, and pulled a paper from his pocket. The paper was Jim's latest report on amateur baseball activity. Here are the figures, just as Jim gave them.

ORGANIZATION	1970 TEAMS	1971 TEAMS	INCREASE IN TEAMS
Little League	32,648	53,624	20,976
Boys' Baseball	8,178	9,159	981
Babe Ruth League	11,204	11,816	612

American Baseball Congress	2,621	2,926	305
American Legion	3,340	3,499	159

In the older-age programs, the figures were:

Babe Ruth Seniors			
(16–18 years)	922	1,128	206
AABC–Connie Mack			
(17–18)	1,104	1,058	−46
AABC–Musial			
(Unlimited)	800	878	78
American Legion			
(17–19)	3,340	3,499	159

The figures speak for themselves.

They show 87,588 teams in operation with 1,310,608 young-sters enrolled in these national programs alone.

Not counted in the listings are the 12,740 high schools, 529 junior colleges, and 958 colleges that participate in organized competition; nor are figures available on the hundreds of park leagues, municipal and industrial leagues, and the thousands of sandlot and small-town teams operating informally across the nation.

It is conservatively estimated that well over six million young-sters between the ages of ten and twenty played baseball in organized competition in 1971. The number has been growing steadily, and there is no indication of a falloff in 1972 or years to come. Certainly, from a participation standpoint there are no signs of baseball's physical break-down or early demise.

Thank you, Mr. Gallagher.

JUST FOR THE RECORD

Professional sports measure success by spectator support rather than participation. Participation is valuable as a developer of talent, but it's the box office that greases the wheels of progress and, to quote a phrase of my boyhood, "makes the mare go." Recently thumbing through various sports statistics, I jotted down the official 1971 paid-attendance figures, as announced by the press associations. Here they are:

BASEBALL	AMERICAN LEAGUE	NATIONAL LEAGUE
	11,868,560	17,324,850

(Not including the World Series and All-Star Game) .... Total 29,193,410
FOOTBALL 10,076,035
BASKETBALL 7,831,542
HOCKEY 7,965,310

Looks like America likes professional sports. Beyond that, no comment.

HAPPINESS IS PLAYING BALL

When it comes to picking the "happiest" player I have ever known there is only one candidate. It has to be Ernie Banks. His "nice day for a game" greeting is a personal trademark that will never be forgotten. It is not only unique, it's 100 percent sincere. In warm weather or cold, in sunshine or in rain, winning or losing, Ernie was always the happiest man in uniform. In the happiness stake, he wins by a furlong. There is no "place" or "show."

Among executives and officials, my candidate is Warren Giles. Most men connected with baseball are rabid fans. Warren is a triple-special. At World Series and at All-Star games, I think I get as much kick watching Warren as I do the performance on the field. When the game starts, he doffs his coat, rolls up his sleeves, and settles down to some plain and fancy rooting. He is the very epitome of everything that a loyal fan should be.

As most fans know, Warren was within one vote of being elected commissioner. He would have been a good one. No doubt of that. But as I've remarked to him half-kiddingly on occasion, I don't think he would have been happy. It would have been necessary for him to give up his rooting privileges and hide his enthusiasms under an austere cloak of neutrality. That would have been his toughest moment, and his most difficult assignment. Don't misunderstand. I know that he would have done whatever duty required. But he wouldn't have been particularly happy in the doing. However, that's conjecture. His record speaks loudly. He has been a great league official; his opinions have carried great weight in baseball's councils, and he has stood firm in the game's battles. And, above all, he has retained his rooting privileges! In my book he wins the title of baseball's "happiest executive" hands down. No contest.

Here are some offbeat observations that come to mind as I thumb through the clippings and memos that have accumulated through the years. Maybe they will answer a few of the questions that fans constantly ask. These are personal opinions, of course, and in no way represent any poll or official finding.

Most aggressive player. Of all the players I have seen in action, Ty Cobb was far and away the most aggressive. His every move was a challenge, and every game was a battle.

Player with greatest fan appeal. Undoubtedly Babe Ruth.

Greatest pitching performance. Don Larsen's perfect World Series game against the Dodgers, October 8, 1956. They say it's impossible to improve on perfection, but that's exactly what you do when a perfect game is achieved against the almost unbearable pressure that comes with the World Series.

Best World Series performance by an individual player. Brooks Robinson's play against Cincinnati in the 1970 Series, both in the field and at the plate, was the greatest individual exhibition I ever witnessed. Pepper Martin was great in the 1931 series, but Robinson was spectacular.

My greatest World Series thrill. A tough question. One experiences many thrills in fifty years of World Series play. As I look back, however, I guess it was Bill Mazeroski's ninth-inning home run against the Yankees in the final game of the 1960 series. That blow gave the Pirates their first world championship in 51 years. It came on the final day of a seven-game series, before a cheering, overflow horde of hometown fans who had about given up hope. Certainly, it came with dramatic suddenness—and I'll have to stay with it as my greatest thrill.

My favorite "bad boy." I interpret "bad" as referring to the player who battled the most with umpires, was most often fined, and was always ready to do verbal battle on the field or off—that has to be

Frankie Frisch. During my National League days we had a lot of lulus—men like Leo Durocher, Charley Grimm, and Casey Stengel. All of them are certainly qualified candidates in the "favorite bad boy" sweepstakes. But Frankie was something special. Maybe I fined him and suspended him the most, but somehow I liked him the best. With a low bow to the others, I still have to pick Frank. He was and is, my favorite "bad boy."

One other award. The leather medal for the best double-talker in all baseball history goes to Casey Stengel for his stellar performance before the Celler Committee. It was a tough challenge. Congressmen are, by profession, experts in the art of dissembling, and that committee was made up of champions. But that didn't bother Casey. At the end of two minutes, he had them completely befuddled; after ten minutes they were in a semicoma; and when Casey delivered his peroration they could only shake their heads and pray for early adjournment. I don't know what Casey said, but whatever it was, he said it with emphasis.

Mickey Mantle was the next witness, and he really put the frosting on the cake. In an attempt to restore the committee's sanity, Chairman Celler, with solemn dignity, turned to Mickey. "Mr. Mantle," he asked, "would you give the committee your opinion on the problem we are discussing?" Mickey pondered for a moment. "Well," he replied with equal solemnity, "I agree with everything Mr. Stengel said."

That brought the house down. Casey had won his spurs. The congressmen knew they had met a master.

JUST FOR THE RECORD

Did you know that baseball has a college education plan, open to all youngsters who sign a professional baseball contract before or during their college career?

The plan provides for payment of $1,000 a semester for a period of eight semesters—payment to be made to any accredited college or trade school that the player may select—covering tuition and living expenses as billed by the college. It becomes effective upon notice from the school of the players acceptance and enrollment. The plan is noncancelable by the baseball club and becomes void only if the player fails to pass his work or voluntarily gives up the project. Transfer of contract or release of the player does not affect the educational agreement.

The plan was first instituted in 1962. Since its inception, some 1,800 players have taken advantage of the fund for one or more semesters. So far baseball has paid out more than $2,500,000 in educational costs under the plan. The whole program is handled and supervised by the commissioner's office. As a result of the plan, several players have already been awarded degrees while still actively engaged in baseball.

To me the plan is adequate answer to the critics who complain that professional baseball, by signing players out of high school, are interfering with the player's right of education. That's bunk. Because the average player has to be carefully trained and developed before he can qualify for major league service, and because that training cannot be obtained through college competition, prospects must be signed and their development program started at an early age.

What is affected is athletic eligibility, not educational opportunity.

And the eligibility rules are made by the colleges, not by baseball. If the colleges want to offer athletic scholarships to promising athletes, that's their business. If they want to interpret eligibility rules to make a professional in one sport automatically ineligible in all sports, that's their business, too.

As a man who has spent his whole life in the professional athletic field, I have great respect for amateur competition. Certainly the man who is paid to play baseball, and who has the advantage of professional coaching and opportunity to play more often than his amateur brother, should lose his amateur status so far as baseball is concerned. But why that should bar him from amateur football or basketball, I can't understand. Certainly the professional football player can maintain his status as an amateur golfer, the star professional basketball performer still rates as an amateur in tennis and the world-champion baseball pitcher is only an amateur among amateurs when swimming competition starts at the local pool. But that's the rule colleges have established—and that's that.

What I object to, along with most baseball men, is the holier-than-thou attitude of a few college officials who cry "educational interference" when they really are indignant over athletic competition.

That baseball does sign high school prospects, regardless of college athletic desires, admittedly is true. That baseball is deliberately interfering with or denying any educational right is completely false. Fans are entitled to know of baseball's educational plan, its financial provisions, and the way it works. They can draw their own conclusions.

Storm Clouds Ahead

In recent years, baseball's business structure has gone through an operational revolution. It started with the move to bring black players into the major leagues. Fan sentiment was divided, and both sides expressed themselves vehemently. It turned out to be a teapot tempest, and within a single season the fans, with a minimum of bluster, accepted the new order.

Then came expansion, viewed by many as a financial chess game, and something that brought a flood of adverse publicity and fan protest. That's understandable. A fan's loyalty to baseball, and his allegiance to a particular club and its players, is emotional rather than economic. Sweeping changes in an established order upset him no end. It's like robbing a bird's nest. Take one egg and the birds scold and raise Cain. Once the robber has gone, they forget their anger and return to the nest. But remove all the eggs, and the bird's in complete panic.

That's the way it was with baseball. Too many eggs were removed too suddenly. Too many nests were left entirely barren. Fans were not concerned with the economic necessity of the moves. Neither were they interested in any long-range benefits that might accrue to baseball through the expansion program. They were emotionally upset. They resented the changes, and, like the birds, they showed their resentment with loud squawks that reverberated from ocean to ocean.

Unfortunately the problem, in my opinion, is not yet entirely solved. True, the big hurdle has been cleared. Expansion has given professional baseball an updated territorial structure that should stand for many years. But within that broad structure, there are mistakes to be rectified and changes to be made. Fans and critics should steel their emotions to more franchise switches before the program is finished.

For instance, five major league clubs today are centered in one state—California. That California is our most populous state, and still growing, is a matter of record. That it is a progressive state and the gateway for international trade and commerce is also beyond argument. But the location of five franchises—roughly one-quarter of the existing twenty-four—in one state is economic overcrowding. I don't know which franchises will move, or when, or where. Nor do I mean to imply that changes will start in or be limited to California. The situation there is cited to emphasize a point, without putting the finger on any particular club or any individual city.

In launching a huge expansion program, whether in sports or industry, problems are sure to arise—problems that can only be rectified through a laborious process of trial and error. I have faith in baseball's establishment to correct these mistakes as they occur. I am equally sure that the vast majority of fans, alerted to these problems, will recognize that any moves are part of a broad program to bring baseball abreast of the times, both economically and as a truly national institution.

Since the major leagues expanded to twenty-four clubs, two changes have already occurred. The Seattle franchise was transferred to Milwaukee and the Washington club moved to Dallas. There will be others. But fans can take heart in this. Once the mistakes are rectified and the errors corrected—a matter of a few years—baseball will be set for a long run. Clubs will be able to concentrate on developing championship teams, unhampered by policital pressures and economic threats. Fans will once again peacefully turn to the sports pages to study the box scores without the blaring headlines of franchise movement or rumors of baseball's economic bankruptcy to stir their temper and send their blood pressure rising.

Won't that be a happy day!

Memo from a Diary Entry

Today's sport pages report many feuds between sports people. A is battling with B; C hates D; so-and-so isn't talking to blank. Reminds me of a song from the musical *South Pacific* entitled "You Have to Be Carefully Taught." Hating takes a lot of concentration and time. Busy men can't afford it. Disagreement? Yes! Argument? Certainly! But hatred? That's reserved for inanimate objects. One can hate an unfair policy, or a bad law, or a malicious practice. But to "hate" other humans, whether groups or individuals, causes ulcers and nervous breakdowns. Guess the haters are either unemployed, or not paying enough attention to their own jobs. Otherwise, they couldn't have time for hating.

Livening the Game

A lot of suggestions are being made these days for changing the basic rules of baseball. One critic suggests changing the rule to allow a batsman to take his base on three balls instead of four. Another would shorten the base line from ninety feet to eighty-nine feet. A third suggests lengthening the time-honored pitching distance by six inches. And so it goes.

These would-be reformers put forth many arguments based on the premise that the game is too slow or too dull, that the defense overpowers the offense, or vice versa, that the public is interested in higher scoring rather than expert finesse. All the suggestions are well meant. In a sense they are a tribute to the game. The suggestors must be fans with a deep interest, else they wouldn't take the time necessary for their suggestions.

I'm not a confirmed reactionary, and I believe that dogged devotion to status quo can be fatal. I favor imaginative and progressive thinking. But suggestions to change the basic character of the game are completely illogical. For years, scientists have marveled at the mathematical precision of baseball. The balance between offense and defense is competitively perfect. To change diamond measurements by as little as six inches, engineers assure us, would affect the whole balance of the game. To grant a runner first base on a three-ball count instead of the present four would take away from the pitcher his greatest asset— the ability to pitch to corners, and to match wits with the batter. All the traditions, all the continuity of offense and defense, all the strategy of team play would be affected.

Maybe the game is too slow in the eyes of some critics. Undoubtedly there are thousands of people in these United States who have no interest in baseball or who prefer the smashing bodily contact of football or the blinding speed of basketball or hockey. That is to be expected.

No sport can be all things to all people. The fact remains that in 1971 (the latest season for which official figures are available) some fifty million people paid admissions to watch some level of baseball, in addition to the six million youngsters between ten and twenty who took part in organized amateur programs.

Don't think I'm opposed to all change. Changes are being made constantly in the playing rules of baseball and all sports. For instance, Leonard Koppett of *The New York Times,* in a recent column, suggested that it would be to the benefit of pitchers and hitters alike if the rules were changed to let a predesignated hitter bat for the pitcher whenever that worthy was due to hit. Such a rule, Leonard points out, would enable a pitcher to continue in the game, and at the same time would give the offensive side a continuity of attack that would please spectators. If that suggestion were adopted (and this is not in any sense an endorsement) it would have one virtue. It would not destroy the basic mathematics of the game. Also, it would afford an opportunity for pitchers in a close game to stay in there to a decision. That I'm sure most fans would like.

But I fear I have belabored the point. Very simply it is this. Speaking as an old fan, I'm "agin" any change in the basic setup of baseball. A vast majority of fans, I think, feel the same way.

A LOOK AHEAD

Gazing into a crystal ball is a popular pastime with most sports, and baseball is no exception. All during the winter, and even after opening day, fans dream their golden dreams of pennants and championships. Yesterday's disappointments are forgotten, and tomorrow's reality tinged with hope and softened with enthusiasm. Before every All-Star game or World Series, fans cloak their emotions in hope and their dreams in the panoply of victory.

I, too, am a fan, entitled to my dreams and hopes along with the others. It's a privilege that tradition makes mandatory. Here's what I see for baseball, and other sports, fifty years from now.

By that time (circa 2020) the major leagues will have expanded from 24 to 32 clubs, operating as four separate eight-club leagues. There will be an agreement with football that will eliminate much of the confusion of cross-scheduling and overlapping play. Baseball will return to the old 154-game schedule, with postseason playoffs culminating with the traditional World Series. The baseball season will be shortened, with the season opening in mid-April and all competition, including the World Series, ended by October 7. Whether or not the four-league schedule will include interleague play, the crystal ball does not divulge.

By the year 2000, there will be no weather problems. Domed stadiums will have taken care of that. By then, expert engineers and scientists will have come up with new construction ideas and new materials to enable municipalities and private corporations to build covered, year-round, all-sports structures, at less than the open structures of today. That will help solve the overlap problem. With a domed year-round stadium fixed schedule dates can be set in advance with no fear of postponements because of weather. All sports will accept likely cities without thought to latitude or the problem of sectional play. It is entirely possible, too, that a moveable dome can be devised that could be opened or closed as weather conditions dictate.

The thought of expansion immediately brings up the problem of which cities would be available for the new teams and how to supply these teams with players of real major league caliber. If moves were contemplated today, these would be matters of deep concern. However, if present projections and present trends are accurate, these problems will solve themselves by the turn of the century.

Cities are growing at phenomenal rate. Statistics predict that by the year 2000, our population will increase by a minimum of 25 to 30 percent. I am not shilling for any particular city or territory. But cities like Miami in the South, and Omaha, Denver, and Salt Lake in the Plains area, and Phoenix in the Southwest are growing by leaps and bounds. The Northwest, by the time expansion comes, will offer the Seattle-Tacoma area for serious consideration, or even Portland or Vancouver as prospects. Washington, our nation's capital, today is without baseball. Cities like Toronto and New Orleans already are in the market.

A lot of folks, even now, are talking of international baseball. When that time comes Toronto, Mexico City, and Havana (even Mr. Castro can't live forever) will be ready and willing. As for playing strength, I don't worry. Increased population will take care of that. Figures show that for every good job there's always a capable and ambitious man waiting around to fill it.

One other thought. By the time a new century rolls around, I'm hopeful Congress will have ceased investigation; the Supreme Court will have decided sports privilege and obligation under Federal statute, and concise, understandable ground rules will have been laid down under which sports can operate. At the same time, I hope sports are not included in the Off-Track Betting frenzy, or harassed by any widespread legalization of betting. Not that I'm opposed to betting per se, or blind to the fact that it exists. I'm not. But sports and gambling simply do not mix. And rules legalizing gambling on a broad scale only add to the sports policing problem, by destroying the most effective weapon we have in protecting the honesty and integrity of our competitive team sports.

Also, I hope Congress does not see fit to put sports under any special sports authority. To do so would only add to an already complicated problem, and add one more to the already overcrowded list of governmental agencies that serve no particular purpose. The result will only be to further complicate the problems of dedicated men who through the years have done a pretty good job of keeping sports clean and palatable for the American pubic.

In my dream I see something different. In the next fifty years, I see sports expanding. I see laws made clear and ground rules established under which sports can operate with dignity and proceed with confidence. And in baseball I see this and succeeding commissioners returned once again to the functions originally ordained. I see the commissioner as a judge and arbiter, respected by press and public, with full authority to protect the honesty and integrity of the game he rules. I see a commissioner relieved of petty annoyances and criticism by rules and procedures that recognize the power and dignity of the office and at the same time define the obligations of leagues, and clubs, and owners, in simple language that the fan public can understand.

Of course, it's only a dream, but a happy one—and a fit ending for what is intended to be a happy book.

EPILOGUE

We live today in a frantic age of skepticism, and doubt, and suspicion. Cynics delight in flouting traditions and destroying old concepts. Yet they offer no plan as substitute or no promise of better things. Homely virtues are laughed at, and established customs scorned. Expediency is the new yardstick in the affairs of individuals and of nations.

We face economic problems and we face political problems. We have racial problems and we have moral problems. Selfishness, and skepticism, and faultfinding, and carping criticism have assumed frightening international stature.

Somewhere, sometime, somehow some individual genius will come up with a solution. I confess I am not smart enough even to hazard a guess as to the answers. But this I do know:

A world at sixes and sevens demands sanity and understanding. There is a crying need today for sentiment, and tradition, and dreams. Those eternal verities of honesty and truth, of fairness and compassion, of sympathy and understanding, still play and will continue to play an important part in our lives so long as mankind exists or the world endures.

235

If ever we become so blasé that children are denied their idols and adolescents no longer encouraged to dream; if the time ever comes when sentiment is replaced by fear and the memories of yesterday are lost in the nightmares of tomorrow; if the time ever comes when we lose our sense of humor and can no longer laugh at our own foibles; if the time ever comes when men no longer find time to play, and the love of friendly sports competition is swept away by the selfish manipulations of self-seeking opportunists—

Above all, if the time ever comes when your sons and mine no longer go to bed to dream their dreams of greatness with a football alongside them in bed, or a baseball under their pillow—then something real, something worthwhile will have gone out of our American way of life forever.

I'm a dreamer and an optimist.

I don't believe that will happen.

Please don't let it!

INDEX